As if by Chance

As if by Chance

Journeys, Theatres, Lives

David
Lan

ff

FABER & FABER

First published in the UK in 2020
by Faber & Faber Ltd
Bloomsbury House
74–77 Great Russell Street
London WC1B 3DA

First published in the USA in 2020

Typeset by Faber & Faber Ltd
Printed and bound by CPI Group (UK) Ltd, Croydon, CR0 4YY

The right of David Lan to be identified as author of this work
has been asserted in accordance with Section 77 of the Copyright,
Designs and Patents Act 1988

A CIP record for this book
is available from the British Library

ISBN 978–0–571–35779–6

FSC
www.fsc.org
MIX
Paper from
responsible sources
FSC® C020471

10 9 7 6 5 4 3 2 1

For Nick, obviously

Contents

'Remembering is the woof
and forgetting the warp.'

Walter Benjamin

Thanks and apologies

This is not the book I intended. When I left the Young Vic in the spring of 2018 I sat down to record and describe the pleasure I had taken in my friendships with the writers, actors, directors, designers, stage managers, producers, board members, casting directors, technicians, architects, fundraisers, outreach and marketing experts with whom I had collaborated over almost twenty years. I anticipated page after lyrical page about, amongst others, Sue Emmas, Nicola Thorold, Julia Horan, Caroline Maude, Kevin Fitzmaurice and Lucy Woollatt.

Almost at once and quite unexpectedly my great-uncle Symon and my great-aunt Shlovka ambled into the room. When, ten months later, I stood up again, the book had become what it is.

It's a *memoir*, a work of memory. Lacking notes or diaries, I've written as accurately as I can, with sufficient confidence (or self-delusion) to have changed only one name.

Judy Daish is my long-time agent and close friend. Jud Cornell is implicit in almost all the Cape Town sections, as is Patrick McKenna in everything to do with YV. Tom Lyons kindly listened to me talk some early ideas. I wonder if Andrew and Filip are downstairs. Dinah Wood of Faber & Faber said 'Yes, it is publishable' and then published it. Huge thanks to everyone who makes an appearance.

London, July 2019

In the days before I ran a theatre . . .

When I was a playwright and a free man, I kept all the drafts of everything I wrote, notes, scraps of inadequate description, bits of speeches I thought too long or poorly conceived, arranged on my laptop, folder inside folder. As you opened one and then the next, cascading down and down, it created the sensation of an advance ever deeper into the mystery of things.

Now whatever I place in a folder on this my company laptop seeps through the screen into a soupy tide swirling away down some grey memory plughole. I've never any idea where anything is. So actual pieces of paper are placed in a pile *right over there* on *that* side of my desk where I'm sure to come upon them at the ideal moment. Then I'll reply or read your play or do whatever it is you've asked me to do.

So piles volcano up and lava down and wire trays are found from which torrents pour and, one by one, the sheets are flipped onto their backs to receive my scribbled reminders of that important email, that most urgent phone call.

'Stanley who? Do I know a . . . ? What does it say?'

My genial assistant Andrew Hughes puzzles.

'Saturday, is it?'

'That's tomorrow. No, it's Salisbury! Am I going there?'

'I think it says "something". You've written down "some – thing".'

He grins showing his teeth.

An actor or writer or director enters the room.

'Hi, um, are you in the middle?'

Never for you, dear actor, writer, director. You cut a path through this thicket of thorns. You're my hero. You set me free.

Ranevskaya I want to sit in this room for a tiny moment longer. These walls, I feel I've never seen them, never taken them in, or the ceiling, I feel I could stare at it forever, it all seems so precious to me.

Trofimov Come, everyone, let's sit for a moment. (*They sit for a short while.*)
Let's go! It's almost time for the train to arrive.

Anton Chekhov, The Cherry Orchard

One

The Magician's Assistant

What Does That Represent?

Song and dance

In the pot on the stove a hunk of beast is bubbling. Aunty Shlovka climbs up onto a stool, so squat and small she has to stretch high in her yellow slippers to see over the rim.

From the doorway, I admire the rain spattering on the tin roof – ping, ping!

'Shlovka?'

'Ah'm cooking der food!'

With a metal spoon she jabs down into the bubbling.

'Shlovka?'

'Symon, ya hearin' me?'

The lofty shoemaker shuffles in, his dry face fleshless, blotched with pink. He points a leathery finger.

'Vich chil' is dis?'

It's a shack in a shtetl in the old country. It's a cottage in Cape Town, the promised land. Or is it a dream?

When her hair is loose it hangs like a curtain around her feet. Now it's coiled tight on her shiny head. He's a crunchy biscuit, she's a lemon dumpling.

'Sugar lump, sing for uncle. Ya shy in fronta him? Vot a silly. He won' bite ya, see, he got no teeth. Show him, Symon! Look, gums only, poor ol' man. Sing fa uncle, sing fa him.'

I make a tense jigging movement, up down, up down, tapping my feet.

My dad's handsome, my dad's tall
Ho ho!
His name's Joe, that's all.

Symon laughs through his papery nose.

'Haw haw! Jossi's firs' born, no?'

'Not firs' born. He's gotta older sister.'

'Firs' born *son*!' His sharp nails pinch my cheek. 'Show ya tongue.' He sticks his fingers between my teeth. 'Oy, vet an' pink. Ya like aunty's cookin'? Shlov!'

'Ya talkin' mit me?'

'De meat's cooked good? Come, Jossi's boy.'

He jerks me high, hauls me onto the table.

'Here ve got someting tasty!'

I kick out, break from him, stagger here, there, dash out of the room into the rain-washed street.

I start awake.

Laurence is kneeling beside my bed running warm fingers through my hair, enchanted by the pleasure this gives him.

I fold back the sheets and tiptoe into my parents' bedroom. It's early dark. They seem asleep, turned hard away from each other.

'Ma, can a friend come with us to the beach?'

'What time is it?'

'Can he, Ma, can he?'

'Oh, if you like. I wanted this to be one day just for us. Joe!'

She prods him so sharply I feel it.

'Dave wants to bring a friend with us. What do you think?'

Laurence is in the doorway, his shaggy hair haloed by the acid sunlight. He's twelve, that's two years older than me. The buttons of his summer shirt are open. It's dangerous and thrilling.

4

Oh come in! Don't come in!

'Darling, if you want to ask him, ask him.'

I scamper down stairs, through the front door aching to call his name, knowing that would give away a secret. He's nowhere. The grass is cold and wets my feet. The sky is wounded grey. I shout his name in silence. *Where are you?* The air is heavy and still. He's gone. It's a relief.

My sister Sonny and I are eating cornflakes with chocolate milk. The phone rings in the hall.

'Hello? Who is it? Dad!' Singing it with rising inflection 'Da-a-a-d! It's-for-you-hoo!'

Ma shouts 'I've told you not to shout! Come upstairs if you've something to tell us. Who is it?'

'It's Jupius or something.'

I can't see her but I feel her shoulders fall.

'Shall I tell him to call back later?'

'Joe, it's Julius. Put the phone back, Dad'll take it upstairs.'

Our maid Edna calls from the kitchen

'Come, child, finish so I can clear away.'

Sonny looks up. Is something bad on the way? I shake my head.

Ma comes down in her puffy dressing gown, face powdery, no make-up on. Dad's invited his new accountant, wife and son to join us.

'They're not free till later so we won't leave at eleven, Edna, we'll go at twelve.'

Something tightens in me, something else I might have had is lost. Edna sees.

'No, Dave, it's fine, the sun is shining, you have the whole day, there's not a breath of wind.'

She's cutting crusts off sandwiches, wrapping them in damp napkins.

'Leave it now, didn't you hear what I said? They'll dry out. Put them in the fridge. Lovely breakfast. Yum!'

She smiles at me and Sonny and goes back upstairs. We cheer ourselves up with songs from *The Goon Show* we heard on the radio last evening.

> *I'm walking backwards for Christmas*
> *Across the Irish Sea.*

Edna hates Ma telling her what to do.

'Go both of you into God's sunshine, leave me in peace.'

Our gardener Alpheus has come in through the back door which leads from the yard into a short corridor. On one side's the laundry, on the other the dank room where Edna lives. He rarely comes into the kitchen when we're there. He's old, perhaps late twenties. He calls out while he's raking leaves

'Hello, Master Davey'

which is embarrassing if my friends are there but I make them understand, yes, he's a servant like the ones they have but I know his name which shows he's really my friend.

'Hi, Alpheus, how's things?'

He grows marijuana down the end of the garden by the rubbish heap.

'No, madam, that's a tobacco plant. *Nicotiana.* I'm an experienced gardener, madam, I guarantee you that's what that is.'

He drops into the metal chair. This is shocking, sitting down with white people. He never does this.

'Haai, Alpheus.' This is Edna. 'My brother, what's wrong?'

He works for us Tuesdays and Fridays. I only see him in the ragged overalls he leaves hanging on a nail on the door of the shed. Today he wears corduroys and a crisp white shirt. Who irons it for him?

'Can I please see the madam?'

'What's the matter, Alpheus?' This is me. 'Can I help with anything?'

Sonny's seen enough to make her fearful.

'Come on, I can't hang around all day.'

Heading for the front room, she calls up the stairs 'Mommy!'

Alpheus' big eyes search for mine, his jaw muscles flexing.

'My daughter's gone, Master Davey.'

Darkness covers the face of the earth.

'Last night she had a fever. Her head was paining her. I woke in the very early morning. I shake her. What could I do? Nothing.'

Edna tries to embrace him. He shakes her off.

'Haai, David! I knew his child. She was a beauty, I'm telling you. The world has lost a marvel . . .'

Ma's dressed now in a scarlet skirt, her colour.

'Yes? Where's Sonny? Dave, why do you look so miserable?' Her voice deepens, mellows. 'What's happened now? Is something wrong, Alpheus?'

I escape through the servants' door into the garden. Is Laurence somewhere? He could be watching for me in the shadows. I hide in the dark of the bed of Christmas flowers. They loll on their long necks. I search for him.

Dad's film-star handsome, towering, big chest, thick black wavy hair, soft ivory fingers that bang out honky-tonk on our upright piano. At weddings and bar mitzvahs he conquers the dance floor, licking smiley lips, singing along in Yiddish or in American or in any language, trotting, gliding, so at ease at speed. He loves to tell long jokes to strangers in the hot streets, Jews and wary Afrikaners, shopkeepers, businessmen like him, sharing his views on science and economics, how great the future's going to be, for us, our country, our galaxy. Ma backs away into some tidy place. Sonny and I roll up our eyes and kick our heels.

Julius and Marcy and their son aren't waiting where they're meant to be.

Ma says 'It's boiling in this car.'

'Wind down the windows.'

'I have, obviously. Let's go. We'll find him on the beach.'

Or not, which would please me. Ma cradles my baby sister Debbie on her lap. We're squashed onto the back seat, me, Sonny, my seven-year-old brother Jeff, Edna who's come along to help look after him.

Edna says 'David, sing that song you like so much, you sing so nicely.'

I sing badly. I don't want to sing. We're speeding now. Hot air streams in. I wonder where Laurence is and who's with him.

Ma twists round to face us. 'We're all together, we should be having fun. I don't know what's wrong with us this morning.'

Sonny wails 'It's afternoon already.'

Edna says 'Seems to me, everyone got up on the wrong side of their bed.'

Dad sings, the others join in.

> We're on our way (we're on our way)
> To anywhere (to anywhere)
> With never a heartache
> And never a care . . .

Ma says 'Come on Dave at the back.'

Just as Ma and Edna are helping my brother out of the car, Julius walks up, his fat son Daniel staggering backwards, squinting at the sun.

'Oh no, Joe, no, my friend, I wasn't waiting on that corner. We were on the corner opposite as we arranged, by the greengrocer. They had such beautiful pawpaws, Danny went in and bought us half a dozen. You didn't see us? That's surprising to me, everyone knows my car, the only one of its year and make currently on the streets. But we're here now, which is all that matters, isn't that so? Daniel, my boy, don't stare, it's not polite. Good afternoon, Jeffrey.'

Jeff wears a metal brace holding his spine erect. It rests on his hips and ends in a rubber pad under his chin. A yellow shirt conceals the metal uprights. He walks jerkily, his head at a crazy angle. He has only two expressions, scowl or grin.

Daniel's hair is shaved off, under his eyes are purple rings. He says 'What's the matter with your brother?'

Sonny calls out 'Ma, I'll be back in a bit, ok?'

'No, not ok. Where are you going?'

'To find my friends.'

And she's gone. She looks eighteen though she's just a year older than me but she's safe on this beach where everyone's Jewish except the raincoated man with a camera who'll take your picture if you pay him and the other who treks the burning sand barefoot selling cool drinks and orange lollies.

Edna and I lay out rugs. We scoop up sand and pile up cushions to make a throne for Jeff to sit in comfortably.

Julius and Dad lounge in the shade of the beach hut we rent, at once caught up in each other's concerns like they're a current affairs programme on the radio and they've switched each other on.

Ma sits, legs splayed, dragging her scarlet dress over her head. Her fingers catch in the straps. I disentangle them. Her swimsuit matches her shade of lipstick.

'Dovidol!'

Tall, strongly built, beaming, her soft arms held wide, Granny is here in her powder-blue one-piece swimsuit. 'Lou, what took so long?

We're all here, Louis, Barney, Jackie, all mine brothers. Not Max, he don't care for swimming. Come down the beach where we are. We got *plenty* sun umbrellas.' I realise now, *that's* what we forgot to bring.

Ma kisses Granny.

'But how did you know we were coming?'

'How do I know?'

Her laugh is soupy sweet juice bubbling.

'I know . . .' She looks up and down the beach. 'Because Joe phoned to tell me you're making a picnic and will I come. It wasn't my plan to be here. Sunday for me is bowls, you know what I'm talking, the tournament, I don't say I'll win the trophy this year again but could be if I practise every week, you agree with me? Joe wanted us all to be together, hey, Joe, you like to be with your family, don't you, my Jossi?'

Dad waves, keeping his distance.

Ma doesn't want me or anyone to see how angry she is.

Granny asks 'How's Jeffrey?'

Ma snaps 'If you want to know, ask him. He's sitting over there.'

'I'm asking *you*, darling.' She looks deep into Ma's face then bends low, which for her isn't easy. 'Hello, sweetheart.'

Jeff grins. 'Hello, Gran.' He gives a shamefaced smile. It's hard for him to move much. Gran kneels and kisses him.

Dad lopes over.

'Joe, this was meant to be a day for just us to be together.'

He shrugs, big-hearted Joe, his arm around Ma's lightly toasted shoulder, his ivory hand on her freckled skin. He whispers to her, sexy lips smudging her flushed cheek. She wrenches away, stands seeing nothing, staring out, raging. But nothing embarrasses him.

'Where's the girl? Edna, move everything down the beach to where my mother is. Dave, help Edna.'

Ma asks Gran 'What time did he tell you to be here?'

'Mine watch is in mine bag. I slip it off for swimming.'

'He didn't phone anyone today. When did Joe arrange to meet you here?'

'Why you're questioning? Is something wrong for me to see mine son?'

Ma's beautiful face is so ugly it makes me clamp my teeth.

'When Jos was by my place last evening—'

Ma's face judders. So he was *there*, was he? She has no one to share this with but smiles at me as if to say 'Don't worry, kid, you're on my team.'

'—he said today you'll be here roundabout half past one maybe?'

Edna, feeding Jeff ice cream, shakes her head.

'Such a lovely day, such a shame to spoil it arguing.'

Ma yells 'Edna, what did you say?'

Gran says 'Your girl is very cheeky.'

Ma yells 'Do what the master told you to.'

Dad, shoving me, 'I told you help the girl.'

But I'm away, running, running, shouting back

'I will in a minute, I'm going for a swim'

heading in a straight line, it has to be a dead straight line even if I need to leap over blurry shapes heaped on towels on the sand. I'm good at running. Last term I won first prize for long jump to everyone's amazement. But I misjudge a leap.

'Look at him! Got a kick like a goat!'

I turn and see sharp teeth, a trickle of blood . . . But straight line, straight line, on and on . . .

> *We're on our way (we're on our way)*
> *To anywhere (to anywhere) . . .*

The tide's far out. I'm pounding the damp white sand, kicking through the piss-warm foam and into the surge, ankle-deep, thigh-deep, it's slowing me so I hurl myself up, up and plunge in.

Laurence is far out in the high rolling waves, strong brown arms flung out before him, body-surfing. I break the surface, stare at the boy whose shaggy hair I glimpsed. It isn't him . . .

It's me now, fifty years later, body-surfing the waves which are so much higher than I ever thought they'd be. I guess I never went this far out as a kid. Cresting high above my head, their muscle thumps me, tumbles me. I still adore to hand myself over, to feel

'My god, this time I'm actually drowning.'

My friend Arthur who died of AIDS told me that one day when he was already quite ill he swam far out into the waves at Manly Beach in Sydney where he lived as he did every morning but that day he felt how weak his breathing had become, how small his lung capacity now is. He's a doctor so at once he knows what it means. He swivels round towards the shore.

'Shall I make for home?'

He turns to the horizon.

'Perhaps today I'll just keep swimming further and further . . .'

Even this far out I can see without my glasses the beach-hut blobs of red, blue, green. Is that the one we used to rent? They're brighter colours now and lined up at a different angle. The beach is rowdy, joyous, carnivalesque. There are a few white faces. Where do we Jews swim these days?

I turn to the horizon, then back to the shore.

'Shall I make for home?'

Do nothing, let a world-wave lift you, whirl you, pound the holy shit out of you, dump you helpless in the piss-warm foam on the hard damp sand.

Special effects

Shakespeare in a park. A tiny English actor hams his way through Bottom.

> *Then die, die, die, die, die*

We bounce about with laughter, nothing will ever be so funny as long as we live – nor in fact is it. The next year his Shylock is suave and full of dignity.

> *If you prick us, do we not bleed?*

'What a great actor' we all agree in the car on the way home. 'Each time he looks so different, he can play anything.'
And an actor, as we all know, is what I'm going to be.

Lois, my ma, known as Lou or Louie, sometimes wrote what she thought of as 'light verse' for special occasions, birthdays or one of her children passing an exam.

> *Even then I knew it was less than sublime,*
> *the syntax busting apart*
> *with verbs down to the end of the line shoved*
> *which, as it helped the rhyme,*
> *she maintained was allowed.*
> *Of her literary ability she was proud*
> *and by her verses the recipients were deeply moved*
> *so, all in all, it was proof of her goodness of heart.*

I wrote a poem

> *It all began with the sheriff's son*
> *Who was in jail for debt . . .*

and recited it, with actions, at the Eisteddfod, but I had muddled the 'free choice' section with the section for 'set poem' so came away with nothing. The next year I entered with a marionette and, though there was no special section for puppetry, won the gold diploma. Ma bubbled over like boiling milk. I told her I was going to write a play.

'That's a good idea. First write it as a story then I'll help you turn it into dialogue.'

You'll help *me*?

I started a novel, filled half a notebook, then forgot about it but had noticed how the act of writing itself makes you aware of detail, of how things connect or don't connect . . .

Dad came home from abroad with a gift for me, a box of conjuring tricks.

'Here we have eight silver rings, all separate from each other. *Ching ching!* Do magic passes. They've linked to form a chain!

'Sim-salabim!'

With his beautiful hands Dad can make or repair anything. Mine have no facility. At school at carpentry I lurk at the back with the other hopeless cases. But

'This silk is sky-blue. I tuck it into this kitchen tumbler which as you can see is empty. Now keep your eye on the blue silk. One, two . . . It's pink! And this one's green! And red! And yellow! Now where's the blue? There she goes!'

A blue dove flies into the air. Or, in this version for younger magicians, an origami bird is pinged towards the ceiling. From Davenports of London you could order hundreds of 'magical effects'. I had cards printed.

> *David M Lan*
> *Magic and Puppets*
> *Children's parties a speciality*

Ma would drive me to homes in our neighbourhood, chat with the mums while I entertained their eight-, nine-, ten-year-old kids. She was tall and slim – in her school days she was 'Louie the lamppost' – slightly gawky in her shyness but sombrely handsome. There'd be clumsy moments as we climbed back into our car.

'But, Lou, how much should I pay him?'

'He's my child. You don't need to pay him anything.'

Ma's sister Mavis was a stage manager. That year, her Christmas show was *Aladdin!*

> *Peking Town, Peking Town*
> *The lights, the sights,*
> *the gaily coloured*
> *lanterns*

The actor who played the wicked magician Abanazar had stubby fingers that made him useless at conjuring.

'I have an idea,' said Aunty Mavis.

'And now,' said Abanazar, 'my young assistant will cause great feats of magic to occur.'

Sim-salabim!

Dialogue

Night after night, Dad and I sit up all hours talking and talking. Apartheid, the accumulation of capital, poverty, Gandhi, Lenin, Zionism, war and peace (and *War and Peace*) but, especially, independence in Africa. Every week he read the *Economist* and *Time* magazine and was moved and intrigued as country after country rolled headlong towards freedom. Barefoot doctors, schools under baobab trees, self-reliance, democracy, giant dams thrown across thundering rivers, *ujamaa, uBuntu, négritude*. He understood what

15

the odds were and what a struggle it would be but was enchanted by it all and wanted me to be.

'But, Dad, if their plans go wrong, millions of people will have nothing to eat. And what about the villages flooded by those dams? How do you think *they* feel.'

He'd press his arguments hard – the individual and the collective, the pragmatics of altruism, *realpolitik* – eager to see how deep into moral despair he could lead me. Hot tears would flow. He enjoyed that the world seemed real to me though all I actually knew of it were Edna, Alpheus and the raggedy kids kneeling in the dust playing games tossing pebbles in the air down the end of our street.

'I want you to understand this, you especially.'

'But, Dad, if people *don't want* their land to be collectivised . . .'

Now Nkrumah, Kenyatta, Nyerere had the chance to achieve tumultuous things for Nigeria, Kenya, Tanzania. It was the logic of history that they should succeed. And if they failed as Patrice Lumumba, the assassinated first elected president of Congo, had failed, well, millions would starve. That's how the world is.

Ma storms down from their bedroom.

'Come on, Joe, this is now ridiculous! You know he has to be up early for school.'

Her voice is shrill. She feels as I do, a discord – why, long past his own bedtime, does he prefer my company?

Star actors

Ma's mother told us Cary Grant was our cousin. Her family came from Vitebsk, the famous largely Jewish city then in Russia, now in Belarus, where Chagall was born, though Ma's mother herself was born on a ship halfway to Liverpool. An aunt of hers was a sister of the mother of Cary Grant. Their name was Lichtenstein. They

settled in Bristol and changed their name, so now he was Archie
Leach. From there he'd gone to Hollywood. He was our third cousin
twice removed or maybe thrice, it's never clear how you calculate
these things.

Nick still says

'Shall we watch that Hitchcock film, what's it called, you know,
the one starring your cousin?'

'*North by Northwest*? No, I've seen it too often.'

'Oh, alright then. How about *Bringing up Baby*?'

'Oh yes he's great in that. He's the best, old Archie Leach.'

Sales and marketing

Dad had hoped to study medicine but Mottle, his father, had died
of cancer in 1956 before he had even turned fifty so Dad had to
take care of Golda, his mother, his brothers, his sister, us and, to
some degree, the four of his mother's brothers who'd followed her
to the new country. They all kept shops clogged with old furniture.
Golda's shop sold bicycles and 78 rpm records. Bing Crosby, punc-
ture repair kits, Rosemary Clooney, The Ink Spots, spare pumps,
Beethoven symphonies. Dad took it over and

Sim-salabim!

it was a family outfitters. In an adjoining showroom he sold
chairs, tables, settees, rolls of carpet, fridges, stoves and the first
ever affordable washing machines. He'd sweep in and out of board
rooms, synagogues, sports clubs, parties, Mr Enterprise, Mr Heart-
and-Soul, Mr Vitality, well known for his innovative advertising

'This pram is ugly but it's cheap.'

He'd sign up for lectures at the university, the archaeology of the
Middle East, 'What's new in World Philosophy?', asking killer questions from the back row.

'But has no one noticed the similarity between the underlying structures of Spinoza's philosophy and quantum mechanics?'

He revelled in orchestral concerts and the film society but what he loved was leading his team of fervent young 'coloured' men, searching their faces and their ledgers to find the one – he needed only one – who might one day take over from him and, meantime, share his burden. It wasn't easy.

'I had high hopes of my deputy manager so I gave him time off to learn book-keeping. Comes his first exam, he fails and, you know what, he just gives up the whole thing. At least now he can never complain it's apartheid that holds him back. Poor chap must live with reality – he hasn't got it in him. Heartbreaking, isn't it?'

Saturday mornings, Sonny and I'd serve in the outfitters. She sells dresses and underwear, I sell shoes and school uniforms. I'd see Dad, in weekend short-sleeved shirt, out in the sunny forecourt with his sharply dressed young managers who'd started with him on the township beat, ringing doorbells, collecting the tiny sums each customer has pledged to pay each week. They splutter with laughter as he taunts them, victim by victim, with tales of their errors and weaknesses.

'Yes, Mr Lan, you get it, you understand so well how life by us is. We'll strive to do better. We want to please you, I know you know that we do.'

Towards the end of long mornings we'd perch on the counters with Sheila, our manageress.

'Yes, my dear, the ANC are banned but they're so busy, those fine ladies and gents, infiltrating here, there, everywhere. Their violence can break out at any time, honest to god, you can't predict how or when. And now there's an even more dangerous crowd. David, you're a reader, you must have seen in the papers about Poqo blowing up railway lines. No one knows where they come from or what their intention is but they strike without mercy. People like us, we just want to all live together.'

'Yes, we do, Sheila, you've said it right,' chorus her saleswomen. 'It's a crying shame, that's what it is.'

We wait for an hour in Dad's airless Chevrolet Impala. At last he climbs in, throwing his briefcase next to Sonny who's sulking on the back seat. She'd arranged to meet 'friends', as she calls her new boyfriend, at half past two. We're so late for lunch Ma will be furious. With Dad we're always late for everything. His left leg jiggles as he drives so I know he's thinking hard about something.

'Dad, do you want to hear a joke Sheila told me?'

'My god,' Sonny says, 'you're not going to tell him *that one*!'

But it's a good one for me because I think I know how to characterise both voices.

'Mrs Van der Merwe is worried about the violence everywhere so she says to her maid

'"Gertie, you've been with us for *years*. If things got bad, you wouldn't harm us, would you?"

'"Oh no, madam, you're so good to me, I'd *never* do such a thing."

'"Oh, I'm so relieved to hear you say that, Gertie."

'"Oh, you mustn't worry, madam. I've made an arrangement with Millie next door. I'll cut the throats of her madam and master and she'll climb over the fence and do you and the master for me."'

Before Dad turns off the engine in our driveway Sonny's gone. In the hall, he tears the wrapper off the new *Economist*, reads it closely at the dining table while calling to Edna to bring in the meal. She slouches at the back door smoking, throwing cigarette ends at sparrows, ignoring him. Ma's stretched out on her rose-coloured quilt fiercely reading her new Agatha Christie, *At Bertram's Hotel*.

'Where were you?'

'Don't ask, Ma. Where do you think? Talking, talking . . .'

'Don't be rude about—'

'Ma, I'm telling you, his guys were desperate for him to go home, I could tell, but he'd rather be anywhere rather than . . .'

Her face goes blank as Edna taps on the door and saunters in.

'And, you know, David, today your ma made her special Malay curry out of the recipe book. Now the sauce is just a crust on the base of the dish. I feel for her from the bottom of my heart. How he treats her is a tragedy, my child, that's what it is.'

Poetry

Our house is ugly, functional, newly built. It faces a noisy city street but backs onto a lonely pocked and pitted lane, morning glory weaving through high hedgerows.

One Sunday Dad says

'Let's you and me take a walk down the road at the back of the house.'

Jeff's pet ridgeback noses along, rubbing up eagerly against our shins.

'I have many things to worry about—'

'What kind of things?'

'No, no, that's what you always do, you try to take control of a conversation. Now you have to listen to me. You, my boy, are my biggest problem.'

'Me? You're kidding. Surely it's Jeff?'

'Will you listen to what I'm saying? We know how to help him and we're doing that. But you—'

'Dad, I don't know what you're—'

'You told me you think you're homosexual. Is that true or not true?'

'Yes, I did but not because I'm worried about it so I don't see why . . .'

'How you can know such a thing at the age of fifteen I don't know but if you think that and if you're not sensible enough to be worried about it then that certainly worries me. And, come on now, think about it logically. If you're not worried why did you tell me about it?'

'Because I thought . . . I'm not ashamed of it. Dad, you and me talk about *everything*.'

'It was no surprise to me.'

'No? It seemed like it was.'

'I knew there was something wrong.'

'Honestly, there's nothing.'

'There is, Dave. What in god's name happened to you? It's my own fault.'

'What is?'

'Letting you spend all that time in theatres. I should have put my foot down.'

'That has nothing to—'

'All actors are homosexual.'

'That's not—'

'Don't lie to me! I know about this. On a school camping trip our sports master came into my tent and stroked my hair. If I'd let him go on, who knows what would have happened to me? I'm not blaming you but you're my responsibility.'

And now I'm extremely tense and I think

'But this is *me*. Whatever else you want me to do, tell me and I'll do it but this is what makes me special, don't mess with this.'

The thoughtful Jewish psychiatrist gave me a cup of tea and a biscuit, then spoke quietly from the other end of his sunny consulting room.

'I'm quite clear what your father's opinion on this matter is but I'm rather more interested to hear how *you* feel about it?'

In and out in half an hour. Dad was furious. The fool had made the situation worse. But somehow I'd succeeded – and by doing what, exactly? I was reading Sartre's *The Age of Reason* so I knew my duty was to choose the pattern of my own life. And also Genet's *Our Lady of the Flowers* so I'd no doubt how I'd choose.

At weekends I'd tell Ma I was meeting friends from school and take the bus to the only cruising ground I knew, a promenade alongside a city beach. Gary, a hairdresser, took me to his tiny one-room flat and suggested we do unexpected things which I was happy to and interested in without being especially excited about them. For a year or two he cut my hair and didn't charge. I wrote my first sonnet about him.

> *You saw me lonely on the shore and thought*
> *That what I wanted was a hand to hold*

From time to time I'd sneak out of the house and work on all-night technical rehearsals for musicals at the city's biggest theatre, the Alhambra. We'd wait until the last film showing was over (*The Guns of Navarone, The Shoes of the Fisherman*) then haul in scenery for *South Pacific* or – this is now the mid-1960s – white singer-dancers blacking up for *The Black and White Minstrel Show*.

> *Mammy, how I love ya*
> *How I love ya*

Keith, the rapscallion set designer, had plans for spectaculars he intended to produce one day.

'The curtain goes up, the stage is bare, what the hell is going on? It's a massive disappointment, but then . . . a single spot snaps on –

pow! – and out of nowhere a solo human figure appears. He sings a bar of music, then one more. Then silence for a beat. Another beat. But then . . . wham! – lights! wow! – the stage revolves and it's overflowing with dancers, musicians, tumblers, jugglers . . .'

He wanted me to work with him.

'I really can't, you know, I'm still at school.'

'Don't worry, that's ok. If I smell talent on someone I can wait for him.'

He ran a trapeze troupe of bleach-haired beach boys whom he trained to global standards. You'd climb a rope ladder, stand on a tiny wooden platform, he'd yell

'*Pret!*'

You'd bend your knees, then thrust out at the swing as it hurtles towards you in a weighty upward curve, grab it with the palms of both your hands, make a wild, sprawling, looping, lurch out into thin air

'I'm definitely, definitely joining a circus!'

then be hurled back and your heels *crunch* on the tiny wooden platform.

'No, no, I bloody told you, David, damn it, when you swing back you have to lift your fucking feet.'

Actors, trapeze artists, stage crew would pick me up in sports cars after school, drive off into a nearby wood, amuse themselves for a few minutes by fumbling with my dick. It was dangerous and exciting *and it was my life as I chose to live it* but it wasn't what I wanted. What I longed for was sex with my school friends but I couldn't talk them into it.

I was pretty certain that Arthur was gay. He was tall, bony, rugby-mad and an expert on the French Impressionists, especially Bonnard. He got on well with his parents and they with each other which seemed extraordinary to me. Perhaps it was because they weren't Jewish? Perhaps that's why I fancied him? Late one night I climbed over the wall around his parents' house, crept to his bedroom, found him asleep, sat on the edge of his bed . . .

'David, what the fuck are you doing here? Oh yes, I said I'd lend you my Apollinaire biography.'

Our favourite poem by Apollinaire was

> *Under the Pont Mirabeau flows the Seine*
> *And our loves*
> *Must I remember them?*
> *Joy always followed after pain*

I wrote poems every day, sometimes going too far.

> *A thin taut wire runs through the house in which I live*
> *and I must walk along it, holding arms outstretched*
> *to keep my balance. For if I fall, if the slightest fly*
> *lights on me and I stoop to brush it off and then try*
> *to stand again, the wire will bend and snap . . .*

When the magazine containing this was published, Ma was so distressed she went to bed. I knocked on her door.

'Dave?'

Half rising from her rose-pink quilt, un-made up, haggard as a sea creature, she held out the puke-coloured magazine.

'Is this how living here is for you? Tell me the truth.'

'No, Ma, really, Ma, it doesn't mean that at all, it doesn't mean anything, Ma, it's only a poem, Ma, honestly.'

Acting

My all-boys junior school staged an Edwardian musical *The Arcadians*. I played the innocent maiden Chrysea.

'The lie? What is . . . the lie?'

was the high point of my part, our drama teacher, Margot, pulling faces in the wings as, once again, I failed to speak up. The headmaster, a bald-headed violist known to all as 'Sally', doubled as the show's MD, conducting from the piano. He was renowned for putting his hand remarkably far down the front of blond boys' trousers. At the photocall I was invited to pose solo in my purple taffeta.

'But what does that represent?' queried one of the lady teachers.

'It represents Lan,' Sally said.

At high school, Denis was two years ahead of me but we were both desperate to put on a play so we became close friends. We rehearsed *Zoo Story* by Edward Albee. He was altogether bigger than me so he played the blowhard Jerry. I was Peter the wimp. Jerry has all the long speeches.

'Denis, can't we skip this bit for now?'

'Absolutely no way. It's Jerry's most self-revelatory monologue.'

'But it's so *long*. It goes on for pages.'

'It's complex. It's subtle. It has a strong emotional curve. I need to work my way through it.'

'Yeah but meanwhile I'm sitting on this bench doing fuck all. It's great for you, it's so damn boring for me.'

One day it was suddenly crystal-clear that what our school lacked was a play-directing competition. We put up a notice inviting entries.

There were two – Denis and me.

In the library we found volumes of one-act plays. He chose *Playgoers* by Arthur Wing Pinero, a snobbish piece about Edwardian household servants having a night out at the 'the-atre'. I directed *The Crimson Coconut*, a silly-ass farce about anarchists in Soho by Ian Hay. He acted in my production, I in his. We were allowed one performance in front of the school. The English staff sat in judgement. The winner was me.

So now I had to organise a prize. I decided on seats for *Once in a Lifetime* by George Kaufman and Moss Hart which was playing at a local theatre and caught a bus to town to buy the tickets that would be presented the following morning at assembly. Next day when I dressed for school they'd vanished. Where the hell had I put them? Then it occurred to me that no one need actually *see* the prize. I put an old exam paper in an envelope, sealed it, wrote on it 'Play Directing Award' and a few hours later, to tepid applause, accepted it graciously.

What is real in this hall of mirrors?

Sim-salabim!

December 1969. Finally finished with school, Denis and I travelled to London. Our plan was to pay for our jaunt by interviewing famous theatre folk and selling our exclusives to local magazines. We wrote to ten selected luminaries. All replied, eight agreed – nine, in fact, but Alec Guinness wrote in his own tidy hand to say he'd be out of town for the festive season but would be quite willing to meet if we were still around in the New Year. Sadly, we replied, we wouldn't be.

We'd borrowed a reel-to-reel tape recorder. Over two weeks we interviewed Trevor Nunn about his exciting plans for the RSC of which he was the newly appointed artistic director, the great socialist actress Sybil Thorndike, then eighty-seven, who, warming to an anti-apartheid theme, described how much she adored her old pal Paul Robeson

'If I see him I throw my arms around his neck and give him a great kiss on the cheek',

Paul Scofield whose honey-and-vinegar voice, recorded in the lounge of the Waldorf Hotel, was indecipherable on the tape above the rattle of tea cups, Tom Stoppard wry and courteous to two scruffy schoolboys, one plump, one toothpick-thin, who quizzed him on the themes of his intriguing new play then playing at the Old Vic, Peter Brook beneath the Christmas tree at his home off Kensington Church Street—

(Fast forward twenty-two years . . .

'Now, can you explain why I have a curious intuition that we may have met before.'

'Umm, well, Peter, it's an odd story actually . . .')

—and Nicholas Wright, or Nick, artistic director of the Royal Court's newly opened Theatre Upstairs. I'd read in *Plays and Players* about his avant-garde seasons but, even more to the point, he came from Cape Town so we were keen to hear how he'd risen to do what he now did.

We interviewed Nick in the tiny dressing room that doubled as his office. On the other side of the thin wall Peter Gill was rehearsing his new play *The Sleeper's Den* with Eileen Atkins sprawling on a wide, low bed, anguished amidst the sheets.

It was a wintry day. When I left, I forgot my umbrella. When Nick tells the story he says I did it on purpose. Possibly. Also that I tried to pick him up while I was interviewing him. Whether or not this last is true, I needed my umbrella. It took a number of phone calls to the stage door to ensure that when I came by to fetch it the artistic director would, as if by chance, be in.

By the time Denis and I got home to Cape Town, most of our

tapes had escaped their black plastic reels and were fatally crinkled. We listened to what we could. None was transcribed. By then I, for one, had more urgent things to think about.

Ma's father Ben came from Riga, 'the Paris of the East'. He was apprenticed to a furrier and tailor and in that way learned the skills he lived by. The firm he founded in Cape Town he called 'The Nobility Fur Company' though it was a one-man band. Unlike the ebullient huggers and kissers on Dad's side, Ma's team were corseted and fashion-conscious. In studio photographs of the 1930s, Grandma Fay and her twin sister Rose are glamorous flappers with bobbed hair and rosebud lips. Grandpa Ben, broad-faced with barley eyes, sports a stylish double-breasted blazer, white flannels, spats.

He was gruff in his old age, given to barking 'Fay! Fay!', though he didn't actually want her or need anything, while engrossed in the *Racing Times* under a wall-wide, gilt-framed oil painting of a peasant woman, babe in arms, struggling through banks of snow. He'd acquired it as settlement of a gambling debt. Everyone hated it.

One day back in old Riga he'd received the crisis news that he was to be conscripted into the army. For a young Jew, army life was brutal. He had to get away but his name, Mordechai Fagan, would be listed among those prohibited from leaving the country, so his father bought the papers of a young man named Benyamin Carklin who had died before he was due to be called up. One evening Mordechai dressed himself in the suit he'd made to his own measurements telling his boss it was for a customer – and then Benyamin presented his new papers at the docks, boarded a vessel bound west for Liverpool and set off into the Baltic Sea, into the blue . . .

I first heard this story decades after I'd engineered my own evasion of conscription, achieved with far less elegance but with no idea I was following family tradition.

I was white, I'd reached the call-up age of seventeen, my country needed me. I was due to board a packed train full of rowdy schoolboys and be hauled off to a camp near Potchefstroom, a small *voortrekker* town in the north-east. I was to be there eleven months and then be liable for a month-long camp each year for the next ten. I couldn't go, I couldn't possibly do this, obviously.

I'd heard there were boys who'd wangled their way out but I'd never met one and I hadn't a clue how to go about it. The Anti-Conscription Campaign set up to defend boys unwilling to fight in racist wars wasn't founded till many years later. Probably there were sympathetic folks who might have advised me on what my options were but I'd no idea how to find them.

Ma and Dad dropped me off at the station on their way to a movie with friends.

'Look after yourself, hey.'

'Give those bastards hell, will you do that for me?'

'Which bastards are you talking about?'

'Any of them, all of them.'

'Aren't you going to kiss your Ma?'

'Oh great, he's gone, now there's more room for us on the back seat.'

'Do it, man, kiss her.'

'Bye, Dave.'

'Christ, Joe, what kind of child have you brought up? Is he going to just go off like that and not say goodbye or anything?'

I was outraged by their casualness. Perhaps they thought marching and following absurd orders would dent my self-regard, my cockiness, perhaps even be a cure for homosexuality? Oddly perhaps, I didn't ever describe to them how I felt about going. Or perhaps not so odd. What's to say except

'It's a fascist army!'

At school our Latin teacher had served in the Second World War in the North African desert. He was a slight, bony man with a mild face that never showed emotion and a jaw that twitched. Without knowing what we were talking about, we ascribed the frozen face and the twitch to shell shock. In *Caesar's Gallic Wars* he found copious cues to lecture us on the virtues of giving our lives for our native land. At last I could take no more.

'What value can there be in dying for your country? I see no sense in it. Surely it's better to *live* for your country and to try to make it a better place for everybody.'

The class tittered with embarrassment. Now I'd put my smartass Jewish foot in it. The brittle ex-soldier stared out through the window into the infinite sunlight. His jaw twitched. He swivelled his head and gazed, marble-eyed, at me.

It's way past midnight. The light in the carriage throbs with howling louts, jangled guitars, playing cards mightily slapped down
  'How*zat*?!'
show-offs leaning halfway out of windows to smoke forbidden cigarettes and double-forbidden dope.
  'Look, the cunt's showin' his fuckin' arse! Woo woo!'
shrieking in anguish for no articulable reason
  'Fuckin', fuckin', fuckin', fuckin' . . .'
  plucking at each other's genitals in spiky parody of sexual predation.
  'Ha! ha! I touched his fuckin' dick!'
It was, in a way, fun or would have been if I'd allowed myself to do other than curl away in a corner and hatch a plan. At this point in my life, all I knew of the world is that an audience will accept whatever you place in front of it provided it's placed there with *élan*.
Hours before dawn, the train pulls in. We're lined up on the

platform. We wait an hour. Another. Someone somewhere howls bloodily at you if you move. It was beach weather back home, I'm wearing a short-sleeved shirt. It's freezing. Fuck this.

Light through the morning haze. Trucks arrive. We're driven to a camp, lined up again, this time to be given coffee, get examined by a doctor, have our heads shaved.

My line approaches the medical shack. In my hand is a half-full cup of coffee. I'm exhausted and dehydrated, that's the theory anyway. As I faint, the cup flies out of my hand and splashes a doctor.

Thump!

They help me up.

'What the fuck happened to you?'

Plan going well.

'Don't know . . . Where am I . . . ? What's going on . . . ?'

Quick medical check.

'Give him some water. Nothing the matter with him.'

Head shaved, issued with kit, led off to a dormitory as Gunner 68351048 of Battery 43, 4th Field Regiment.

'You've got just two fuckin' hours to sleep so keep your hands off your cocks. Say "Ja, Sergeant."'

'Ja, Sergeant.'

Well, this isn't working. First parade.

'Get your fuckin' helmet on!'

'I'm trying, Sergeant, honestly, the strap won't buckle round my chin.'

'Jesus, Jesus, the rubbish they send me. Tell your ma from me she'd have done far better to shove a Coke bottle up her *poes* then I'd never have had to deal with a nuisance like you.'

It turns out I'm trying to put on two helmets, one metal, one plastic, one inside the other, at the same time. Now the strap fits. But what do I do with the metal helmet?

'Oh my fuckin' fathers, don't ask me, boy. Shove it where the sun don't shine. Give it here, Jesus F Christ!'

He hurls the helmet into the air.

'Watch where it lands, fool. Pick it up after parade. Remember you're fuckin' responsible for it!'

An hour of stamping. My helmet wobbles, my boots are the wrong size, I can't find a way to stop my rifle dangling off my elbow. It's hot. I haven't slept. I've had nothing to eat.

Thump!

Some underling shoves me through the door of a hospital ward and hurries away. As he runs I hear him shouting viciously. Nurses bustle but ignore me. I wait. I lie down on a bed. When I wake it's afternoon. Food arrives. When it gets dark, I open the sheets and get in.

In the morning my suitcase is by my bed.

It feels essential that I don't look round but I can hear there are other boys in the ward, I've no idea how many. They're talking Afrikaans so I can't understand what they're saying. They take no notice of me. I've no sense at all of how big the ward is.

Breakfast arrives. I don't eat anything. I have to pee. This is the moment of crisis. Honestly now, this is crazy. Am I going to continue with this for ever? I go on staring at the corrugated ceiling. I really have to pee.

On the way back from the latrine, I fall over. I lie on the ground. Someone has to do something. Perhaps no one will? Ever. Then what do I do? If I stand up, it's over. I can't think of anything. A nurse comes out, a black woman in a green uniform. She gently helps me up.

'Shame . . . Shame . . .'

Yes, I am sort of ashamed of what I'm doing but I'm in over my head. She guides me to my bed and abandons me.

Over the next few days I become so expert that when I fall, even crashing down onto concrete, I hardly feel anything. The boys in the ward, hard-muscled young farmers who are actually ill – though what *is* real in this hall of mirrors? – take pride in keeping their eyes skinned

'Oh, look, Dave's on his feet, is it going to happen? My god, look, there he goes!'

and catching me before I hit the deck. There's not much else to do apart from boisterous flirting with the white nurses and masturbation.

No doctor visits me. Nurses enquire

'And how are you doing today?'

and that's it.

My suitcase was full of books. I have a clear, well-focused middle-distance image of myself lying in a rusty steel-frame bed reading the Penguin Classics two-volume edition of *War and Peace*.

In the evenings the boys would gather round my bed and describe their astounding sex lives.

'By us, Dave, take my word, it's *poes en piel*, cock and cunt, rain or sunshine, every day, every damn day.'

'So how are you surviving in here?'

Snake eyes dart round the room, mocking lips, tiny adjustments of the head meaning 'Fuckin' imbecile question . . .' meaning 'Ask the fuckin' nurses, man, they'll tell you how we boys deal with this situation . . .'

Has anyone told Ma and Dad I'm ill? On the way to the latrine I'd spotted a pay phone. Every day I planned to call them

'Ignore whatever the army told you. I'm ok, honestly'

but I was afraid the line was bugged. I could write but what if my letters were steamed open? Which was, yes, paranoia but I'd had no contact with anyone official. I'd no idea what authority thought about what was happening to me.

One afternoon two wounded soldiers are wheeled in and surrounded by high screens. In the real world, a thousand miles away, a secret war was escalating. South West Africa, held illegally by South Africa as a colony, is fighting for independence. To the north in Angola three armies struggle to throw out the Portuguese. China backs the FNLA, Moscow the MPLA and Richard Nixon's State Department finances UNITA. For them, the prize was Angola's gargantuan reserves of oil and minerals. For South Africa the priority was defending its borders from the *swart gevaar*, the threat of blacks taking power. My farmer friends warned me that as soon as my cohort had completed its basic training

'You'll be sent up to South West, man. Then, my god, you'll get fucked up so good like you never in a million years can even begin to imagine the possibility of getting fucked up so bad as that.'

As the days go by, more wounded are brought in. The ward hears rather less of cucumber-sized pricks and how sex increases your brain power.

'I can prove it. Ask me any question, Mr Brain Box, I'll tell you the answer, ask me anything.'

The young doctor sent to care for the wounded finally notices me. He's short, wiry, blond, his sweet weak face deep lined with tiredness, his blue eyes shot with red. He drops into my bedside chair, stares into my face like he's trying to see right through and out the other side.

'So you're the useless fuck who's wasting a bed.'

He glances at my medical chart then shows it to me. It's blank but my backing group provide a commentary.

'Every time he stands up, doctor, he just falls over flat. Every time, every time. We're all so worried about him.'

They're serious about it but they're giggling. He takes my pulse but he's not interested in that, he's shutting the others out, creating a circle of intimacy.

'Boy, what's going on, hey? Don't risk arsing about. You've got one chance and only one. You can speak softly but you have to tell me.'

I say nothing. I'm praying he doesn't pull back the sheets and find gripped between my knees the Penguin Classics edition of *War and Peace*.

In the evening he brings me a Coke, sits on the bed, looks me hard in the face for a while and then begins.

'Ok, so I did the research, I'll tell you what's happening here. A year back at this camp two of your kind—'

English speakers? Jews? Queers?

'—complained they were being driven too hard by their commanding officer. They reported sick. Their sergeant is trained to ignore sissies' moaning so he sent them on a march with heavy packs. It was a hot day, unusually so, or that was the sergeant's excuse. Heat stroke. *And* he left them lying in the sun. What else could occur but acute dehydration and then the inevitable?'

One of the boys has sneaked up and been listening.

'But what happened to the sissies, doctor? Did they pass over to the other side?'

The doctor glares at him but won't be persuaded to say the D word. He turns back to me.

'Which is why they're not so keen to take risks with types like you.'

After a week I'm summoned. I dress. A soldier guides me through a part of the camp that's luxuriant, avenues of tall green, palm-like trees. We reach a concrete block. I'm led into a high, wide, almost empty room. There's one small desk behind which, huddled together,

sit three elderly uniformed men. Another with a typewriter on his
lap glances at me.

'Engels or Afrikaans?'

'English, sir.'

'Are you Lan?'

'Yes, sir.'

'L – A – N?'

'Yes, sir.'

'Are you Chinese or what?'

'No, sir.'

The elderly soldiers mutter amongst themselves. One writes on a
card and hands it to the typist.

'Alright, Lan, go.'

Which means?

'Get out!'

I leave the room. The soldier's there.

'Come.'

But where to?

'To where you were fuckin' put when you fuckin' arrived in this
shithole.'

I've no idea about that – or about anything.

'Where am I bloody supposed to take you then, fuckwit? Ok, ok.'

We traipse all over the camp. I'm guessing, I was only ever out-
doors for half a day, but I think I recognise my dormitory.

'You have to return every fuckin' piece of kit. Get on with it!'

It was all there in my locker except the helmet that my sergeant had
hurled into the air. If I can't find it, will they keep me here for ever?

There's no one in the dormitory. On a bed down the other end I see
a helmet. Is it the right type? Who cares? I steal the helmet and then
see on a bed in a far corner two soldiers sleeping in each other's arms.
Or perhaps they're not asleep. Or perhaps there's only one of them.

'What the fuck are you staring at? Who are you? Does that belong to you? Then why stick it in your kitbag?'

I shove the helmet on my head, calmly gather my things, hand in every item of kit, get a receipt, get an exit chit, fetch my suitcase from the ward. My old friends want to hug me goodbye but I can't let them, who knows who's watching?

At the front gate

'Which way to the train station?'

The guard indicates.

'How far?'

'In a jeep twenty minutes.'

'Is there a jeep I can get a lift in?'

Too long a pause.

'What exactly are you asking? Are you not supposed to be leaving? If you were, there'd be a transport arranged for you.'

I flash my chit and set off down the track. I walk. And walk. And for the first time in weeks I don't fall over. And every moment I think

'This is obviously a trick, they're hiding behind trees, when they see I'm ok they'll pounce. If I don't fall over, they'll know it was all acting, I'm a damn fine actor, they'll arrest me, haul me back, they'll send me to South West Africa and I'll die there.'

The train station is deserted. By some compression of time, it's still very early morning. Late in the evening a train draws in.

I walk into our house. Ma's in the kitchen, having her breakfast cup of coffee, reading. All the way walking up the road from the station I'd rehearsed

'So, Ma, did you and Dad enjoy the movie?'

She puts down her book, *Setting Free the Bears* by John Irving.

'You're back? You didn't write. You promised me you would.'

I go up to my room. I unpack my suitcase. I try to stop acting.

You grow up looking at one particular tree outside your house. It's your tree. For you it is 'tree'. Your sky is 'sky'.

Later in life your tree, your sky appear in the songs you write or in your dreams. They're your place in the world and you can't think of them without being at some deep level 'you'.

Some people find they're also deeply who they are in the shade of other people's trees, bathed in the light of other skies. They are the free.

Angels

1998

Jonathan Dove calls.

'I've been asked to write an opera on the theme of Tobias and the angel. Do you know the story? It's in the Apocrypha. I don't know if you've written a libretto but I wonder if you'd like to write this one for me?'

He played me the love duet from *The Cunning Little Vixen*. Two foxes meet, fall in love, settle down and have children in one page of quick-fire dialogue.

'I'd like a libretto like that, please.'

He set to music what I wrote except for one section I reworked over and over until words appeared for the themes he was already hearing. As Tobias arrives on the crest of a mountain, the mountain sings

'*Nothing. Nothing. Nothing. Nothing.*'

And he asked for three extra lines, each of seven syllables with the rhythm

dee dee, dee dee, dee dee DUM

If you write a play you write your own music. A librettist is the magician's assistant. Your job is to create a strong structure – start the story *here, this* should happen before *that,* end *there* – and to keep the dialogue as simple as possible but no simpler.

A 'church opera' for combined forces of professionals and amateurs, the Almeida Theatre produced *Tobias and the Angel* at Christ Church Highbury in Islington.

A youth (*tenor*) goes on a journey over high mountains. In the course of his travels (*adult chorus*) he overcomes many obstacles including a giant fish (*children's chorus*), he exorcises a devil (*baritone 1*) who has possessed his future wife (*soprano*) and he gains the knowledge he needs to heal his blind father (*baritone 2*). He is able to do all this only because he receives unexpected help from a stranger who turns out to be an angel (*counter tenor*).

Teaching: we rely on well-meaning strangers to help us find our way.

November 1999

The room is shaped like a shoebox and cluttered with battered desks, wobbly chairs, a row of swamp-coloured filing cabinets over *there*, piles of scripts on the floor over *here*, posters on walls, charts spattered with stickers and annotations.

Sitting at a small circular table, L to R, are Jenny MacIntosh, elbows on table, knees tucked in, Patrick McKenna, seat pushed back and angled enhancing his perspective, Martin Smith, chair of board, relaxed, leading this job interview, Katie Mitchell, seat at right angles to table, facing me four-square.

Martin begins.

'You do understand that, were you to be given this job, you would find that it consists of many parts? Three primarily. To direct productions, of course, though it will be a matter of discussion how many of those you do. Then, to run the theatre from a practical perspective, I don't mean administratively, I mean executively and, of course, artistically. And, finally, and I mean finally in two ways, both in terms of my remarks but also in terms of our various attempts to achieve a positive result with regard to the appalling state of this building, to get it *refurbished* or, to put it more strongly and, naturally, depending on how much money can be raised, at least in part by you, *rebuilt*. This is clear to you?'

'It is.'

January 2000

Each morning I bicycle from Westbourne Park to Waterloo, a dew-bright journey, slightly downhill, through three parks, the glory of the city. As I begin to take the measure of this job, the cycle home, slightly uphill, becomes more than I enjoy late every evening. The janitor of the flats behind the theatre spots me looking for a parking place for my little white car. He kindly offers that for £5 a day I can park in their driveway if I'm careful to pull in neatly against the wall.

One morning a scrawny muscle man howls

'Why the fuck d'you think *you* can park over there, hey, mister, I'm *talking* to you?'

'I've an arrangement with your janitor.'

'That so? Pay him cash in hand, do you?'

'Yes, why.'

'What's he look like?'

'Big guy, face like a potato.'

'Oh him. Bleeding chancer. *I'm* the jannie of this property!'

'Then who's been getting my money?'

'Get your car *away*! Watch what happens if I see you about here again.'

March 2000

A friend calls to say he's seen an Arts Council list of priority the-atres. We're not on it.

'Is this a setback or a disaster?'

'What do you want me to say? It's obviously not good.'

When I don't know what to do, I have three angels I can ask for help. First, Nick Starr, executive director of the National Theatre and regular Sunday-morning badminton partner. Second, my old Royal Court Theatre boss Stephen Daldry, now directing movies but still an occasional Saturday-night clubbing partner. Third, Nicholas Wright, *my* Nick, ex-artistic director of the Theatre Upstairs and the Royal Court, playwright, director, literary manager of the National Theatre and my long-term boyfriend. Stephen would say

'Don't ask me, ask your Nick and do whatever he tells you.'

Sorted.

May 2000, The Room

The fabric of the building, the wiring, the plumbing are all in such a poor state the borough wants to shut us down. One night, mid-show, rain drains in through the roof fusing a lighting board. The backstage areas and offices are squalid, sweltering in summer, in winter impossible to warm. Years later, a senior officer of the Arts Council told me

'Until recently, if a bulldozer had gone down your street and razed your theatre to the ground, no one in this organisation would have shed a tear.'

I hadn't known things were as rough as that. Even so, it was clear we needed to build an argument as to why our theatre should survive.

Most theatres are two rooms. *There's* the place for the audience, a single tier of seats, raked more or less steeply, or many tiers – two, three, four – stacked one atop another. And *here's* the stage, or the 'stage house' as architects like to call it thereby including the wings, the backstage areas, all the unseen territories.

Our theatre is one room.

It's a room shared by everyone, actors and audience in easy reach of each other. At its heart is the original 1970s concreted-in thrust stage with fixed tiers for an audience of four hundred on three sides including a tier above cradling two rows. This works fine on many occasions but our room's wondrous proportions, derived from Leonardo's *Vitruvian Man*, really start to sing when used *against* the built-in thrust but *with* the underlying architecture, say, fully in the round or with a traverse stage cutting through or in the infinite number of other shapes and configurations that tumble into the mind once you forget (in practice, *build over*) the concrete that's inherited from the past. If you think of our room as a 'found space', events occur, stories take shape, discoveries are made as if by happenstance.

Room as mind.

Standing at the entrance, I'd say to directors and designers

'Imagine no one's ever thought to perform a show here. How would you use the room? For starters, *where would you put the stage?*'

In recent times many shows seen at YV had been produced by other companies and designed to tour to two-room theatres with prosceniums. The potential of our single room was unrealised. So a first decision was 'no more imports'. We have to take control of our repertoire, which means produce, or at least co-produce, all our shows. But we don't have anything like enough money to do this.

And then . . .

Obviously we need and love playwrights, I'm one myself, but no theatre in London was focusing on directors – and as I'd barely directed anything I, for one, needed to learn, so it made easy sense to decide to think about directing collectively. Even so, we'll not be the cliché of what the Germans call a 'directors' theatre', *Regietheater*. We'll be an actors', writers', directors', designers', audience's neighbourhood theatre plugged into the world. Or at least we'll give that a try and see how it goes.

December 2000

Dick Bird's cross-cutting diagonal stages for *The Three Musketeers* slice through the space like crossed swords. The fights swirl around the young audience's ears. I persuade the *Evening Standard* to send a photographer.

'Ok, let me get this straight. You brought me down here to take a picture of a returns queue?'

'I'm so sorry, you're quite right, I got over-excited.'

Our handsome d'Artagnan poses in his jaunty hat. He makes page six. So, Mr or Ms Arts Council, in what sense is this theatre not a priority?

February 2001

For *Six Characters Looking for an Author*, Richard Jones wants to make the auditorium feel like a small Italian opera house. Our bench seats are humped into storage. The audience perch on gilt chairs and the angle of the seating rostra swivels by a small amount, just enough to disorientate everyone.

'Where's the main door into the auditorium gone exactly?'

At a fundraiser I call the YV

'The only great theatre built in London in a hundred years.'

'And the Cottesloe?' sings out Stephen.

Oh, ok, yeah, thanks, that's helpful.

Spring 2001

Jude Law says he'd like to play Doctor Faustus in Marlowe's play.

> *Philosophy is odious and obscure.*
> *Both law and physic are for petty wits.*
> *Divinity is basest of the three,*
> *Unpleasant, harsh, contemptible and vile.*

'Tis magic, magic that hath ravished me.

Yes, he probably *is* too young for it but when we did *'Tis Pity She's a Whore* together he was spectacular and he brings such gladness of heart and lightness of spirit to everything he does. I reread the play. It seems a cathedral with some of the walls fallen in. Do you play it with a large cast or as a one-man show? And how to do Helen of Troy?

Is this the face that launched a thousand ships?

It's such a snippet of a part will a good actress accept it? Or do you use a video image? Or cut it? It's all too difficult. I can't direct this play.

The Lottery awards us £250,000 to develop ideas for a new building. We convert a quite large toilet into a conference room. We launch an international design competition. Steve Tompkins wins. He and his team (Roger Watts, Toby Johnson) spend weeks listening to actors, directors, designers, technicians, audience, our staff, our neighbours and after some months they distil it into a model that has beauty, boldness, authority, informality, wit.

Early summer 2001

In France, in the sun. I'm reading *Doctor Faustus* one more time before calling Jude and jacking it in.

Ok, so what if it's an empty stage, the only thing on it a wooden chair that can be used in many ways and . . . it has a high back which . . . flips over revealing a mirror and Faustus sees his *own* face, which happens to be the face of the world's most angelic young actor and *there* suddenly Helen of Troy *is*.

But the real problem is this. Acts 1, 2 and 5 are hard to understand but when you track your way across the speed bumps of the language, Faustus' wrestling with conflicting conceptions of power and knowledge feels modern and monumental. But Acts 3 and 4 seem scrappy. Why, once the devil has given Faustus power over the whole cosmos does he fool about teasing popes and eating peaches? I don't get it.

Jude and I meet David Mamet at a Soho hotel.

'Would you be interested in writing us two new acts?'

'Don't say another word. Honestly, no, no, no. I'll do it. One hundred per cent. And if I tell you, if I say, if I buy into, if I commit, to the both of you, not only Jude, who I adore, you get what I'm saying?, but to you too, both of you, to your theatre, to deliver, say, Tuesday, Tuesday just as a for example, then Tuesday I will deliver. It's so, so *clear* I can't tell you how formed, how *clear* in my mind it is, already, this idea, *clear*, like that, right away, ba boom. You have dates for this?'

We do.

'No fuckin' way could this be better. I'm committed. It's a great, great idea, my friends, and I'm your man.'

Long before Tuesday, he called.

'You know what, unbelievable, I've a better idea.'

'No, please—'

I foolishly don't say

'—we *have* a great idea. We don't need—'

'I'm going to write you a new play. A new work, one hundred per cent original but with its toes in that great original material. It'll be terrific for your theatre, believe me, my friend. It's *clear* in my mind, the whole narrative, I can see it all, and you know what?, the moment I woke up this morning I started writing.'

So, great! 'We're doing a new play by David Mamet.' Though, also, occasionally 'But we really like the Marlowe.'

So, also great! We'll do the two plays in repertoire.

Ba boom.

Late summer 2001

What will our 'capital project' cost? After other recent theatre rebuilds, how much cash is still out there?

Patrick McKenna, now our board chair, agrees that on the build itself we can spend £7 million – but when you add consultants' fees, rent of temporary offices etc., closing/re-opening costs and so on, you need £5 million on top of that. So it's £12 million altogether.

The Arts Council sends a consultant round to tell us that we should lay off everyone and rehire when we reopen. We've only just built a strong team but, even if we hadn't, obviously we don't want to do this. A theatre company *is* its people.

'Dear Jude, will you be patron of our fund-raising campaign?'

'Dear David, I've been coming to your theatre since I went to school at Alleyn's in Dulwich down the road. I'd be delighted.'

Stephen says

'At a time like this when you need to raise lots of cash you should do comedies. How long since you read *Rookery Nook*?'

The new *Faustus* play doesn't arrive. Meantime it has occurred to me that, if we're doing both plays, I need to figure out what to do about Marlowe's two scrappy acts. I reread and after a while, to my surprise, they stop seeming so scrappy . . .

I call Mamet's agent. I get the intern.

'Who? How do you spell that? L-a-m and afterwards? Oh. Ok, David's intensely busy just now. I don't want to blow smoke up your ass but, you know what, if I get a moment, and I may over the next coupla days, if it looks like it may be copacetic I'll put it to him. He does know about this? Tell me again the name of your movie – uh, play?'

September 2001

Rufus Norris directs *Afore Night Come* by David Rudkin which is set in a pear orchard. Ian McNeil's design is strings of lightbulbs looping down to suggest rows of trees laden with fruit. Rain will pour through burning lightbulbs which therefore must be watertight. A glassblower in Italy promises to design and deliver them by our first preview.

It's the first preview. No lightbulbs. Our head of lighting flies to Italy, flies home with a large wooden crate.

Ralph Koltai, *doyenne* of theatre designers, calls it

'One of the great conceptual designs of the last fifty years.'

At the *Evening Standard* Awards Rufus wins Best Newcomer.

The new play arrives. Is Mamet's *Edmond* the best play of its generation? Possibly. But this new Faust play is talky, abstract and, as far as I can tell, pointless. The part for Jude, then thirty, is a middle-aged Harvard philosophy don.

I'm standing on a patch of waste ground behind the theatre. I hesitate – perhaps the play isn't *that* terrible . . .

'Mr Mamet is entirely in the middle of an extraordinarily complex rehearsal process but, yes, he is expecting your call and will likely come to the phone momentarily.'

I tell him we're not doing his play. He screams at me.

March 2002

Jude plays Doctor Faustus in the play by Christopher Marlowe. Richard McCabe plays Mephistopheles.

In the next Lottery round we receive the maximum £5 million. So now there's just £7 million to find . . .

Late 2002

A speech to the National Endowment for Science, Technology and the Arts.

'What we hope for is a theatre that replicates the experience one can have at certain, long-established street markets. A pound of cherries is weighed, tumbled into a packet, the price is paid. Then the stall-holder tosses in an extra handful.

'That's the feeling we're after. A gift creates a special kind of relationship because what goes around comes around, call it good karma, call it enlightened self-interest, call it generosity.

'State theatres built of marble proclaim: these relationships are eternal, this is how the world *is*. As did our Victorian commercial theatres. The rich and powerful enter through ornate portals and sit close to the stage. The poor troop in round the back, climb uncarpeted stairs and watch from high up, safely out of the way.

'Hard-wired into the design of our theatre will be the belief that everyone is of equal value, that nothing and no one is here for ever. The proportions will be humane, the materials elemental – wood, glass, metal, stone. They splinter, they wear, they rust, they can be replaced, as we all can, as we all will be.'

July 2003

The set Ultz designs for Richard Jones' production of *Hobson's Choice* shows Hobson's draper's establishment on two levels – *there's* the shop and, underneath it, *there's* the workshop in the basement of the building. Our whole auditorium is hoisted up and turned into a rather bland village hall while the stage itself is raised so high that the actors enter through a doorway that usually leads onto the upper audience level.

Act 3 centres round a wedding. The audience leave the theatre and cross the street. The wedding scenes are played on the stage of a nearby church hall. Then we all return to the theatre for the final scenes.

Summer 2003

Energised by a hugely generous gift from Patrick, we've raised £5 million from trusts and foundations. We hold a press conference.

Jude launches a public campaign for the £2 million we still need. Meantime our Board has accrued sufficient confidence in the whole enterprise to let us commission the building.

April 2004

For Luc Bondy's production of *Cruel and Tender*, adapted by Martin Crimp from Sophocles, co-produced with the Vienna Festival and the Chichester Festival Theatre, we've rearranged the auditorium so that the stalls rise up to join the circle in a single tier. We've reconfigured the theatre in a dozen ways but never yet like this.

After the final performance I make a speech.

'Hello. Thanks to absolutely everyone. Goodbye. We'll be back shortly.'

We have a party and hand out sledgehammers but don't manage to knock down much of the building.

2004/2006

While our theatre is being rebuilt we continue to receive our grant from the Arts Council which just covers the salaries of our full-time team but with no theatre of our own in which to produce we can't earn anything through the box office and all our fundraising is aimed at the campaign for the new building. We've no money to produce shows – but if we're not producing shows, why should anyone believe in us enough to donate to our campaign? And anyhow, we're a theatre company, producing shows is what we do.

While trying to figure that out . . .

We realise our builder doesn't grasp our architect's intentions or even, to an alarming degree, the detail of his design. What they do understand they're not in sympathy with.

'Surely this tatty old brick wall will be plastered over, so what does it matter if we scrawl all over it in indelible ink?'

No, it's a gorgeous palimpsest the patina of which expresses the long, complex existence of this simple but sturdy and now repurposed edifice. Great theatres exude the scent of history.

When I'd briefly met Stuart Lipton, then chair of the Commission for Architecture and the Built Environment, he'd generously said

'If you have any problems, here's my number, call me.'

So I go and see him and he says

'I have just one question. Is it a tidy site?'

'Oh, interesting. No, actually, it's chaotic. They leave tools and other equipment all over the place. And they never hit targets. They seem to take pride in missing them.'

He leads me over to the window of his central London studio.

'So many buildings. Big ones, small ones. Can you see even one that isn't finished?'

'Oh, interesting. No, actually.'

November 2005

Kindly organised by a city banker on our board, we hold a fundraiser at the Bank of England in a palatial, plushly papered meeting room. Heading off down a cavernous corridor in search of somewhere to pee, I run into who else but the Governor himself Mervyn King.

Unaccustomed as perhaps he was to coming across folk, even after hours, wandering his precinct not only sans suit and tie but clad in black trainers and black jeans, his follow-up to answering my opener 'Where's the gents?' is

'And who are you?'

'We're in the room across the way there holding a fundraiser for a theatre.'

'And what's your role in this?'

'I'm artistic director.'

'And what kind of theatre would this be?'

'A small one in Waterloo, not too far away, it's almost your local.'

'And the purpose of your fundraiser, would I be correct in surmising, is to supplement such monies as you receive from the government, is that it?'

'Well, yes, that's it but also, as it happens at the moment, to refurbish the building.'

'If I had my way the government wouldn't give a red cent to any of you.'

And off he went.

February 2006

Paul Russell, my technical director, asks for a meeting. The planning team gathers. Our new building will have two studio theatres as well as the rejuvenated four-hundred-seater which can now achieve even *more* configurations.

'In terms of design in the new building, is there anything to which we will say no?'

An interesting question. Our policy has been that we never say 'no'. And we never compromise, though we may reconceive. If you can't achieve Plan A, you certainly don't want Plan B, you need to come up with parallel Plan A.

Inevitably it has been tough for his team, endlessly treating our auditorium as a 'found space', virtually building a new theatre for almost every show. But what does he want me to say? He knows our mantra

'Let the artist lead.'

'Maximum artistic risk, minimum financial risk' is another.

No, his real question is

'With three auditoria, are you and Kevin (Fitzmaurice, my executive director) aware of the resource we'll need to make the new building sing?'

Well, yes, or possibly no, but can we ever allow our new theatre to teach us the one word we've always resisted?

'So we say no to nothing? Is that it?'

March 2006

The artist Clem Crosby has created a series of 126 oil paintings to be installed behind a metal mesh on the facade of the main auditorium. We think it's the biggest studio painting in the world. Possibly.

Clem says

'From afar the theatre is a shimmering silver facade but on closer inspection the subtle language of the paint becoming apparent through the mesh encourages a double reading. At night the paintings become the main focus. I knew they had to work within the visual noise of Waterloo. When creating them in my studio I had no intention of matching them up in any preconceived order.'

I'm finishing a quick chat on my phone with Kevin about sales for the first season and about to watch a new play at Battersea Arts Centre. He gets a call on his other line.

'Kev, I have to go, it starts in a minute.'

'Hang on a tick. Now don't worry about this, there's nothing for you to do. Steve says the bloody builders have left two crates of Clem's paintings outside in the street and there's no security.'

I call Steve. He says

'I've been down to the site, called, banged, yelled. Don't worry, I'll go down later and sleep next to them.'

In the cab, I get through to the site manager at his home.

'Yeah, well, I accept it's not desirable but there was no room for the crates actually on site and, after all, the panels are insured.'

I too call, bang, yell. I so don't want to sleep with the paintings but I can't let Steve do it. At last the guard emerges from his tiny caravan.

'Of course I've been here all the time. No, I didn't hear anyone shouting, that must have been when I was patrolling inside the building. Yes, of course, I'll keep an eye on the crates right through the night especially as there've been four break-ins over the last week. It's all good, I'm doing my job, no need for you to worry about anything . . .'

Blog: August 2006

'Over the two years the YV has been closed we've co-produced twenty-four shows that played all over the world in thirty-one cities. We've learned many lessons from and with our many co-producers. The key learning is the value of collaboration, the search for mutual advantage – "what do I want to produce that I can persuade you you want to produce with me." Treating each other as our strongest resource is the future – is, in fact, everything.

'When we closed our old building, we produced *Tobias and the Angel* in St John's Church, Waterloo. Now we're doing it again in a more ambitious production to open our new theatre. Having more than a hundred of our neighbours, old and young, on our stage alongside professionals in this our first show is the most powerful way we can think of to say to the world

'"This theatre is yours as well as ours."

'Experts on "community shows" advise that the strongest performance is always the first one so we're opening to the press without any previews, which is of course quite a challenge.

'As to the building itself, there's a burglar-alarm test tomorrow morning at six-thirty. As of now, some of the doors haven't had their safety catches screwed on yet. Does that mean we won't be able to do the test? Does it matter? None of us on the YV team have ever done anything like this before. Learning, learning.

'All performances of *Tobias* are sold out but many seats have gone to those who helped with the rebuild and people with freebies sometimes (frequently) don't show up. Will the opening performance be half-empty?

'Another thing that's gone wrong is that I forgot to write this blog and now it's seriously overdue. At least *that's* taken care of.'

September 2006

According to our technical designers, the only buildings more complicated than theatres are hospitals. To ensure that our electricity supply is adequate to run all our systems, they must all be tested at the same time: the air handling, the theatre lighting, the sound system . . . The procedure is: turn every power source to maximum then boil a kettle, see what blows.

The most effective way to do this is to put on a show. We ask the *Tobias* company to take part in a cabaret. Our head of lighting's brother is a close-up magician. We discover that one of the guys employed to paint the outside of the building plays the guitar rather beautifully so he's roped in to sing a song he's written.

Pupils from Johanna Primary School with whom we've worked for years have made a short film *The Young Vic: Our Favourite Place*. We show it because we all find it moving but also to test our new projectors and screen. In the middle of everything, the fire alarm goes off – as planned, we're testing that too. Evacuated into the street while, as it happens, it's drizzling, the audience grin as though even this is a special treat.

October 2006

We're a week from opening. The building looks great, sunlight bouncing off the contrasting surfaces. Our cafe's been open three days. People actually wander in off the street and order coffee and then actually drink it.

The *Sitzprobe* for *Tobias* is happening, the first time cast and orchestra try out the whole score together. The room is bursting with ten actor/singers, twelve instrumentalists, forty in the adult chorus, sixty young people who sing the birds and the giant fish and the river, Jonathan Dove composer, David Charles Abell conductor, John Fulljames director, Ben Wright choreographer, Alex Lowde designer. It sounds momentous and glorious.

Late into the night, John and his lighting designer Bruno Poet are in the auditorium plotting cues ahead of tomorrow's first technical rehearsal. When I go in, just a few lamps are burning. They're playing about making large lemon splodges on our newly painted earth-red walls.

That afternoon we'd invited theatre people from all over London to tour the new building. I'm nodding and smiling

'Oh, do you think so? Yes, isn't it?'

but thinking

Isn't it time to give someone else a turn at running this joint? I think I've done enough of this.

11 October

Opening. Steve goes round with a tiny paintbrush touching up everything. Various people comment

'Aren't you a bit previous? It's still a building site.'

'Ah, no, this is what it's meant to look like.'

The audience of four hundred are gathered in the foyer, we're twenty minutes from speeches, the fan that inflates the giant fish has died. Someone conjures up two more, neither with enough power to inflate the damn thing.

'Does it work yet?'

Now a microphone used in the show is on the blink. It's only needed for two moments but we can't start speeches till it's fixed.

'Ok it's working.'

I'm out in the foyer about to clink wine glasses. We get a radio message, the monitors that the chorus need to be able to see the conductor have gone down. Oh, hang on a minute, someone unplugged them. They're plugged back in.

Speeches.

Peter Brook and Jude Law cut a ribbon.

We all troop in.

It begins.

I watch two minutes and come out for a drink . . .

It's over.

Applause. Curtain calls. Jonathan the composer and John the director take a bow as do I the librettist. We leave the stage. House lights up. They're still clapping. The audience is on its feet. The cast come back on. More curtain calls. The cast leave and the stage is empty. The applause goes on.

Standing to one side, I realise that if I were now to walk into the centre of the stage, the audience will go quiet. They'll sit down again. Then I can say something. Then the audience will get back on its feet. It's not rehearsed but I'm confident that the lighting operator will know what to do and bring a light up on me. I have to choose exactly the right moment.

The moment is coming . . .

It's almost here . . .

Go now.

Go now.

Go!

Now!

I stay where I am.

'Nothing. Nothing. Nothing. Nothing.'

Two

Scene Changes

Some directors will tell you that what they like best about directing is the scene changes. It's a neat way of cutting through the claptrap, aesthetic or quasi-political. And it gets an easy laugh. '*They* may think they're going to change the world, *I'm* going to change the scenery.' Perhaps it's a relief to an audience to be told

'Relax, nothing that ensues will be hard to take. Theatre, above all, is craft. *Stand by, two, three*' – lights dim, stage revolves, a dark-clad stagehand hurries on to place a glove on a chaise-longue – '*four seconds and five . . .* Lights up!'

Where is meaning in theatre? Is meaning the cheese in the toasted sandwich? Or is it a three-course meal? Is it the raw materials? Who was it that grew the wheat or tended the lamb, how were they paid, how did the food arrive on your plate, in what style is it cooked and how served, who's serving it, who's paying for that, who's at the table and who isn't and why aren't they?

I sometimes think stage design should be taught as a branch of philosophy.

Realistic design in grand opera conventionally consists of palaces, prisons, pavilions built of granite, marble, steel. Great love will end in death, the stronger the love the more inevitable the disaster, nothing can prevent it, that's how the world is. But an empty stage is never empty of meaning. The platform on which the Isango Ensemble of Cape Town play is heavy, wooden, steeply raked. They hump it along wherever they tour and it's worth the effort. Before a word is heard it declares 'We make our own meanings, we control our own destinies.'

In scene 10 of *A Streetcar Named Desire* there's a feverish party. Tensions that have built up over months erupt. Stanley assaults Blanche. The room is a wreck. Curtain. Scene break, during which stagehands (bump, bump) reset the scenery. Curtain up on the final scene. '*It is some weeks later.*' The room is as it was at the start of the play.

In our production of *Streetcar*, directed by Benedict Andrews, designed by Magda Willi, there was no stage curtain. All through the show Stanley's apartment slowly revolved with the audience looking in on it from all sides. After the assault, all the actors in the company trooped on stage. Silent, respectful, they swept up, reached down torn paper lanterns, emptied dustbins, remade beds. 'Our community is implicated in whatever violence took place, we can help restore order but we can't influence what happens after that.' Then they departed. Those who remained went on with the play.

Four-fifths of the way through Sam Gold's production of *Fun Home*, designed by David Zinn, a bare white wall flies out and we see for the first time in detail the house into which Bruce has poured all the love that might otherwise have gone into his relationships with his wife and children. Then all the actors enter and fold what had seemed to be solid walls in on themselves, leaving Bruce in a massive black emptiness – the depression in which he will, at last, throw himself in front of a speeding truck.

In our adaptation of *Wild Swans*, Jung Chang's autobiographical history of China in the twentieth century, director Sacha Wares and designer Miriam Buether suggested the tortuous progression of forty years of revolution by designing the show's five acts in discordant styles. A chorus of workers effortfully, bodily lugged the scenery about, transforming their nation and our stage.

Whatever you represent, it is your custom to represent
it in such a way
As if it were happening right now. Enraptured
The silent crowd sits in the darkness, transported
From their everyday life: [...]
[...]
What happens here, is happening
Now and just this once. [...]
[...]
Your spectator is sitting not only
In your theatre, but also
In the world.

Bertolt Brecht, *Portrayal of Past and Present in One*

Cape Town, 1970/1971

I was released from the army just in time to sign up for an arts degree and an acting course at the university, both to be completed over three years, academic lectures in the morning, acting classes in the afternoons and evenings.

Officially, you could only get into Philosophy 1 in your second year. I went to see the head of department. Blah blah blah. They let me in. J. M. Coetzee taught the modern novel – Henry James, Joseph Conrad, Graham Greene. He was so mordant and dour we knew he was special though he hadn't yet published a novel of his own. Some of us were invited to his home where we'd sit out under the vines on the veranda and talk about intersections of art and politics, for instance the meanings of the word 'labour' in 'Among School Children' by W. B. Yeats.

Labour is blossoming or dancing where
The body is not bruised to pleasure soul,
Nor beauty born out of its own despair,
Nor blear-eyed wisdom out of midnight oil.

Years later I ran into him.

'John! Good to see you! Long time. I have to say, I really loved *Life and Times of Michael K*.'

'I'm sorry, I have absolutely no memory of you.'

What we acting students were after above all else was authenticity, which was what black people had. How to get it? By going on demonstrations against the laws that caused black and 'coloured' people to be thrown out of their parts of town now declared 'for whites only', improvising on the themes of *The Caucasian Chalk Circle* with young people from 'black townships' Langa or Guguletu, arguing about which was 'the more relevant to our situation', Jerzy Grotowski's *Towards a Poor Theatre* (objections to communist Europe) or Peter Brook's *The Empty Space* (objections to capitalist Europe), eating magic mushrooms, sleeping on the beach, taking part in 'sit-in' protests against various forms of racial discrimination, trying to get your straight friends into bed and sometimes succeeding, marching through the centre of town holding up 'Down with the Bantu Education Act' placards, being chased by police into St George's Cathedral which we believed was sacrosanct but proved not to be when they invaded it and beat up some of us with batons though not too seriously, hauled some of us out into the street, arrested some under the terms of the Riotous Assemblies Act, jailed some though not for very long, some not me.

Black and white students acting together on the same stage, in the same production of *Henry V*, sharing the same dressing rooms

. . . For us, for me, that seemed authentic. But we went back to our comfortable homes while they went where? Was it *all* acting? Yes, no, possibly.

In my Italian classes, to which I paid scant attention, a single line of Dante sang out to me.

> *Tra li lazzi sorbi si disconvien fruttar*
> *Li dolci fico*

I thought it meant 'a sweet fig will never thrive among bitter fruit'. I'd repeat it to myself, seeing in it a justification for leaving the country. But my Italian was rubbish. That's not what it means.

And then Nick arrived. To visit his mum, to direct *Drums in the Night* by Bertolt Brecht and *Uncle Vanya* by Anton Chekhov but really, or so he always says, to see me. I was nineteen, he was thirty-one, burnished with flowing gold-red hair, zipped tight into a rock star's red suede jacket. He moved into the hippy house I shared with our earth-mother movement teacher Tessa Marwick, my closest friend Jud Cornell and various highly strung, anorexic, dope-smoking drama students. He and I shared a mattress on a bare floor tucked into a high bay window. Being openly gay in that country at that time – wasn't *that* authenticity?

London, 1969

This is Sussex Gardens off the Edgware Road where I rented a room in a bed-and-breakfast for the two weeks over Christmas I spent in London as a schoolboy showbiz reporter. In the jagged skyline of pebble-dashed, time-warp buildings it's hard to differentiate but I think *that one over there* is a window of the room where Nick and I first shared a bed. It was freezing, of course, and he was warm and funny and not at all insistent and, after jokes and cuddling, had no need to be. His Christmas present to me was *Ward Number Six and Other Stories* by Anton Chekhov.

'*Dear David, Happy Christmas 1969. Nicholas.*'

1972

Here just across the walkway from the Thames is the ground-floor flat in Hammersmith Nick rented when, a few days before Christmas, I came to London to live with him. *This* low-ceilinged, pine-panelled back room is where we gave a first-night party for Sam Shepard's *Geography of a Horse Dreamer* which Nick produced in the Theatre Upstairs. Lanky Sam in an eau-de-Nil T-shirt puffing at a roll-up before a wide glass window beyond which, in a tiny enclosed garden, stands a peach tree with two ripe fruit. *Here's* our stuffy front room – faded Turkish carpet, boxy beige settees – where Nick, Bill Gaskill, David Hare, David Aukin held the inaugural meeting of the Joint Stock Theatre Company.

I applied for various courses. The one I really wanted was the one I got into, a B.Sc. in Social Anthropology at the London School of Economics. It didn't start till the autumn. Lots of time to read Freud and Marx, to write plays and hang around theatres till then.

Here's where we tacked down an urgent strip of carpet backstage in the Theatre Upstairs an hour before the first ever performance of *The Rocky Horror Show*. I pass the tacks, Nick taps them in.

At the Royal Court Theatre you were either out or you were in. You could relate to the core family in many ways – as one of the informal company of frequently appearing actors, as friend of someone on the staff, as artistic friend, as friend of artistic friend, as wealthy supporter, as board member/city gent, as star, as celebrity, as intriguing guest who was as likely to be toff as riff-raff – but the only ones who mattered were the big voices of the early years:

John Osborne, Edward Bond, David Storey, Christopher Hampton. Loyalty to the first-born was everything. If they wrote a play, the Court would do it. So what if it wasn't their finest work, if few people would buy seats. Hard truths must be told about England.

On the walls of the general office hung a photograph of a jubilant Royal Court contingent on one of the anti-nuclear Aldermaston marches. Of course the Court was of the left, not communist or Worker's Revolutionary Party but muscular Labour. Socialist. So they read the torrent of new plays that tumbled in always hoping for the opinionated, the argumentative, the contrarian. With interest in your work would come waves of affection and long hours in the fug of the Royal Court Tavern and meals at Como Lario round the corner or Parsons in the Fulham Road or, if they were seriously considering producing your play, parties in comfortable South London homes with Buck's Fizz and Haydn concerti on original instruments drifting out into the drystone-walled garden or it might be Dizzy Gillespie or *Sticky Fingers*, and you'd go to all the Court press nights with film stars and movie directors and star King's Road photographers or couturiers and, occasionally, rock stars who tended to dematerialise during the first interval.

Appalling stories trickled in from foreign parts. Christopher Hampton had a play done somewhere in Germany. They paid no attention *whatsoever* to his stage directions, they cut or transposed *whole scenes* . . .

If you were twenty with no claim to attention except as a significant somebody's boyfriend, you had to keep on your toes.

'Why is *he* here? He doesn't even know who *Tony Richardson* is!'

But it was mostly crazy fun. In Patsy Pollock's always jam-packed casting office, Lindsay Anderson, frustrated by not finding an actor to play the hippy student in *Life Class* by David Storey, points at my mountainous afro.

'Patsy, darling, I don't know *why* you're not listening to me, are you listening now, *marvellous*, he should look like *that*, like him! Actually, what *about* him? Who *is* he, with the ridiculous hair? Can he act?'

Oh yes, I've studied acting, I'd love to do it, seriously.

'Can someone take a photograph? We need an actor who looks *exactly* as he does. Oh he's *Nicky's friend*, what's he doing in here? Out you go, do you mind dreadfully?'

What they adored, what you had to learn to value as deeply as they did, was the auditorium itself, the intimacy of its four hundred seats, how powerfully the human form displayed itself within the neat proscenium, how its lack of stage depth and wing space meant designers had to summon up all their inventiveness – though not *too* much as the stage was thought most elegant and effective when there was almost nothing on it. Cavaliers in their personal lives, as artists they were Puritans.

And, of course, if they rejected your play, the Court was your enemy. It could only happen because you'd been intrigued against. You felt you'd been tossed into the wilderness which, in effect, you had. There were few other major theatres to which you could take a new play.

In 1973, using a pseudonym, I sent in a short play *Painting a Wall* based on time spent during school holidays in a Cape Town theatre paint shop and received a not discouraging note turning it down. It was produced by the Almost Free Theatre in Rupert Street, Soho. I wrote another, *Bird Child*, based on my student days in the hippy house in Cape Town. Anne Jellicoe, now the Court's literary manager, took to it. Artistic director Oscar Lewenstein gave the thumbs up. Nick resigned from running the Theatre Upstairs so he felt free to direct there a play by his twenty-two-year-old boyfriend.

Romeo and Juliet

Iceland, 2003

As I walk into the long, narrow corridor of the cafe in the YV, a young, thickset, ice-blond Icelandic holds out a file of press cuttings and letters recommending a show he wants me to fly to Reykjavik to see.

'I know people have to try hard to persuade you to fly all over the world to see their shows.'

In the eighteen months I'd run YV no one had tried to persuade me to fly to any country.

'I think perhaps you've heard of the actor who wrote this letter? He was in Iceland filming. We have a major film industry, you know this? He came to our show the one evening he had free. I think you know Reykjavik is a major theatre city?'

He grins, half-mocking my provincialism, the shining tip of his tongue nipped between gleaming Viking teeth.

The arrivals hall in Reykjavik is a masterpiece of joinery. The walls, the floors, the hanging, jutting staircases are a massive puzzle box created, apparently, by piling up layer on layer of strips of pale glazed wood.

Through immigration, through customs. All I have is my shoulder bag so I'm first out through the swing doors. Where's Gisli, the director of *Romeo and Juliet*? I've no idea what he looks like. That can't be him, that can't be him . . . Ok, he's not yet here which is fine as it gives me a moment to hang about and take in that extraordinarily handsome couple snuggling against the wall, so lithe and blond and glowing, what are they, models?, film stars?

They see me eyeing them, confer, cross the hall to me.

'This is my wife Nina. She plays Juliet. Of course you know I play

Romeo as well as directing. So, welcome to Iceland! We're going to give you the best time you ever had.'

Which they did.

The long road through the night to the city is like the negative of an ancient photograph. How can there be no trees? Is that a house? It seems to be some kind of shed. But what *is* that? Is that really the coastline? Is that the sea?

'Our company has no money to pay for a hotel but you can stay in the house of one of our actors. How many nights will you be with us?, only two?, well, that's great anyway. He's sleeping with one of our other actors, I mean sharing her house, no, actually he's sleeping with her, ha ha, so he's never in his own house anyway. It's a gorgeous small place with a view of the original harbour, one of the oldest houses in town, it's made of corrugated iron, the roof, the walls, but it's quite warm. Is that all fine with you?'

They all keep horses in stables near the theatre.

'We can go out on horses tomorrow in our lunch break. You ride, don't you?'

I've ridden twice, once very briefly at a gypsy fair in Hungary and once in the Himalayas in Nepal near the Tibetan border. Going up, the angle was so acute I kept sliding out of the saddle so I climbed the mountain trudging alongside my steed mile after flinty mile. On the way down I clung to the horse's mane, cannoned up, thudded down as the unfettered beast hurtled mile after flinty mile to the bottom leaving *my* bottom a mass of bloody bruises.

They're so charmed by this story I tell them about the time slip.

'I can see my guide far up the track ahead of me then – what the fuck? – it's like a hard cut in a film, no time at all has passed and he's way down the mountain behind me. How do you explain that?'

'Tibetan magic! Amazing! You've had *such* an interesting life, and you're quite young still. Fine, we'll ride tomorrow.'

'But do we have time for this?'

'We have time for everything.'

Strolling past Hallgrímskirkja, the sky-jabbing bone-white church in the town centre, skirting the lake they call Tjörnin, the pond, you're in a play by Ibsen.

'Oh, look, there's the Mayor. Good morning, Mr Mayor, when are you coming to see our *Romeo and Juliet*? We love him, he sees all our shows. Good morning, Mr Master Builder. He's the one who's designing the apartment block we're building. You don't make much money out of theatre in this country.'

Iceland's economy is flush. These kids are entrepreneurs, go-getters, throwing off waves of positivity. I'm a mug, I acknowledge it, easily beguiled, always have been, but even knowing full well how hard they're working to get me to like them they seem to me warm, eccentric, delightful.

And so is their show. Gisli and Nina play their romantic scenes high above the stage on trapeze. *Love is in the air.* It's a circus in every shade of scarlet and crimson edged with silver and gold – clowns, fire-eaters, tumblers, jugglers, a genius acrobat child who does serial backflips. The acting is broad but has a larky sincerity. Despite all the cutting of the text and the goofy interpolations, by some rough-house legerdemain the original play is still somehow there.

It's exactly what I'm after: central repertoire directed with energy, authenticity and a deep love of the play. There are drawbacks. The ideas are brilliantly sketched but not many actually land. Despite the trapeze, it lacks lift-off. And it's in Icelandic.

'After the show, we're going drinking in a new bar sculpted entirely out of ice, the whole room is ice, you get me?, cray-zee. We're thinking of taking it over, you know, buying it. Or maybe we'll start one of our own. Will you join us?'

Obviously.

'Tomorrow we'll take you to the Blue Lagoon. You honestly cannot come all the way to Iceland and not swim there. The chemicals in the water are so health-giving.'

After the ice bar, we're in a downtown coffee shop recently opened by one of the company.

'So tell us, what do you think? You know the London theatre scene. If we take our show there, do you believe we'll succeed?'

Next day, Gisli and I are on the high roof terrace of a restaurant at the edge of town gazing at the moonscape countryside.

'Look, can you see how that road bends, there, do you see it?, right over there, ok, it's not a bend, it's more of a kink. You know why it's there?'

'No. Why's it there?'

'Because when they plan a road in this country, the engineer is careful to draw the route so they never dig in any spot where the little people live.'

Ok, so let's have a think about this.

I'm about to make my first big, mission-defining and also expensive commitment to these one-year-out-of-drama-school unknowns playing an English classic in a language no one understands and their director believes . . . ?

'But do *you*, Gisli, I mean actually you yourself . . .'

'Are you asking if I believe in the little people?'

'Yes.'

'I see. Well, I'm Icelandic.'

'Meaning?'

'Well, you've been to mystical Tibet.'

'Well, no, I haven't actually . . .'

'My friend, how can I explain this to you?'

Over the next decade I went back to Reykjavik time after time. One time, still having no spare cash for a hotel, they arrange for me to stay in a student hostel during the holidays. By then I'd done the drive from the airport so often I didn't bother to check in advance where the hostel is. As I approach the town I unfold a map and suddenly find myself on a raised motorway that winds up and around and up again. I realise I've gone wrong but the road's so narrow there's nowhere to pull over and it's still winding up and around, though at least now I've managed to pull the map open – when my mobile rings. It's Stephen so, of course, I talk to him while searching for the way, consulting the map, down the raised roadway, up another, until

'Stephen, sorry, this is idiotic what I'm doing and bloody dangerous. But don't go away.'

I shove the map on the floor, take the first turning, it doesn't matter where it leads. At last I find a verge, park, finish talking to Stephen. Right. Breathe. Think. Pull the map off the floor. So now, where I'm trying to get to is . . .

Exactly where I am. *Exactly.*

There on the far side of the street is the hostel. Outside are the actors waving at me.

'You see, you took care of us, the little people are taking care of you.'

None of them believes it, it's hilarious, they're teasing me but . . .

Is it just that I've fallen in love with all of them, the whole company, which I know (yes, I am a mug but not *that big* a mug – no, I *am* that big a mug) was their plan and they've carried it out to perfection? Well, if they've made *me* fall in love with them and their *Romeo and Juliet* . . .

'Gisli, I think we can get your show to be really good. It's really good already but we can get it even better. If we do, it will be a big success in London. The question is—'

'What is the question? Quickly, my dear, my heart is beating very fast.'

'Will you work with me on it?'

He has no hesitation, not for one heartbeat.

The Magic Flute

South Africa, 2007

I'm in Athlone, a suburb of Cape Town, in a church hall just across from where Dad's shop used to be, where as a kid I sold clothes on Saturday mornings, where a shop called 'Lan's' still is.

Music director Mandisi Dyantyis is coaching the musicians and singers

'Yis, yis, let's go, two, three!'

Mark Dornford-May, founder-leader of the Isango Ensemble, in search of a music director, heard from his wife Pauline Malefane, Isango's lead singer, about the dreadlocked young man who trains the choir at her church. Over weeks he's recreated, bar by bar, the orchestral parts of Mozart's opera for eight marimbas: two soprano, two alto, two baritone, two bass. Before these rehearsals, none of the company could play marimbas at all. Now they pound away stylishly.

In a back room, a sub-group is translating the libretto from the German line by line, humming the tunes. The original is rhymed, a literary convention no African language has. I can help with this. For three days I sit in my hotel room facing the wall using all the cribs I can download. I try to write with a Cape Town accent, putting in local references.

When Isango began seven years ago with a production of *The Mysteries – Yiimimangaliso*, fifteen hundred people from all over the country were auditioned. How hard it is to say 'no' when the likely consequence is that a family won't eat. Rehearsals must end an hour before sunset to allow time for the long bus journeys back to the 'townships' where most of the company live. Darkness brings danger and the streets are poorly lit.

Mandisi raises his pencil.

'Two, three . . .'

Simon Rattle heard a performance.

'Mozart would have been surprised and then delighted' – which captures it exactly. It takes a moment to adjust, then you grin. It's deeply touching and slightly jokey, as though the score is being made love to and at the same time gently sent up.

They finish. Whoops of pleasure. They've learned just the first half, it feels complete, a real accomplishment but

'Great, guys,' says Mark, 'now let's learn the rest of it.'

And I think

'Are you sure about this? Won't that be too much of a good thing?'

But he's right. In performance an odd thing happens. They play the first half of the overture and the audience is rapt. It reaches a climax, it sounds as though it's over, applause begins. But the music continues. Thrown off-balance, the audience suddenly gets it: this is not a gag or a pastiche. Because now the music gets more difficult and the players need real skill to carry off its bouncy poignancy. Can they sustain it? Prolonged applause and, sometimes, stamping. And when you look round the auditorium you notice few dry eyes.

What is being applauded? If the Royal Opera House chorus sang transcriptions of Xhosa or Zulu songs, would the audience be as moved? I think they would, almost, and for the same reason, the evidence that, at a profound level, we can share with strangers what matters most to us, our greatest achievements of self-awareness, self-knowledge, individually and collectively.

But Isango-style sharing has a special value. These performers come from poor people. Their audience knows this but they can't condescend to them because the artistic achievement is so high. Talent is not embedded in DNA, it's not a force that will realise itself come what may. It's a relationship – with a parent, a teacher, a friend, a book, a performance. At YV we found ways of creating such relationships with thousands of those who surrounded us. When we put our neighbours on our stage alongside leading actors and musicians, each enhanced the other's experience as well as that of their audience. Everyone's game was raised. To make shows in and for the most diverse city in the world, we needed to engage, in our own way, with 'other people' in 'other places'. Hence this Mozart with these courageous South Africans in whose company we learn each day something new about the challenges of being human. Who cares that this *Magic Flute* received a Laurence Olivier Award for Best Musical Revival? Their harmonised roar when they won gave the answer. We all do.

To co-produce across boundaries of geography, politics, language is difficult and expensive. Is it worth it?

In the church hall in Athlone they're approaching the last moments of the piece.

> *The sun has arisen*
> *Goodbye to the night*
> *The whole world is shining*
> *In glorious light*

Then comes the world-joyous final chorus. I dial my office in London and hold up my phone.

'Listen to this! Just listen to bloody this!'

A Season in the Congo

Congo, 2013

Aimé Césaire, the activist author of *Return to My Native Land*, was one of the great poets of *négritude*. I'd somehow heard about his play about Patrice Lumumba, the first democratically elected president of independent Congo, written in the 1960s, but I couldn't find a copy. Then, when I'd given up looking, I happened across it in one of those thick, themed American collections, read it and knew we had to produce it but who could direct it, who could play the leading role? It's a poetic patchwork of satire, naturalism, quasi-documentary, not all the scenes of equal quality but written with a fervour that gives it the urgency and elegance of an object in flight. And it has an answer to the mystery of who murdered Lumumba. It was the CIA, just as we always suspected. I'd read it from time to time over the years but then put it aside. It's *really* hard. One day, one day.

At the party for the last night of our *A Doll's House*, Joe Wright appears at my elbow.

'Hello. I really love your theatre. I'd like to direct a play here. Is it alright to say that?'

'Of course it is. Do you know what you want to direct?'

Big shrug, arms spread wide, hands to heaven, a cheery smile.

'Shall we have a think?'

I watched all his films. If I needed convincing, *The Soloist* did it. This gorgeously acted story of a homeless virtuoso musician living under the freeways of Los Angeles is perfectly engineered yet torrential and heartfelt. I sent him *A Season in the Congo* but at once regretted it. He'd never directed a play in the professional theatre and this one is so difficult.

I call him.

'Joe, have you read it? Ah, that was quick. Well, look, I think we should forget about it anyway. I've got another idea, there's a terrific three-hander by David Mamet that hasn't been done for a while . . .'

'Too late,' says Joe, 'I love it. I love it, I love it and if you let me do it I'll get Chiwetel Ejiofor to play Lumumba. In fact, I sent it to him and he's *extremely* keen. By the way, what are you doing this afternoon? Can you visit me in my editing suite?'

He shows me the current cut of the ball scene from his film of *Anna Karenina* choreographed by Sidi Larbi Cherkaoui.

'We'll get Larbi. He'll do it, I know he will.'

Of course, this onscreen ocean of dancing aristos is nothing like what we'd need but it's superbly achieved and anyway I know that Larbi's a great choreographer from seeing many of his works at Sadler's Wells.

Well, I always say that at YV we take leaps in the dark. And I've totally fallen for Joe's slightly pushy charm and his vast cultural reference and his larkiness and of course his expertise. And he *loves* the play.

'Ok. I'm in.'

Chiwetel tells me Oxfam have asked him to go to Congo to help draw attention to the work they do there protecting some of the hundreds of thousands who've been damaged, traumatised and displaced by the decades-long civil war. Joe's going too.

'Oh, is he? And me?'

The refugee camp Oxfam wants Chiwetel to visit is in one of the most volatile war zones, near the town of Goma in the extreme east of the country. The only way to get there is through Rwanda. We fly to the capital Kigali and drive in convoy to the border. We go so fast all you see through the window of the jeep is a blur but our route seems to be along the tidiest country road I've ever seen, perfectly tended houses and huts, brightly dressed villagers politely waving. Until the border, that is.

Some travellers, including us, are exhaustively inspected by heavily armed officers who seem to take for granted that our passports and papers will be fraudulent and interrogate them page by page. Others wander freely across beneath the crude metal archway that separates Congo from Rwanda.

On the Congo side, whole streets have been swallowed and vomited back up as hard-baked swirls of black spit. It's lava that poured down into the town when a volcano on the hillside erupted. We visitors think

'Wow, what a powerful metaphor for a war-torn country' but these weird, acute-angled rollercoasters are also actual streets and the townsfolk have to carry on their lives in a landscape that, I guess, never stops seeming like a dream.

We eat at a camp run by the United Nations High Commission for Refugees. A weary, crewcut UN officer asks

'Do you understand where you are?'

'Ummm, I kinda think I do . . .'

'You have no idea, buddy. You're in hell. This town is on the edge of the abyss.'

In the morning we drive west for an hour into the interior. The camp is on a plain between low hills. We meet the youthful Oxfam team. They guide us around, explaining how electricity for the camp is generated, how drinking water is piped in. Chiwetel is filmed and photographed looking cheerful and delighted to be there beside camp officials and then surrounded by small crowds of old people, adults, kids. It's like someone's pressed a slow-motion button on all of them. A few are willing to share details of what they experienced. Each catastrophe has a different beginning but the same end.

Some can't speak. They gaze into the far distance, into nowhere, eyes long dead, gently rocking or shaking their heads.

Some have been sheltering in the camp for most of the past year, some fled here yesterday when they had word that yet another armed militia was hastening towards their village, towards their house, towards them. Loss, loss, loss, they've all lost so many things, the most precious things, children, family, parents, everything. The rows and rows of plastic, canvas, cotton tents repeat over and over again and again, to the edge of the plain, and ascend the hills.

You think

'I've wasted my life.'

You think

'I was wrong, evil exists.'

You think

'When I get back to London, I will raise money to send these people agricultural tools, sewing machines, cloth, they need the best food and clean water obviously and the school needs books, they'll surely be here into the next harvest, they need seed.'

On the drive back, the road edges a cliff and we spot what seems to be a military lookout. We're somewhat apprehensive not to say alarmed but, hey, this is a research trip, we have to see everything. Standing on a roughly built wooden platform jutting way out over the valley you see green, green, green all the way to the far horizon. It's perfect for surveillance. There's a Y-shaped pole stuck between the planks presumably to help steady a rifle or a machine gun. This lookout has clearly been abandoned. Or has it? Chiwetel emerges from a tumbledown hut holding a camouflage jacket.

'Fuck! Let's get out of here.'

We do, Chiwetel taking the jacket which he puts on over his own clothes.

'I'll wear it in the play.'

He doesn't, as it turns out. He needs no *appliqué* of authenticity. As Lumumba he gives a performance like a cliff face. Is it an actor or is it the actual Patrice up there, great brain, great heart, struggling like a titan against a thousand enemies, seen and unseen? Joe's production is muscular, expansive, thrilling, submerging, exuberant, penetrating, raucous, violent, sensitive, mocking. Larbi's choreography fuses actors and dancers into a non-stop evocation of violence and victory and resilience in the midst of disaster. At its heart is Chiwetel's passionately bitter-sweet defence of a statesman of gigantic courage up against odds that, in the end, killed him. We travellers know that the refugees in the camp outside Goma, fifty years later, still pay the price of his defeat.

We almost made a film of it. Enough money was found for a month-long shoot in Kinshasa. And then, for one reason or another, it didn't happen. *Tant pis.*

Simply Heavenly

The US, 2003

In the final chapter of *Not Since Carrie: Forty Years of Broadway Musical Flops*, Ken Mandelbaum writes about three musicals which he believes would have been commercial successes had not fate intervened. I produced two of them: *The Human Comedy* by Galt MacDermot and *Simply Heavenly*.

The 'book' of *Simply Heavenly* is by Langston Hughes, the great poet of the Harlem renaissance. It's based on a series of newspaper articles he published in the 1940s about Jesse B. Semple, a resourceful young man, somewhat depressed by his circumstances, trying to make a life and a living in Harlem, New York City.

I couldn't find a recording online, on eBay, anywhere. I rang Upper Circle, the now defunct Covent Garden shop that specialised in musicals.

'Do you have a recording of a show called *Simply Heavenly*? Well, have you ever heard of it?'

'I'll look in the catalogue. If it ain't there it don't exist.'

It ain't there.

Ok, so perhaps it was never recorded. Would there be sheet music, I wonder? Where should I look for that? But the Upper Circle guy's still on the line.

'Don't run away. You happen to have called at exactly the right moment. There's a gentleman who comes in from time to time who knows everything there is to know about musical theatre. He's in our basement right now. I'll run down and see if he knows anything.'

Footsteps down staircase. Footsteps up staircase. Second set of footsteps up staircase.

'Yes, and who's this?'

'My name's David, I run the Young Vic.'

'But do you *do* musicals? I haven't *heard* of any, not that *recently* anyway.'

'I want to do musicals if we find the right one. Have you heard of a show called *Simply Heavenly*?'

Long pause for reflection.

'I *believe* I have that at home. I *believe* it is in my vinyl collection. I have *thousands* of musicals in my vinyl collection. I *believe* the one you're in search of is amongst them.'

'Wow! What a lucky break. Can I borrow it from you?'

'I'm afraid I *never* lend out anything due to extraordinarily *painful* experience.'

'Well, can I come and listen to it at . . . ?

'No, no, no need for that. I won't charge you more than a fiver for it. Let me take down your address. I can *picture* where the Young Vic is but tell me where it is *exactly*.'

The music by a certain David Martin was jazzy, nostalgic, brash and fabulously tuneful. On the record sleeve there was just enough information to track down an agent. I phoned. No answer. No email address. I wrote an actual letter. I heard nothing.

I was in New York for some other reason so I took time off to go and talk to the agent which wasn't easy as the numbers had fallen off all the doors in that particular run-down Lower East Side street. You had to count your way down from the corner. 197, 195 . . . 171, 173. This bell must be for 173c. Possibly.

You're buzzed at, you go in, you turn sharp right, you climb the narrow wooden stairs observing that no one's had time to sweep the floors since the 1950s. By now the steps have branched off so far to the right you must be in the next building. The landing is the size of a door mat. Five offices open off it.

'Hi there. I believe you're the agent for David Martin?'

'No, we got your letter but we didn't answer because we have no idea who that individual is.'

'Ah, ok' – showing a photocopy of the record sleeve – 'it says here that . . .'

'Hang on there just a minute, darlin'.'

She makes her way over to a filing cabinet, opens drawer after drawer, flicks adroitly through files.

'No, no, no, no and no. I'm so deeply sorry about that and about the long distance you've travelled to discover precisely nothin'.'

'But do you have any information about him?'

She folds her arms.

'Darlin', we've not had cheques in for that particular name in eighteen years. That's how long I've been here and I've no notion of who or where or even whether any such songwriter any longer exists – if he ever in reality did.'

Each song is so different from the rest that, yes, we'd wondered if the show had in fact more than one composer. Perhaps they'd devised the name 'David Martin' to represent all of them collectively?

'We've no comment to make 'bout that.'

'If he or they ever show up, we'll be delighted to come to some arrangement.'

'Darlin', what you got is a deal.'

I asked Josette Bushell-Mingo if she'd like to direct the show. She said

'I'd rather do *Antony and Cleopatra.*'

She said

'I'd much rather adapt two novels by Ben Okri.'

She said

'Well, I've booked Clive Rowe and Ruby Turner.'

The world (or at least the *Daily Telegraph*) said 'You are swept along on an irresistible wave of joy.'

It was the first show we moved to the West End.

Annie Get Your Gun

The US, 2009

The Rodgers and Hammerstein Organisation on West 28th Street also looks after all the musicals written by Irving Berlin.

'Is *Annie Get Your Gun* available?'

'We'll get back to you.'

They got back to me.

'It is.'

So I went to New York to describe to Ted Chapin, the long-time shepherd of an ever-increasing flock of masterpieces, what we're imagining.

'You know Richard Jones' work?'

'Especially *Titanic* on Broadway and his celebrated revival of *Into the Woods*. Indeed I do.'

'Of course, we won't be able to have a full orchestra. We don't have the space even if we had the money.'

'I do know your theatre.'

'Oh you do?'

'The productions these shows get, they can be great or they can be godawful but they're usually put up more or less the same as when they were first produced fifty, sixty years ago. I know, we all know they must also be seen through the lens of today. I'd go so far as to say we need, occasionally, new-style productions if they're to speak to a new generation, if they're to live.'

'Ted, it's so good to hear you say that. This will be a new-style production. For a start, our idea is to have the score played on four pianos.'

'It's a great score.'

'It's the greatest.'

'You'll need our music team's approval.'

'We'll want more than their approval. We'll want their scrutiny.'

'Who do you have for the job?'

'Jason Carr.'

'Oh, we know Jason. Good choice. He's extremely musical. And who do you have in mind for Annie?'

'Jane Horrocks.'

'Very interesting. Can she—?'

'She can.'

'Then all's well.'

'The thing about this show is every song is genius.'

'Yes, they truly, truly are. Irving never wrote better. One of his granddaughters lives round the corner from your theatre in Waterloo, did you know that?'

'No, I didn't. That's amazing! We'll get her in.'

'I'll drop her a line. She'd love to come and see it, I know she would.'

'What a happy chance. Of course, we want to do every one of the songs.'

'That's the correct thing to do. Their placement in the show is perfect.'

'But we might want to make a few changes to the book.'

'Ah. Yes, you would, wouldn't you. Well, there may be some advice I can give you about that . . .'

The late Dorothy Fields wrote the lyrics of dozens of evergreen songs such as 'The Way You Look Tonight', 'A Fine Romance', 'On the Sunny Side of the Street', 'I'm in the Mood for Love' . . . And she wrote the book of *Annie Get Your Gun*.

I met her son in his basement apartment in the West Village and suggested that, though his mother's fabulous work has just the right quantity of sprightly dialogue . . .

'Some of the jokes, just a few, are a bit out-of-date or obscure and, sir, here's the tricky thing, the gags about Chief Sitting Bull now seem somewhat racist.'

'They either are racist or they're not. How do you mean *seem*?'

'They are racist.'

'Oh come now, these are hardly serious comments. They're gags. It's a musical comedy. Musical comedies have gags.'

'We can't use them.'

'I'm sure I don't agree.'

'I've done research on Sitting Bull. He was a Sioux, chief of the Hunkpapa Lakota. He led his people against the US cavalry—'

'Every incident contained in this musical is true.'

'Yes, I get that but . . .'

'The Sioux were defeated, you know that? They were almost

totally wiped out. It was a terrible thing. You know your American history?'

'Well, some . . .'

'Sitting Bull made the best of the lousy situation he was in. He became a performer in Buffalo Bill's Wild West Rodeo Show. He met Annie Oakley. If you've done research, as you say you have, then you know that everything my mother put in the show is historical fact.'

So we agreed that Richard and I would mark up a script with our suggested excisions, there wouldn't be many, though we might suggest one or two simple rewrites, invisible mending, no more than that, and we'd send it to him.

'We adore the show. Why else would we want to do it?'

'For the reason most people put on shows.'

'Sir, I personally will not make any money out of it. Put it this way, there's fifty other great shows we could choose.'

'Well, perhaps you'd be better off choosing one of those.'

It's a year later. It's a preview. The packed house is laughing, whooping, applauding each of the genius, humane, quasi-mythic songs in Richard's trademark quirky, psychologically pitch-perfect, wry, self-satirising staging.

Dorothy Fields' son is sitting in the circle of the theatre at a little wooden desk we've specially installed for him. Under a shaded lamp, biro in hand, script in a ring-backed binder, he interrogates page after page, checking that each word spoken is just as his mother wrote it apart from the few that, after multiple heated phone calls and abrupt emails, he's agreed we can remove or rewrite or rephrase.

In the interval we're in the small room off the foyer. He's actually yelling. *He is so angry.*

'I absolutely did not agree to this!'

Or to that!

Or to the other damn thing!

And we're feeling

'Of course he has the moral and legal right. He owns his mother's racist jokes, they all belong to him. And, after all, he is quite properly doing his duty by her as her literary executor. And no doubt he loved his mother who, unlike mine, was one of the greatest lyricists ever. But come on now, it's just a silly musical – about what? Annie Oakley overcomes sexist prejudice to become the world-famous sharpshooter she always longed to be. Or something. Whatever happens in this production, no one's going to die. Surely? And in ten weeks' time this show, like every other, will be just another poster scraped off the wall . . .'

'Yes.

'No.

'Yes.

'I'll talk to Richard.

'Possibly.'

There he goes down the street away from the theatre for the final time, crossing Waterloo Bridge towards his Covent Garden hotel, towards the taxi that will whisk him off to Heathrow first thing tomorrow morning, he'll be thirty thousand feet closer to the sky, then at JFK, then back in NYC and his basement apartment in the West Village.

In his memoir *Finishing the Hat*, Stephen Sondheim describes Richard's production as

'Quite wonderful.'

I'm pleased to say that Irving Berlin's granddaughter agreed.

Alive from Palestine

Israel/Palestine, 2002

After the Six-Day War in 1967, Dad's two younger brothers left Cape Town for Israel. Sam, the older of the two, worked as a doctor. Sydney joined the army. A year later, Dad took Ma and Sonny and me to visit them. It was clear at once that Ben-Gurion had taken Dad's measurements and run up a country precisely to suit him.

'Everyone you meet is so *engaged* with life, they *plunge* their arms in up to their elbows and when they argue, boy oh boy, they take the bull by the horns and give battle. Even the old boys sweeping the streets are full of *joie de vivre* because they're sweeping *their own streets*.'

Sydney was posted to a territory the Israelis had captured from Syria, the strategically crucial Golan Heights. In Cape Town, as kid brother to a flamboyant man with great curiosity about everything, he'd battled to find a bit of ledge to stand on. On this hard-won mountainside, in olive fatigues, his big heart in his barrel chest overflowing at this unexpected visit, laughingly brandishing his Uzi over his head, he seemed to have found himself, a real man amongst real men.

I didn't buy any of it. Which was inexplicable. In this young country a new kind of society was being built. Didn't I claim to be a socialist? During the summers, Jewish kids would arrive from all over the world, learn *yivrit* and pick grapefruit on a kibbutz.

Dad said

'Explain why you don't want to do it. You'd meet the kind of people you like, with crazy ideas.'

Back home, an elderly rabbi called me in.

'It may seem to you that we're secure in this country but for us there can be no safety until we're in our homeland *Eretz Yisroel*.

Don't look away, why do you do that? Until then, surrounded on all sides by danger, we need strong leaders. From what the principal of your school tells me you could be such a leader. Are you with us? It's time you made a decision about this.'

I doubt I said 'no' to his face but the people I was 'with' hung round dodgy nightclubs called Darryl's and The Ace of Spades in the narrow streets down by the harbour. On the journey back from Israel, I'd gone into the last gents before boarding the plane and strapped beneath my shirt books that were banned in South Africa: *The Thief's Journal* by Jean Genet, *Special Friendships* by Roger Peyrefitte.

In June 2001 the London Festival of International Theatre brought Amir Nizar Zuabi's *Alive from Palestine* to the Royal Court Theatre for one performance. The *Guardian* said

'How often do you see a piece of necessary theatre? These "stories under occupation" fall precisely into that category. We are used to the idea of theatre as a diversion. Here it is fulfilling a more import-ant function of bringing us the news.'

I didn't see it and I couldn't get hold of a full script – perhaps there wasn't one – but by reading a print-out of the English surtitles I felt I'd got enough of a sense of its quality. I called friends at LIFT and at the Court.

'Do you plan to bring it back?'

Amir Nizar, then twenty-five, had written, directed and designed the show for the West Bank theatre Al-Kasaba in the heart of Ramallah near the beautiful old walled vegetable and fruit market. At the time the show was created, the occupying West Bank police forbad gatherings of more than three people. It was impossible to rehearse a conventional play in those circumstances so writer/ director and actors created this one out of a series of very brief

90

scenes, each with no more than three characters. Say what you have to say and get the hell out of the danger zone.

'*This is how our life is.*'

There was satire but far more anger and distress at how Palestinians had lost control of their day-to-day existence, at how the world knew nothing and seemed to care less about how they lived, at how nothing of their experience of occupation was of interest unless it could be splashed in violent headlines.

We scheduled eight performances which quickly sold out and, in the end, played eleven. We could have gone on for weeks if we hadn't had another show booked in.

Protestors stood on the pavement holding placards denouncing what they saw as anti-Zionist propaganda.

'It's so cold out here. Why not come inside and stand in the warm foyer?'

They preferred the pavement which I guess was better publicity for my business as well as theirs.

A year or two later, Amir Nizar set up his own theatre company ShiberHur which means 'a small territory' or, more poetically, 'a breathing space'. They had almost nothing, no money, no lighting or sound equipment. I commissioned him to write a play which was the best way I could legitimately use our resources to bolster his.

The new play was called *I Am Yusuf And This Is My Brother*, a quotation from the Quranic version of the story of 'Joseph and his Brothers' which is, of course, also found in the Old Testament. It told the tale of two brothers adrift during the crisis of the *nakbah*, the expulsion of Arabs from Palestine at the moment in 1948 when much of the land between the Mediterranean and the Jordan River was taken to create the state of Israel.

A year or so later we presented Amir Nizar's ShiberHur adaptation of Kafka's short story 'In the Penal Colony', and later still a second original play that we'd commissioned, *The Beloved*, based on the Biblical story of Abraham's sacrifice of Isaac, also found in the Quran.

Each time we worked with ShiberHur, I'd spend time in Tel Aviv where Amir Nizar lived with his wife, the actress Sivan Sasson, and his young son Noor, and also in Haifa where they rented space to rehearse in Al-Midan, 'the Arab theatre' on the crest of the hill above the *wadi* Niznaz overlooking the bay.

If you ask liberal Israelis about Haifa, they say

'It's our most integrated city. Jews and Arabs are more relaxed with each other there than anywhere else in our country.'

Arabs say

'Yes, but the Jews live in the nice houses high on the mountain, we live at the bottom of the hill.'

In fact, Makram Khoury, for decades one of the most admired actors in the Jewish and Arab theatres (in 1987 he was awarded the Israel Prize for acting), a member of ShiberHur and a performer in their Kafka adaptation, lives with his wife Wadiya near the top of the hill.

We sit in his comfortable living room in capacious armchairs looking through his wide picture window out across the Bay of Haifa, which in the past was known as the Gulf of Acre. We can almost see Acre just up the coast. Beyond it is Lebanon and a different reality.

Wadiya has layered the table with glistening red pepper and buckwheat salads, heaped couscous, cheese pastries. And I feel . . .

Why is it that I feel so at home? Because Wadiya reminds me of my Granny Golda? Golda was strongly built but cuddly with a broad, open face just like Wadiya's and an embrace quite as enfolding. They could be sisters, no?, ok, not sisters, cousins, do you buy that? No, because my family are Ashkenazi Jews from the depths of Eastern

Europe who never, in historical actuality, had anything to do with the Second Temple or the Maccabees or the Babylonian captivity or any of those catalogues of courage, violence and anguish. There's nothing remotely 'Semitic' or 'Mediterranean' about them. But, but, but did I ever feel so easily at home in Golda's living room, in *her* capacious armchairs? Or with her many brothers, my great-uncles? Or with Aunty Hadassah, Barney's wife, who in her youth studied pharmacy at the university in Königsberg, a cultured and sophisticated woman? I hardly ever bothered to talk to her. Or to Uncle Louis who fought in the Spanish civil war? Why was I so self-centred, so unjustifiably self-assured, so snobbish, call it by its name? Because they spoke with a funny accent and their voices were pitched in a minor key? I sit looking out at the bay puzzling.

Amir Nizar and I hang around on the pavement outside cafes in the *wadis* of Haifa playing our game. As a passer-by appears I guess her ethnicity.

'Definitely Arab.'

'She's Jewish.'

I'm hopeless at it.

'Well, *he's* Jewish.'

'Uh uh. He's a Druze.'

Amir Nizar's mother was Jewish, a doctor, an anaesthetist, elderly when I met her but still with a long-haired hippy look though her hair was now grey. His tall bony eagle of a father had been a horse dealer and breeder from an aristocratic Arab lineage that once controlled one of the pilgrimage routes to Mecca. Amir Nizar is a past master at our game but then he lives it day after day. Taxi drivers assume from his handsome, more or less 'European' features that he's a Jew and, as they drive, curse those fucking useless Arabs.

'Shooting's too good for them.'

Well, everyone's entitled to their point of view.

Late in the golden afternoon with the low sun bejewelling the sea, Makram asks

'So have you ever visited Acre? No? You're not interested?'

'No, really I am.'

'So why just sit looking at it? It's only an hour away, no more than that. I'll drive.'

We stride along Acre's massive stone embankments that held off waves of crusaders and, some centuries later, Napoleon's hitherto unconquerable army, towards 'Abu Cristo', a favourite restaurant built into the battlements that features in all the tourist guides. As the sun finally goes down, we drink beer, eat fish hooked straight from the sea, talk – mostly about the terrible events now unfolding a hundred miles down the coast in Gaza.

'There are always terrible events unfolding in Gaza.'

'Hush.'

'What?'

'Can you hear that?'

I can hear nothing but the sea slapping the battlements but then I'm rather deaf. What am I listening for? Rifle fire? Bombing? An air raid?

In 1987 I was hired to rewrite a film based on *Under Western Eyes* by Joseph Conrad. The original, set at the turn of the last century on the political axis of St Petersburg and Zurich, of a revolution-ary who betrays his cell and is punished by having his eardrums punctured, tells the story. The film *Streets of Yesterday* transposed the story to Israel/Palestine, the political axis to Jerusalem and East Berlin. To help me understand the politics of that historical moment, the director Judd Ne'eman drove me to a village in the north of Gaza. We looked for the home of a young Palestinian jour-nalist who, the previous year, had been one of the first, if not the actual first, to describe and analyse the *intifada*. He had grasped that there was something more than angry Arab kids throwing stones going on, that this was something significant, that political sensibilities had hardened and set in a new pattern.

All the buildings were surrounded by shining white stone walls. We struggled to find the one where the journalist lived because at that time the Israelis were demolishing houses in the area. No street was like the map said it ought to be.

We found it. We knocked at the whitewashed door. We were let in by a young boy who led us into a white courtyard and then hurried into the dwelling to announce us.

We waited. We were served tea. We waited. It's ok, it's fine, people are busy, this visit is our priority, not his. We waited. Finally the journalist appeared.

'Forgive me, I must have seemed rude. I was caught up in a book, I wanted to finish it before we started our meeting. It took longer than I expected. Were you looked after properly? Accept my apologies.'

He embraced Judd and turned to me.

'You are?'

I said my name.

Silence.

'Would you repeat that please?'

He went back into the house and emerged holding my book *Guns and Rain* about grassroots resistance in the 1960s and 70s to the racist regime in Zimbabwe.

'How strange this is. Your book is the reason I kept you waiting. I had one last chapter to go. I didn't want to stop reading until I'd finished it.'

Lithuania, 2012

During the First World War, my great-grandparents Rebecca and Joseph took their six young children Louis, Barney, Sam, Max, Jack and Golda from Lithuania across the border into Tsarist Russia for safety. On the return journey both parents fell ill in the global 'Spanish flu' epidemic. They died in 1918. Barney, the oldest son, managed to get the children home to Kaunas, the second city of Lithuania, where places were found for them in a Jewish orphanage. Each was taught a trade. Barney was a hairdresser. Jack, the baby of the family, learned cabinet-making. Golda was a dressmaker. Into her adult years she earned her living with her Singer sewing machine.

The man she married, Mordechai known as Mottle, was an intellectual, a Trotskyist, a typesetter, so dark and angular in the few photographs I have of him he looks like he might be from Rajasthan. They were not quite twenty when they married and set out on their journey to the far side of the planet.

In the Soviet years it wasn't easy to visit Kaunas though people went, often on organised tours, but I did no more than think about it. After the Berlin Wall came down you could fly there and back for thirty quid.

In 2012 I was overseeing a series of shows that brought together theatres in London with others in European capitals including *Three Kingdoms* by Simon Stephens, co-produced by the Lyric Hammersmith, the Munich Kammerspiele and Theatre NO99 in Tallinn, Estonia. If I'm going to Tallinn for late rehearsals and the opening, well then, Kaunas is just down the street. And if I don't visit it when I'm going to be flying over it I'll have to face the likelihood that I'm avoiding it.

When asked our name, everyone is our family says

'Lan L-A-N'

or otherwise it gets written as Land or Lamb or Lang or even Lunu occasionally. But registering at the Kaunas hotel I just said 'Lan'. And if they know to spell it, what does that mean? That I'm home? Well, not in this *haute bourgeois* part of the city.

'Lan, yes sir, can I now see your passport?'

To get to Vilijampolė, the ghetto, you walk along the neatly cobbled streets down a steep hill towards the River Neris. You reach a bridge. It's wide enough to take traffic in both directions and edged with metal rails that are painted orange, stingingly bright orange, like someone had a tin of orange paint left over from decorating and thought

'Waste not want not, I'll go paint that bridge.'

You cross the bridge.

The guide book lists Fortress Five, a Nazi slaughterhouse, as a tourist site. It's a short walk up the river to the right as you cross the bridge but I don't want to see it. As you step off onto the other side you reach a wide square. I have only one day here so I'd set out in the early morning with my map of the ghetto as it was in the 1920s. The air is icy but plate-glass clear. At this moment in the history of the world I'm the only living person in this square. Over to the side in the long shadows are two tall commemorative stones, one inscribed in Russian as far as I can remember though perhaps in Lithuanian, and the other in English.

'Here stood the ghetto.'

On the earth in front of one was an outline of a *menorah*, a Jewish candlestick, laid out in petals. The atmosphere was heavy and still but petals are lighter than air, they must have been laid out only moments ago. By whom? Is someone watching? There's no one anywhere. In front of the other stone was the same *menorah* design but this one laid out in glistening chestnuts. Is this done every day? Or if only today, for what reason? It felt like a greeting. Or a warning. So have I gone far enough? Too far? Should I retreat across the bridge?

Guided by my map, I walk the streets. All the houses, warehouses, wood cabins, shops, shacks seem where they'd always been, frozen in time but not abandoned, shutters are open, there are lace curtains in windows, smoke rises from chimneys straight up into the air *but no people*. I start to feel

'I've had enough of this'

when, rounding a corner, I come across the Jewish cemetery. Even here there's no one. The tombstones are gone, they've been carted away leaving grass, six inches high, evenly trimmed. By the tumbledown wall, weeds have grown into those spindly trees you find after a year or two on cleared land, weeds longing for dignity and recognition but without a focused idea of what a tree actually is. There's a low, squat monument commemorating the Jews slaughtered when the Nazis moved in. It's battered, someone's chipped away at it. The date is just legible, 25 June 1941, the day – I imagine it as a moonless night but it might just as well have been bright sunshine – when citizens of Kaunas carrying guns and knives and clubs hurried from their cosy part of town across the bridge. Did my father's father's mother die of 'natural causes' as some records suggest – or was she shot in a nearby street? Her husband and his brother were put on a train to Dachau, recently constructed to hold 'political prisoners', half a continent away, on the far side of Germany.

They left by crossing that bridge. Were they already in a train? Has the bridge a track? I don't think so. Did it then? Or did they have to walk across the bridge? What were they wearing on their feet? Shoes? Boots? Nothing? Were their clothes dry or wet? What did they look at? The River Neris? What did they think would happen next? Was it already an orange bridge?

When I was a kid, on the walls of our dining room hung two matching photographs, an elderly woman, an elderly man, shawls and suits, she with scraped-back hair, coiled into a tight bun, he with a pointy beard and bowler hat, stately studio portraits staring out with gravity and tenderness. How was it for Dad to be gazed upon by his murdered grandparents whom he never met while his first-born son ran about saying or at least implying

'I want nothing to do with all this Jewish shit?'

My dad's handsome, my dad's tall
Ho ho!
His name's Joe, that's all.

Before I went to Kaunas, I googled this ghetto, Vilijampolė or *slobotka* as Golda always called it though that seems to be a generic name for Jewish ghettos in the 'bloodlands' between Berlin and Moscow. I discovered only one Lan L-A-N, a businessman named Gabriel. In his spare time he held down a second job. He was the general manager of a theatre.

Three

That's Enough About Me

'That's enough about me.
What did you all think about my play?'

Distinguished playwright
at dinner after an opening

1

Spirit

1974

The morning after my play *Bird Child* opened I got up early, walked to the newspaper shop round the corner from Hammersmith Bridge, bought the papers, turned to the arts pages and, walking home, read the reviews, then climbed back into bed and fell asleep. When I woke in the early afternoon with the papers scattered round me, I read the headlines. The previous night, 25 April 1974, the *Movimento das Forças Armadas* had staged a coup against the fascist government in Lisbon. The leaders of the bloodless 'Carnation Revolution' immediately declared that all Portuguese forces would be withdrawn from all its colonies – Guinea Bissau, Angola, Mozambique.

1979

I've completed the B.Sc. at the LSE, I've had two years writing plays, now I want to get back into anthropology and do fieldwork but where to do it? My supervisor Maurice Bloch says

'Get a map of the world, close your eyes, stick in a pin, it's all extraordinarily interesting.'

It seemed to me that what was now happening in Mozambique might be one of the ways South Africa would go when, as had to happen soon, it too achieved freedom. The Portuguese had lost a ten-year war with the nationalist guerrilla army FRELIMO which formed the basis of the new state. In the north, FRELIMO was still engaged in a brutal struggle with a resistance army organised and funded by the apartheid states of South Africa and Rhodesia.

But the south of the country was fairly peaceful. Ruth First, one of the intellectual leaders of the anti-apartheid struggle, was director of research at the Centre for African Studies at Eduardo Mondlane University in the capital, Maputo.

'But why should we let you work with us? What do you know?'

'Not a great deal but I'm interested.'

'Interest is not enough. If you can show you're committed we might allow you in but we're not ready for individual research, I don't know if we ever will be. We have a project on the go, "The African Miner". Hundreds of thousands of our men have worked in the gold mines of South Africa on very, very low pay. What they did get out of it is training. Many are tremendously highly skilled but we don't know how many or who they are. We need to know so that we can plan effectively for our future. Can you suppress your ego enough to join the team?'

Possibly . . .

By chance, I catch a news story on TV about how nationalist guerrillas fighting the Rhodesian state are inspired by spirit mediums. And then, unexpectedly, a deal is done, an agreement is signed at Lancaster House, the war in Rhodesia is over. I apply to the Social Science Research Council for a grant to study the religious aspects of guerrilla struggle in the new Zimbabwe which is about to come into being. They say

'You know, peace doesn't happen overnight. It takes months, possibly years, to come into effect. Field research in these circumstances will be perilous. Without evidence that you will be secure, of course we can't fund it.'

The cheap way to get to Salisbury, Rhodesia was by Aeroflot via Moscow. As I go through immigration in Moscow, one glance at my South African passport and they won't let me in . . .

'We know absolutely what kind of people you are.'

'So what do I do?'

'The rule is absolutely clear. Go in that room.'

'I'm in transit. I want to be in the USSR just one hour.'

'Absolutely no possibility.'

'So what do I do? I can't just sit in a room.'

'Absolutely not our problem.'

In the far wall of the room was another door. I went through into the palatial, glass-walled, light-enchanted halls of Sheremetyevo airport around which I lope gazing out at the rows of silver birches, thinking

'Now what the fuck do I do?'

And then I hear an accent I recognise. What is it? Xhosa? Zulu?

'Hello, brother. You are wandering around like a lost ghost. Who are you?'

They turn out to be ANC comrades waiting for a flight back to their base in Lusaka, Zambia.

'I'm trying to get to Zimbabwe. Because I'm South African they won't let me on a plane.'

'Ah, ah, ah, brother, bad luck. So what will you do? Put a bed under the counter in that bar where you have been drinking and move in?'

'Come with us, brother! Lusaka's just a hop and a jump from Zimbabwe. Once you're there it will be so very easy for you to shove on to your destination.'

They fix me a ticket on their flight and pour me a cognac. As we're about to board the plane suddenly they're cheering, running up and down the lounge, punching the air.

'We did it! I can't believe it! We actually did it! Wow, Jesus, man, amazing news! God, my god, my god!'

JOHANNESBURG 2 June 1980 — Saboteurs who
bombed two of South Africa's strategically vital SASOL

oil-from-coal plants could not have chosen their targets
with more devastating effect. The biggest act of economic
sabotage ever carried out in South Africa underlines
the rapid escalation of the guerrilla war being waged
by militant nationalist movements opposed to the
government's apartheid policy.

Outside their base near Lusaka, they gave me a corner of a hut where young exiles were sheltering, radical schoolkids from Soweto who'd protested against the apartheid education system, been beaten by the police and fled. To my surprise, they talk to each other in Afrikaans, the language of the oppressor.

'But why do you speak the boss' language?'

'Because we're homesick, man. It makes us feel better.'

Zimbabwe, 1981

I flew to Harare, as Salisbury was soon to be renamed, hired a car and drove due north through miles and miles of citrus farmland, oranges, grapefruit, then through never-ending cattle country, one straight road, straight line, straight line, on and on towards the steep escarpment leading down into the Zambezi Valley where, twenty years before, the guerrilla war had begun.

Despite the change of government even then taking place, the final security post was still manned by white police.

'And where are you heading?'

'Into the Valley.'

'You have an intelligent reason to be there?'

'I'm scoping a research project.'

'There's nothing to research down there, man. Jesus Christ. Are you armed?'

'I'm not.'

They give each other looks: idiot doesn't deserve to live.

'No, man, it's just as well. There's too many guns in the Valley as it is. You wouldn't know how to use one anyway, would you? So, yes, a guy like you is definitely safer without a weapon. So go and good luck to you.'

Noon in the Zambezi Valley. The hottest time of day at the hottest time of year in the hottest part of Zimbabwe.

It's Friday, the day sacred to the ancestors. No one is allowed to work in their fields. Circles of men and older women sit in the ever-decreasing shade and drink a rough, warm beer made of sorghum.

'In the time of the struggle,' says my assistant Lazarus who was born in this village, 'our guerrillas used to watch these people with sharp eyes. If someone dug in his field on a day of rest they would beat him, maybe kill him. If it's a Friday and a guerrilla meets the enemy in the bush he'd run away. A gun is made of steel. The ancestors hate steel. There was no steel in the days when they lived on earth. If a gun is used on a rest day the ancestors won't protect him so he'll get shot by a white soldier and then he's dead.'

The temperature suddenly plummets as a wall of rain wheels in from the east. There's a crack and flash of lightning. An old man rushes out from the shelter of a tree.

'Haai! Davey! Go home! Your shirt is dangerous!'

My faded yellow shirt is patterned with red, a colour dangerous to the ancestors. Wear red and lightning will strike you.

'Red is blood,' says Lazarus.

We head off through the downpour. Drenched shirts stripped off, we shiver in the doorway of my hut and watch the sheets of flat white light embolden the sky.

'Did you hear that lightning blew up the police station?'

'Which police station?'

'The big one at Mahaba. They had an armoury there. Everything was blown sky high.'

Mahaba is a village perched high above us on the tip of the escarpment.

'You know no one ever tells me anything, nothing important anyway.'

'Ah ah! So what are you doing here?'

'Learning from you. Tell me.'

'Will you write it down?'

'Depends how interesting it is.'

'I find it very interesting.'

I fetch my notebook.

'It was so crazy. The police stored all their weapons, guns, bullets, everything for the whole region in that armoury. The lightning hit it bull's eye. Kaboom!'

'Was anyone injured?'

'No one. *No one at all.* Which is also interesting. The lightning knows what it's doing. But what is *really* interesting . . .'

'Tell me.'

'Is why it happened. Are you writing?'

'Why it blew up?'

'Exactly.'

'Or why the lightning struck it?'

'I'm explaining to you that the two are the same thing. Long back ago . . .'

Which is how in this part of the world all stories begin.

'Long back ago, that place where the police station now is was the home of an ancestor. For many, many years he didn't come out in anybody.'

By which he means that for a long period the ancestral spirit didn't choose a living person to act as its medium so that, by possessing her or him and speaking through their mouth, it could make direct contact with its living descendants. Every single person who lives here, as far as I can tell, believes in and carries out rituals in honour of the ancestors. Which doesn't mean that they're not also good Christians. Penyas Katsvete, a leader of a local Apostolic church amongst whose family I lived for two years, once explained this apparent paradox to me.

'The Bible says that you must love and honour your parents but it doesn't tell you when to stop. Ah ha! You see?'

Lazarus continues

'Now the ancestral spirit of Mahaba has chosen a medium. That medium comes from far away but of course he wants to take back the home of his spirit. It's his duty now to come and live there and that is what the ancestor wants him to do. But he can't live in that village in a good way if there's a police station on his land, can he? During the war and even before, those police were the enemy of the people. So the ancestor sent lightning to frighten the police and make them leave.'

Next day I hitch a ride up the escarpment on the back of a tractor and ask the not-yet-replaced white District Commissioner to give me his account of these events.

'Damn it, Mahaba is right on the edge of the escarpment. It sticks out like a bunion, not to get too graphic about it. It gets hit ten times every lightning season, naturally.'

'But lightning struck the armoury.'

'Yes, I've no idea how that could have happened. The bolt passed right through the metal grid on a window. But it was pure chance, pure rotten luck, take my word for it. My strong advice to the police is not to budge, not even to think of it. If they move that station, any time that we – by which I mean my successors, whoever they may be – have to push through some unpopular measure, which they will have to, believe me, some wild-eyed prophet will crawl out of the bush and claim that the ancestors prohibit it. They'd be fools to fall for a trick like this but God preserves fools mightily, doesn't he?'

In his files, I found a report written by a police sergeant of a visit he'd paid to the newly arrived medium whose name was Zakaria.

'When we arrived at Mahaba, all of us were told to take off our shoes. We sat and clapped our hands. Then the medium said

'"I do not want to see any buildings here. None. The police must go but all the other buildings the white people built must go as well. This is my home. Every building must be removed. The lightning was just a warning. If what I say is not done, then you're really going to see something."

'The sergeant gave the medium a gift of meat, beans and salt. He explained to him

'"When the police station was built, no one knew this was the place where the ancestor used to live. As you are a spirit medium you should realise we all learn by mistakes."

'"Yes, it is a mistake," said Zakaria. "You must correct it."

'"But you know it takes months to put up a station like this. It isn't possible to pull it down very quickly in just a few days. This matter will be solved but slowly, slowly, bit by bit. Intimidation won't make anything go quicker."

'Then the medium said

'"You must know, I am possessed by a very powerful spirit."

'The sergeant asked to be told the spirit's name but Zakaria said

'"I cannot tell you the name until all the problems of the buildings have been solved. I have travelled a long way to arrive at this place. Now I'm tired. Leave me."'

As I learned more about Zakaria I realised how brilliantly his arrival on the local scene had been orchestrated. By not revealing the name of his spirit until the police station had been removed he'd trapped the local officers in an impossible position.

Throughout central and southern Africa spirit mediums have enormous prestige. The more important the spirit possessing them, the higher the status of the medium.

The local police lieutenant, in those early days of the new Zimbabwe still a white man, was willing to give a hearing to the demand that his station be moved but he was savvy enough to be cautious. If he moved it and then it was revealed that the spirit possessing Zakaria was of little consequence he would look ridiculous. He'd have let himself be pushed around by a nobody. On the other hand, if he tried to avoid that risk and simply refused, he'd be accused of insulting the ancestors and, by extension, all their descendants, all the Shona people, the current leader of whom was, of course, the new president Robert Mugabe.

Late one afternoon Lazarus called out to me from the road that ran through the village. He'd walked all the way down the mountain with a bag of mangoes for his family. As he passed through Mahaba he'd heard, he said, that Zakaria was preparing for a possession ritual.

'Great! When will it happen?'

'Obviously it will be tonight because it's going to be a full moon. Really, Mr Davey, don't you notice anything?'

I packed my tape recorder, spare batteries and a blanket, checked that nothing on the clothes I was wearing was red, and hitched a ride back up the mountain, this time in a bread van.

When the full moon rose, it was obscured by cloud but there was light enough to see that the smoothly curving road leading to the very highest point of the escarpment was empty. Hearing drums I cut away from the road stumbling in their direction across a field, past huts with no one in them, embers of cooking fires still burning, across more fields, more fires, into a small wood and out onto a narrow stony track that winds up the side of the hill.

'So you've come to dance with us?'

A posse of women are ahead of me on the track hauling piles of blankets and huge clay vats of beer. They're looking back over their shoulders, swaying with laughter.

'You're not afraid?'

'What should I be frightened of, mama?'

More laughter.

'You don't know what's going to happen?'

'He knows! He's the one from the village at the flygate, the one who's always asking, asking. He knows, he knows!'

I climb the hillside with the laughing women.

The clouds melt away. Acid moonlight bleaches all colour out of the hillside. At the centre of the plateau are the drummers, each inside his own tumult but together creating a wild but measured cacophony. Around them circle young women jiving, jolting, singing full-throated, hooting. A horde of youngsters dart in and out of the singing and the dance, as if spontaneously, as if by chance, but the pattern is repeated over and over, again and again. They yell to drive on the drummers. It's like a mass rave in an airless warehouse, so oppressive but, in the open air, so free, so joyous and fat with feeling.

All around are fires. At one sits the chief, his headmen and his elders. They lower their mugs into big clay bowls and dredge up gritty beer. He sends a messenger.

'The chief says to ask if you will be making any recording?'

'I will, yes, if that's ok with him.'

'Oh yes, the chief will be so pleased. The night is long. He's an old man now. It's not always possible for him to remember everything. He asks will you bring the recording to a meeting in town at half past four on the eighth of the month?'

114

'Tell the chief I will.'

On the highest plane of a wide stone terrace is a courtyard built for the medium, his team of assistants, his family. For hours and hours there's no one there. Hours and hours of this thrilling – but also often deeply boring – *Götterdämmerung* and then all at once total silence. Sleep conquers the hilltop. Flocks of blankets wriggle and huddle encircling the fires. A child wails complaint. The cicadas. The sweetish scent of green wood burning. The hot night breeze. The honeyed moon.

One of the medium's assistants dashes onto the terrace and cries out. The drummers bounce up, blankets tossed aside. At last the spirit has come.

Zakaria leads the singing. He's dressed in black and white. He jabs his long stick up down, up down. He throws it into the air and catches it without looking.

You see me, you see me

The one who holds up the heavens, that is me

He dives into the circle of dancers, lunging, retreating, hopping, bobbing, growling, choking.

'Do you see our ancestor?'

A schoolteacher is at my side, sweating with excitement.

'That is the one who says if the buildings aren't pulled down lions will come. One time a spirit gave my uncle a command. He refused. Next night we heard growling in the garden. In the morning my uncle's donkey was just a pile of bones.'

You see me, you see me

At four in the morning a new circle forms at the edge of the plateau. Zakaria, now fully possessed, sits on a reed mat. In front of him, kneeling, is his assistant. On either side are experienced mediums who are there as midwives to ease this rebirth of a long dead spirit out of the mouth of his new medium into the world of the living.

The assistant kneels and claps to the spirit.

'Grandfather, we are waiting to hear you. We want to hear your guidance for us. Speak to us. We're weak. We know nothing.'

I've crawled as close as I dare to get a good recording. To my astonishment I see that the medium's assistant is Lazarus.

'Grandfather, help us.'

Zakaria lifts his lizard face, his black goat beard. Softly he chants.

I was the first, the first to come . . .

Clapping. Silence. Clapping.

I was the first, the first to come here . . .

Over and over the same line. Suddenly the membrane breaks and the chant begins to flow. At last, two long hours later, the spirit reveals his name.

I am Mutukuramatenga

I am the father of the oldest of the spirits

I was the first one in this country . . .

No one has ever heard this name before but there is relief. He is a very old spirit and therefore a powerful one. He recites the entire lineage of ancestors and there are so many names it's obvious that Mutukuramatenga must have lived at Mahaba an extremely long time ago. During his lifetime he was the first man ever to live in this part of the country. The police station will have to be moved. Of that everyone is sure.

A few days later I climb the hill again and ask to see the medium. Lazarus appears.

'Hey, Mr Davey.'

'Hey, Lazarus.'

'You didn't know I am the assistant of this medium?'

'How can I know if you don't tell me?'

'Some things you have to find out for yourself, Mr Davey. Do you agree?'

'Yes, you are very wise. I agree.'

'But someone has to tell you what to look for, someone has to open your eyes for you, is that what you feel?'

'Honestly, Lazarus, I'm grateful for whatever you tell me.'

'It was me who brought Zakaria to this place, did you know that?'

'You know I didn't know that. How would I know?'

'Well, now I'm telling you. And you are the only one who knows this.'

'And why did you do it? Will you tell me that?'

He looks at me. He doesn't say 'You really understand nothing' but I hear him.

A young boy appears. Lazarus asks

'What is it, little brother?'

'Is he the one who made the tape recording?'

'He is.'

'Grandfather wants to hear.'

Some distance away Zakaria is gazing across the Valley but I know he's really got his eye on me. Lazarus says

'Mr Davey, your shoes.'

I remove my shoes. The boy has brought two stools. I sit on one, Zakaria on the other. I play the recording all the way through. When I try to fast forward through the silences he stops me. He wants to hear it all – everything. Lazarus whispers

'So now you're doing my job, Mr Davey.'

When it's finished Zakaria says

'So? Ask if you want to.'

'Grandfather, tell me why you have come here.'

'Me?'

'You.'

'Or the ancestor?'

I don't know what to say. He shakes his beautiful lizard face laughing then gestures at the tape recorder with his chin. I turn it on.

'Everything happens by itself. It is not me Zakaria who does these things. I was living in Zambia. That is where the ancestor came very strongly on me. It told me to go to Mahaba. To come to this place I had to cross the Zambezi. The river was in full flood. I put my clothes in a plastic bag. I tied my stick to my side. I set one foot in the water. At once the river stopped flowing. I walked a dry road across the river bed. When I reached the other side the river moved again. I came to Mahaba. I slept under a tree. In the morning a young girl went to tell the chief I was here. He came out to me. I said

'"Now this whole country is ours but this place, this Mahaba, belongs to me. I am the one who lived here long ago. Now I am home. Now the war is over. Now everyone is in the right place. Now we shall live in peace."'

The Soldier's Fortune

2007

I have no idea why I have chosen to direct this terrible 'comedy' by Thomas Otway in the first season of the reopened YV. The actors are wonderfully game and, by the time we open, truly heroic but, all the same, the characters have no reality. The plot is poor. I have zero feeling for it. Who can I blame?

When Nick and I lived in the ground-floor flat of the house in Hammersmith, Peter Gill, one of our few great naturalistic directors, lived on the top floor. Occasionally when the gas ran out and we had no hot water, Peter let me have a bath upstairs. On his bathroom wall hung a drawing of Sheila Hancock in his, no doubt, scintillating production of this dreary farrago. So that's whose fault it is.

As You Like It

2005

While YV was closed for rebuilding, I directed *As You Like It* in the West End. While preparing, I found what seemed a clear mistake in the edition I was working from – a line of dialogue in the wrong place. When you first come across such a thing you think

'Obviously I'm wrong about this.'

Each word of every play by Shakespeare has been argued over by specialists for four centuries. How can a blatant textual error have slipped through the net? I check other editions. The flaw, if it is one, is in all of them.

I happen across Trevor Nunn in a Waterloo cafe.

'Hi Trev. So sorry to interrupt. Ok if I ask your advice? I think I've discovered an error in *As You Like It*.'

'How do you mean "an error"?'

'I'm pretty sure there's a line in the wrong place.'

'There isn't.'

Director of the RSC for eighteen years, Sir Trev has directed almost every one of Shakespeare's thirty-something plays.

'Sorry again to take up your time but can I show you?'

He raises his arms like Prospero in wonder and despair.

'Show me.'

Act 2 scene 7. Orlando has fled the violent city with his aged servant Adam and is looking for the peaceful folk living in the forest. He ventures ahead of Adam, finds Rosalind and Jaques and begs for food.

> *There is an old poor man*
> *Who after me hath many a weary step*
> *Limp'd in pure love. Till he be first sufficed,*
> *Oppress'd with two weak evils, age and hunger,*
> *I will not touch a bit.*

Surely what Shakespeare actually wrote is

> *There is an old poor man,*
> *Oppress'd with two weak evils, age and hunger,*
> *Who after me hath many a weary step*
> *Limp'd in pure love. Till he be first sufficed*
> *I will not touch a bit.*

Trevor pores over the paperback, then gives a quick little to-and-fro shake of his long hair as a diver might when breaking up through the surface of a stream, then he reads it again.

The Daughter-in-Law

2002

In the first decade of the last century, in a miner's cottage in the north of England, Minnie (Anne-Marie Duff) and Luther (Paul Hilton) work out, through struggle, how their deep love for each other can survive the stereotypes their circumstances have imposed on them.

D. H. Lawrence imagined his play would be acted within a detailed recreation of a house like the one he grew up in. In my production, we had on stage almost nothing real. A chair, a metal stove. Apart from these, the stage was empty.

Out of sight, we built a staircase. When Minnie and Luther row, Minnie would thump off stage and up the stairs. Because she was invisible to them the audience could only intuit what she was feeling from the sound of her feet.

Now she's stamping up to her room, now she pauses, now she slips down quickly a step or two, pauses again, one step, another, silence, will she come down into the room and make peace with Luther? No, she's thumping back upstairs. The abrupt shifts in Anne-Marie's physical dynamic expressed all the complexity of Minnie's intellectual unfolding, sight unseen.

A Raisin in the Sun

2001

Lorraine Hansberry's play tells how three generations of a family struggle against history, against the racism of the US in the 1950s to achieve lives of meaning and integrity.

Hansberry writes a lengthy description of how she wants the apartment in Chicago's Southside to look:

> ... *a section of this room slopes backwards to provide a small kitchen area where the family prepares the meals that are eaten in the living room proper. The single window that has been provided is located in this kitchen area* ...

We had none of this, neither walls nor doors. On a raised platform we placed a damaged parquet floor, a square pine table painted white and four white chairs.

In the course of the play the family cook and eat meals, mop floors and so on. What to do about the frying pan, the books they read, the radio they listen to? We designed a small table, painted grey, the top of which was a lift that could be pulled down below the stage. It was set against the back of the stage. Towards the end of each scene, whatever objects had been used – a bottle, a box of matches – would be placed, as if by chance, on this table. As the lights dimmed, the top quickly dropped down, the stage manager removed what had been used and added whatever would now be needed – a hat, a knife. Seconds later, the top of the table shot back into place and the next scene began.

Julius Caesar

2001

After the press night, my friend the director Andrei Şerban embraced me and said kindly

'So now you are artistic director you ask other directors to work at your theatre but actually you do it quite well yourself. Ha ha ha.'

When a show goes well, you can have a bit of a rest. If it's a big hit or if it fails, right away you have to start working again. Success means

'So how can we take advantage of this?'

Failure means

'What wounds must be dressed?'

This, the first show I'd directed as AD of YV, the first of my first season, was a flop. Simona Gonella, another director friend, emailed from Italy

'If you survive this, you'll survive anything.'

I'd had failures as a playwright. The second full-length play of mine to be produced was attacked in the press so aggressively that, while running the YV, I kept the critics away from young writers and directors for as long as I could.

The actor who played Caesar was compacted with rage.

'*We* have to go on doing this night after bloody night. Where the fuck have *you* been?'

'Ummm . . . You know, I also have to run this theatre.'

'To repeat my question, where the . . . ?'

On a desk in the general office I found an opened letter addressed to the chair of the board left where I couldn't help but stumble across it.

'The speaking of Shakespeare in this production is the worst in my long experience . . .'

When a production fails you feel you've conned everyone, especially the actors. You've invited them to a party that prevented them accepting an invitation to another party which would have been far more rewarding and perhaps actually fun to be at. You're guilty – of what exactly? – it doesn't matter, you've taken a part of people's lives and given them nothing in return. You've made them look foolish in front of their friends. You've created a sense of the likelihood that they will experience a life-affirming connection between actors and audience but you had no idea how to get that to happen *and you should have known you didn't,* whose big idea was this anyway? The actors must night after night dig out of themselves their long stored-up soul treasure while you chill at home watching *Spiral* or hang in Soho drinking cocktails with your glitzy friends.

But what of the possibility that in fact you're ahead of the game – aesthetically, politically, morally? Sometimes, ten years later, a stranger says

'You know, I once saw a really original production of *Julius Caesar.* Oh, you're kidding me! Did you direct that? Awesome.'

But the truth is . . .

> *'Now, man, that alto man last night had IT – he held it once he found it; I've never seen a guy who could hold so long.' I wanted to know what 'IT' meant. 'Ah well' – Dean laughed – 'now you're asking me impon-de-rables – ahem! Here's a guy and everybody's there, right? Up to him to put down what's on everybody's mind. He starts the first chorus, then lines up his ideas, people, yeah, yeah, but get it and then he rises to his fate and has to blow equal to it. All of a sudden somewhere in the middle of the chorus he gets it – everybody looks up and knows; they listen; he picks it up and carries. Time stops. He's filling empty space with the substance of our lives.'*

> Jack Kerouac, *On the Road*

You hoped you had IT.
We believed we had IT.
You don't have IT.
We don't have IT.
I don't have IT.

Four

Origin Myths

If you study social anthropology, you find that origin myths all over the world say more or less the same thing. *In the beginning* men made the world. They made society and they made culture so both belong to them. Women make babies, grind grain and wash corpses. That's how the world is.

Ma had hoped to go to university but her father, my grandpa Mordechai-Ben, said

'But why? I see no benefit in this'

so she found a job as a clerk at the electricity board. The office where she worked was right in the centre of town. She enjoyed the bustle, the clatter, the high jinks of a high airy room filled with 'girls'. The work itself, Ma's hand scuttling crab-like down and down the columns of numbers, engaged just enough of her interest. All her life she was a whizz at arithmetic but what she adored was literature, the idea of it, its immensity. She was a daily visitor to the enchanted garden where Cathy Earnshaw, Jane Eyre, Becky Sharp and Miss Havisham meet for Earl Grey tea and iced biscuits. Her favourite poet was Keats

Oh for a beaker full of the warm south

but she lived in the warm south so in the summers the 'girls' from the 'pool' would go out as a crowd and spread plaid rugs for picnics on the lower slopes of the mountain or drive on each other's laps, four to a seat for hours to party on a creamy beach where they'd meet matching crowds of young men, mostly Jewish though not exclusively, amongst whom was *the* catch, *him*, dark, wavy-haired, broad-chested, a bit wild perhaps, swaggering, a bit dangerous maybe, sexually adventurous so you had to be careful but so go-getting and appealing, especially since he grew his Clark Gable moustache which made him seem so much older. He was barely twenty, she just twenty-three.

'*Look* at my waist – and don't think I had to diet to keep it so thin. You can see, not all the girls had figures like that, hardly any.

If this was a colour photograph I think you'd recognise the dress. Or did you? Yes, it's the red one, a bit like Alice in Wonderland, I still keep in the back of my wardrobe.'

'But, Ma, was that when you became pregnant? Ok, you don't have to answer that but can I ask, if you could have – well, of course, you *could*, no, what I want to know is: now, thinking back on it, do you wish you'd chosen differently?'

Pause.

'Not at all. Don't ask me that again.'

Her response to the bleak politics of the 1950s and 60s was to try to live as a good person. Did she stand shoulder to shoulder with the stalwart women of the Black Sash lining the highways protesting apartheid? No, what *she* did was raise money for starving families by baking tarts for fetes, organising raffles and planning quiz nights for which she'd devise all the questions, including the trick ones. There were always bags of barley or pulses in the garage waiting to be collected by some or other charity. Her friend Fred, a member of the banned South African Communist party, lived as a dealer in fine art. When he was on the run from the police, he asked

'Can I leave this suitcase under a bed?'

She didn't hesitate. What was in it? Paintings? Guns? Copies of *The Communist Manifesto*?

'Do not touch it. Forget it's even there. It belongs to Fred.'

For decades she served on the committee of an orphanage for black children. Cradling rescued infants in her arms, a serenity would descend on her like a shawl, a sweetness and, it seemed to me, a longing. She adored having her photograph taken in famous cultural places signifying: this is the kind of person I am. This is *me*. I am a part of this.

'And do you remember *this* photograph? Here we all are in St Mark's Square, Venice, when you kids were in your teens. Can

130

you even see any of us through that cloud of pigeons? Look at this cheeky one sitting plump on Dad's shoulders – and look, Dave, there's one in my hair!'

Later that holiday in Rome I persuaded all of them that the sophisticated thing to do was see Peter Brook's film of *Marat/Sade* which had just opened. Ma worked hard to acclimatise. Dad had soon had enough

'What on earth made you bring us to see this?'

joining Sonny, an earlier escapee, in the foyer where she wondered if it was ok with him if she went off to a nearby club with the *ragazzo* she'd only just encountered.

'Only for an hour, Dad, till that movie's over. I couldn't watch another second, it made me want to throw up.'

Back at Albergo Turistico he yelled all through dinner, called me a fool and her a whore. Some forms of culture bring humiliation to everyone.

Back story

As far as anyone knew, Ma's third child was bobbing, contented, in her inland sea. Just before his birth was due her symptoms turned strange but, by good luck, her doctors had seen similar signs once before and very recently. Just hours after he was born, Ma's second son was operated on and a genetic tic that had jammed his duodenum was repaired. The surgeon made his reputation and my brother Jeff lived.

Then our luck turned. It was 1956, the year of the worldwide polio epidemic. Children everywhere were handed brightly coloured sugar cubes squirted with vaccine. Was this delicate child robust enough to accept the prophylactic or would it hurt him, even kill him?

'With so many factors complicating the situation, even the most experienced physicians find it hard to advise with confidence. So, dear Mrs Lan, we're obliged to place this matter in your hands. You'll no doubt talk it over it with your husband. Then let us have your decision.'

What did they do? Read medical books, get second opinions? Did they hang over the cradle whispering? Did they sit out at night in Ma's garden amid the agapanthus and the hydrangea? How much time did they have? Days? Weeks? Jeff was born in January. Were the evenings still warm or by now was autumn already in the air? Did they walk under high green bowers of chestnut and plane trees or were dry leaves already piled at the side of the streets? Did they find themselves down by the river and, arm in arm, walk the track along the bank and, so as not to have to turn homewards – anything, anything but that – did they gaze into the rushing water and cross the narrow bridge? And did they, as they ended their wandering, go abruptly through the front door, lock it, drink something hot for her, strong for him, undress, cover themselves in light nightclothes, drag back the rose-pink quilt, the white sheet, lie on one of their adjoining beds, heavily entwined for a moment, then he roll away leaving her to reach out, press the light switch, lie wrapped in her own darkness? How could she sleep? He was twenty-seven, she was not quite thirty.

'I've made up my mind. It's difficult for me, as it would be for any parent, I believe. I've held Jeff in my arms and tried to feel how much strength there is in him. So this is my decision and it is mine. I'm his mother and he's my child. Anyone in the world can under-stand that. I don't want him to have the vaccine.'

This is the origin myth of my family's unhappiness as it was handed down to me.

The Glass Menagerie
by Tennessee Williams, directed by Joe Hill-Gibbins

2010

I didn't tend to sit in on all the on-stage technical rehearsals for every show I produced. Long before these begin you know whether the director and their designers are confident of their show's physical language, its rhythm, of the pace it needs. To direct actors requires a complex set of skills but to conjure a show's material life, to blend light, sound, time and inanimate objects with moving bodies, a director has to walk a double high wire of intimacy and discipline, of cheerfulness and technique. So what I'd do is smile a good deal, ensure everyone has all they need for the long dark hours by way of coffee, nuts, sweets and from time to time watch from the shadows.

On the other hand, I'd see every preview and after each I'd muse with the director, sometimes offering many ideas, sometimes not so many.

During technical rehearsals for *The Glass Menagerie* Jeff died so I had to seek out Joe Hill-Gibbins, its director, and let him know that this time, unlike all the other shows we'd done together

'You're on your own.'

'Oh, that's cool. What's up?'

'Did I once tell you that my brother had polio?'

'Oh, I'm sorry, yes, you did. Has something happened to him?'

'It affected his back. I don't think you ever met him, did you? His spine was quite bent out of shape. Anyway . . . In the last year or two . . . If you live long enough, polio moves round your body affecting it in unexpected ways, though *what it is* that moves . . .'

'You're going to see him?'

'For a while he's needed – he needed, now past tense . . .'

'Oh, oh, oh, sorry.'

'He had to plug himself into a kinda pumping machine so he could breathe when he was asleep.'

'The machine packed in?'

'Or perhaps his lungs did. I had a call from his son early this morning. Or it might have been a heart attack.'

'I'm really, really . . .'

'Or both. We don't yet know.'

'How old was he?'

'Four years younger—'

'Wow! *Younger* than you? I'm so, so . . .'

'What I feel mostly, oddly, ridiculously, I guess, is rubbish that I'm walking out on you.'

'Oh, don't worry about us. We're in good shape.'

Which they were. Joe's production of Tennessee Williams' tale of a domineering mother, her disabled daughter, her gay son was a big hit for us, a sell-out success, so what difference would it have made if I *had* been there to muse with him through all the previews?

'So you're going . . . do you still think of it as home?'

Astute question, Herr Direktor.

The Christmas after Jeff was born, Ma, her ma, Sonny, Jeff, me, my cousin Beverley went by train to a village called Tsolo in a faraway part of the country where black people lived and where Granny Fay's twin sister Rose kept a small hotel and an 'African trading store' selling zinc baths, mixed-fruit jam, spades, gumboots, bags of seed. At dawn Rose would lead us through the rain, down deep mud tracks to her ramshackle cow shed. A prancing, grey-haired dairyman would entertain us by squeezing an udder and pinching a teat so arcs of hot milk squirted into our faces splashing our teeth. The hotel toilets were shacks with long-drop buckets out in the fields, the night soil collected by trucks once a week.

Or was Jeff infected with polio before we'd even arrived at Tsolo, or on the train, or even before he'd been carried embalmed in soft blankets down our garden path and out into the street?

Dad wasn't with us. Christmas was the most hectic time of the year in the furniture trade. Or did he have another reason?

The breath in my lungs leaves me. Chest-deep in salt water, gazing out to sea, a wave bumps and trails, depletes.

This idea had never occurred to me.

Of course I knew, Sonny knew, in time we all did that Dad had girlfriends, many of them, but that was *years* later, *wasn't it?* Could he have been screwing other women, his friends' wives, his secretaries, with Ma out of the way in a tiny village at the other end of the country with a sick baby?

A water mountain hangs in air then crashes. *Yes, that would have been just like him. No, I can't, I don't . . .* I'm tipped, turned, tumbled . . . *Yes, no, yes . . .* My feet find sand. I trot to the shore and halt to get my breath.

Possibly.

I dry. I dress. I drive to the house Ma moved into soon after Dad died. She's sitting in her kitchen, not eating, not even reading, the morning paper beside her, folded, pristine.

'Did you have a lovely swim? What a good idea to go to the beach as soon as you arrived. Rinse that awful aeroplane air out of you. Which beach did you go to? Coffee? No, you prefer tea. The water's boiled. And have something to eat. Or later, don't rush, there's no need, he's not expecting you till twelve-thirty. Oh and the maid has pressed your suit. It got creased in your suitcase. Did you think just hanging it in the cupboard would make it fall straight?'

'Do I need to wear a suit to see the rabbi?'

'Darling, you can wear whatever you want. She's also ironed your white shirt. I thought perhaps you might like to wear this. The one you brought is quite loud but of course it's up to you.'

She drapes a dark tie of Dad's across my arm and, still in her dressing gown, wanders through a glass door out into the garden, kicks off her slippers, kneels and digs her trowel into the gravelly earth beneath her lemon tree.

'Come outside, Dave. Dave? Don't sit inside. It's a glorious morning. It's going to be even warmer than I predicted.'

'Can I help you?'

'Help? With what? My weeding? You won't need that jersey when you go out, not even a light one. But goodness, it makes me think, wasn't the sea water freezing?'

She presses her palm into her face as though to flatten it, to smear away all feeling, and here under the branches of the lemon where you might let yourself believe we can't be seen she does what she never did, lets herself slide, no, fall, give up, give way against my chest and folds her arms round me.

The rabbi's shirt is open at the neck, long grey hairs tendrilling, and as he strides towards me, he's tucking it round his paunch into his jeans.

'I wish you long life.'

'Thank you, rabbi. Same to you.'

'Your mother tells me you flew in. From where, from London, yes?'

'When did she tell you that?'

'I just put down the phone to her.'

'You just spoke to her?'

'Why not?'

'Is she ok?'

'Well, depends on what you're asking. No and yes. I speak to her every few hours. I have since your brother passed away. Three times during the night.'

'Really?'

'You think she isn't a religious woman?'

'I never thought of her that way.'

'How do you think of her? You know, at certain times people like me have our uses. How does she seem to you?'

'Well, you know . . .'

'I know what I know. Now I'm asking you.'

'Deeply upset.'

'Yes, well, that's so but it's not yet as bad as it's going to be. The shock absorbs some pain, not all, a portion. How long are you staying? At least a few weeks?'

'I've not decided.'

'Decide. She needs you. She needs all her family. Your sisters are coming, yes?'

'They live in the States.'

'I know where your sisters live. Upstate New York, correct? It takes a while to get here.'

'They arrive tomorrow morning.'

'They'll stay, I know them. Very nice women, very loving to your mother. You're not going back immediately?'

'No.'

'No? What kind of "no"? The kind that means "yes"?'

'I'll stay as long as she needs me.'

'Now don't exaggerate.'

'Rabbi, I—'

'Don't tell tall tales. But you must stay at least a month. Why not? You have a job? Of course but you also have a mother.'

'Look, are there things we need to do?'

'Certainly. Why else are you here? Do you wish to see the body? Yes, I know, it's a tough decision. You may regret it if you say yes, you may regret it even more if you say no. When you've made up your mind, tell me, I'll make a phone call. Otherwise . . . There are some papers to sign. Not many. Getting yourself put into the ground is not a complicated business, not compared with getting yourself through life. Speaking of business, I remember when I officiated at the funeral of your late father . . . You want to sit down? Come inside.'

His office is tiny with a low ceiling and scuffed-up walls and no carpet or furniture except for a heavy table with nothing on it but a box of cotton tips and a clothes rack with a single bar from which hangs a long *tallit*, its edges embroidered with glittering silver.

'I did business with your father. Did you know that? Not in a big way, I'm not a rich man. In fact, to put it correctly, the business that we did was your father's generous way of supporting . . . I won't say the synagogue, though he did that as well. Ok, he helped me personally. I was grateful to him. And always of course it was Joe signing the papers, the contract, whatever it happened to be, along-side me. I sign, Joe signs. Your father was a titan, you know that, don't you. He was a man who should have lived for ever. But that's not how the world is. So, comes his funeral— Do you find what I'm saying offensive?'

'No.'

'Who's going to sign the documents for his burial? I remember so clearly that feeling. Who's going to countersign Joe's documents? I know it may sound silly.'

'Rabbi, you don't remember?'

'Remember what? Ah! Yes. It was you. I'm sorry. It was twenty years ago. It *was* you?'

When I open my eyes, the painfully blunt edge of the grass where it's been hacked by the blade of a lawnmower is the first thing I see.

'Are you ok, my boy?'

'I think so.'

'You want a glass of water?'

'I just needed . . . I hardly slept on the plane.'

'Some fresh air. I'm sorry.'

'It's fine.'

'I shouldn't have . . . You have enough to . . .'

'It's all a bit . . .'

'Unexpected? My boy, in this life the unexpected is what you have to expect. And what you don't expect from a rabbi is for him to say fatuous things like what I just said. Come back in out of the sun. Let's get this over and done with. No need to feel your nice suit pocket for a pen. I have a drawer full of them.'

'What do I need to know—?'

'About the funeral? Nothing at all. It's quite straightforward. The people come in . . . How many do you think there'll be?'

'I've no idea.'

'However many there are, the people come in, I speak, briefly I promise. Then prayers and so on. Oy yoy yoy yoy. They wheel in the body. More oy yoy yoy. Who will the pallbearers be? Do you know yet? Never mind, time enough to arrange it. But you will be one, yes?'

'I will be one.'

'So you're in charge, ok with you? I give you signs of what to do, you follow me.'

'We don't need to rehearse?'

'How do you mean?'

'In theatre we have what we call technical rehearsals.'

'Oh yes, interesting. What happens? You perfect the practical aspects. We can do so if you wish.'

'Is it necessary?'

'Not at all. Life can be a kind of technical rehearsal. I could speak about this in my sermon. Life could be no more than a technical rehearsal but that is what, in my opinion, it should not be. Life should be a big musical show with lights and dancing girls. Is it a good subject for my sermon? It's certainly highly original. My boy, listen to me. You have neglected your mother. You know that? I see a lot of this from your generation but your case is, forgive me but if I don't say it who will and it must be said, exceptional. Why do you think she calls me every three hours? With whom can she share her anguish?'

'I speak to her, of course I do.'

'Once a week? Once a month? Don't bullshit me. You run a theatre in London. Well, no doubt that's a highly prestigious affair, I wouldn't know about that, I've never been there. The fact is she had two sons, now she has one. That son must move back home to be with her. Do you need me to spell it out? She's your mother, she needs you. Are you listening? What are you looking at? The cotton tips? Here's my prayer book, look at it, the pages of course are new but the casing is ancient silver, possibly medieval, from the old country, it belonged to my grandfather and his grandfather before him. You see the engraving in Hebrew? Can you read it? Are you even interested to know what it means? I call you "my boy" but I think you're actually older than me. How old are you? I'm forty-eight. Isn't it time you took full account of what matters in life? It isn't dancing girls. I use those cotton tips to keep the casing of my grandfather's prayer book nice and clean. So, did you make up your mind? Do you want to see the body of your brother or don't you? The men in the morgue will instruct you not to touch the body, not to try to kiss it, him, but whether you do or not is up to you.'

1964

They're off playing ping-pong or bridge. Sonny's at the swimming pool with the sexy, older kids. I'm looking after Jeff. I'd so much rather be finishing reading *A Rocket for the Toff* by John Creasey.

There's a jet of water pulsing out – tick, tick, tick – in a circling arc watering the croquet field. Jeff and I are playing in the harsh sun on the see-saw. He's wearing, as always, his metal brace resting on his hips with a rubber pad under his chin. We go up, we go down, up, down till we're both sick of it.

'Jeff, how would it be, would you find it more exciting if we tried it with you standing up? Come on, just stand straight on your end, you'll be able to stay standing up, right?'

He grins, says nothing.

'Ok, stand, let's try it and see.'

As soon as his side of the plank is in the air, with nothing to hold on to he topples and crashes down. From nowhere Ma thrusts in, croons to him, comforting him, cradling the tender flesh below the metal strut wherever her fingers can edge their way in.

'How could you be so *idiotic*?'

'I didn't mean to hurt him.'

'No? Then why did you do such a stupid thing? You're not a stupid boy.'

I don't know what the fuck I am, stupid, cunning, careless, envious, sorry, resentful, distressed, *so angry with him, with Ma, with all of them* running from the carnage as far as I can, away, away, straight line, straight line, into the high dry grass with its sharp cutting blades at the shadow end of the croquet field.

The Cherry Orchard
by Anton Chekhov, English version by Simon Stephens,
directed by Katie Mitchell

2014

Sometimes it's easy. One morning Katie Mitchell came into the theatre.

'I'd like to do *The Cherry Orchard*.'

As written, from act to act the play moves from room to room in the Gayev family mansion and on their estate. Act 1 takes place in the nursery. Lyuba Ranevskaya returns to her family home after five years away. Act 2 is set in 'open fields'. The family, its servants and other dependants gather near a river. They're so short of money their ownership of their estate, including the famous orchard, is threatened. Act 3 'The Drawing Room', a party during which news arrives that the estate and orchard have been sold at auction. In Act 4 we're back in the nursery. Ranevskaya leaves her family home for the last time.

Katie and Vicky Mortimer, her designer, want to create 'real' rooms. The audience, they feel, should live in this house for a while and get a feeling for its beauty and solidity before it's lost. We don't have the means to achieve two highly detailed rooms as well as 'open fields' so they decide that all four acts will take place in a cross-section of the house so craftily designed that the audience gaze in at a drawing room which leads through wide portals into the nursery, to one side of which you can catch just a glimpse of sunlight reflected off glass doors leading out onto the invisible garden.

Another staging idea was that at the end of each act a screen would be let down concealing the rooms, that it would stay down for just a few seconds and that when it rose some change to the rooms would have taken place to indicate the passing of time, to suggest that some living had happened. Quite late in rehearsals this idea was rephrased. In performance, the first two times the screen rose, the stage looked exactly as it had in the previous act but when it rose for the third time on Act 4, having been down for almost no time at all, the rooms had been brutally stripped. Books, cushions, curtains, bedclothes, carpets, knick-knacks, paintings had all vanished. The Gayev era was over.

In Act 1, when Ranevskaya (played by Kate Duchêne) returns after five years away to the house of her childhood, one of those who welcomes her is the forty-year-old 'eternal student' Trofimov (Paul Hilton) who had been tutor to her young son Grisha when he drowned in the river that runs through the estate. It was because of this catastrophe that she fled the house for Paris where she's lived ever since. On seeing Trofimov she bursts into tears.

> **Ranevskaya** My Grisha. My little boy. My son.
> **Trofimov** Shhh. Please. Sshhh. Don't cry.
> **Ranevskaya** My little boy drowned. Why did that
> happen. Why did that happen to me? Can you tell me?

Even though she moves quickly on to talk of other things – Trofimov's lost good looks, her exhausted daughter's need for sleep – in Katie's production the mother's grief saturated this scene, and every scene. When the memory of the lost child first arose in her, distress smashed against Kate Duchêne's body knocking her down with the force of a great wave. Throughout the evening, that is throughout the months that Ranevskaya stays on her estate, the weight of Grisha's death never lifts. Can she think clearly enough to listen to the plan her estate manager Lopakhin (Dominic Rowan) has come up with to save her estate?

> **Ranevskaya** I'm afraid I don't understand you.

She destroys all relics of her life in Paris but it's not possible for her to imagine a future. She's transfixed in the torturing seconds in which water flooded her child's lungs and his last breath left him. Why did he die? Neglect? By whom? His tutor? Even if this were proved, it's a mother's responsibility to care for her child. Are these responsibilities assigned by culture, by society? No, the link between mother and child is as natural as roots in earth, or it ought to be. Is there some dark flaw buried in her that caused her to fail her son? What distracted her? Frivolous interest in fashionable folk, a love affair, parties, the theatre? Or is her elaborate grief itself a distraction from something else? Is she self-dramatising, wilfully overdoing it? In Act 4 the governess Carlotta (Sarah Malin) mocks her.

> **Carlotta** (*picks up a bundle of rags that she squashes to resemble a swaddled baby*) Oh my little baby. Bye, bye little baby. (*She throws the voice of the baby, making it do a crying sound.*) My poor little babby boo. Mummy won't forget you. (*She throws the bundle back into the luggage.*)

Critics and others sometimes argue that it's the job of a play to ask questions, not to provide answers. But this is the wrong way round. If you *have* answers, if you *know* why life happens as it does, why would you keep it to yourself?

A Streetcar Named Desire
by Tennessee Williams, directed by Benedict Andrews

2014

I'm late. I hurry off the street, turn left into the brightly lit cafe. At the window in the golden sunlight sits a gold-blonde woman who, by chance, at first glance slightly resembles the actress who I'm scanning the depth of the room to find but who – yes, I'm quite sure – is not yet here. Great. I'm not late after all. I've a moment to glance more closely at . . .

'I'm Gillian.' She half stands, releasing a smile into the air, reaching out her tiny hand.

'So sorry I'm . . .'

'Don't be. I'm enjoying catching my breath. I seldom get the chance. Sit. Ha!, listen to me inviting you into your own home.'

'You know this place?'

'I come here all the time.'

'Tea? Coffee? Water?'

'You look anxious. You *were* expecting to see me?'

'People often ask me if I'm anxious, I don't know why.'

'Because you look anxious.'

'No, it's not because of that, honestly, it's because I'm Polish.'

'You're *Polish*?' Now she's laughing.

'No, not really, joke.'

'I get it.'

'It's complicated. I had Lithuanian grandparents.'

'No, I get it. But you know, *I'm* Polish.'

'Anderson? Ah, no, you mean you're anxious?'

Another honey smile.

'I'm happy to be here, I am truly.'

Hamid, the waiter from Casablanca,

'Yes, Miss? I know what he wants, fresh mint tea, always the same. Two fresh mint tea?'

'Ordinary tea for me please.'

'Thanks, Hamid.'

'So—'

'So?'

'So, there are few roles I long to play. Not that I'm choosy. No, I am, I'm lucky, I can be. But *her* . . .' She pulls a clown face, mocking her depth of feeling. 'I think of Blanche not as me, I'm certainly not her, I hope not anyway, but as *mine*. I feel she's been inside me for a long time, since I first read her aged sixteen. I've been desperate to play her ever since.'

'Then you should do that.'

'Yes. The reason I've come to talk to *you* . . . I went to look at other places, other theatres, a few, not many. This is the right place, or *I* think so, for what I want to do with her, with Tennessee's play.'

'And that's because . . . ?'

'Because many fine actresses have played her, my god, everyone wants to, this part, what can I say. I want to do it close up.'

'Got it, we can do that.'

'Not staring through a picture frame. Not remote, declaiming, la la la. Intimate, overlooked, which is what you can do here, I'm right about that, aren't I?'

'You know, I really want to do this.'

She blushes slightly, looks down, sips her tea.

'You want to? Thank you. That's terrific.'

'There's just one thing—'

'There always is. Bless you if there's just one.'

'We'll need to agree on a director.'

'That's fine, you were bound to say that. I've a suggestion.'

'Great. I have one too.'

'I *know* who I want.'

'Ah.'

'What?'

'No, please go on.'

'Who I believe would be ideal for *me*.'

'I get that but I'm going to have to like the idea.'

'I know. Who's yours?'

'Let's speak together.'

'Say both our ideas at the same time?'

'Yup.'

'Great thinking.'

'Ready? Though I think you know who I'm going to say.'

'I hope I'm going to say the same name.'

Benedict Andrews calls from Reykjavik where he lives.

'Magda and I . . . I need to just say this straight, ok? You ready? We've failed to find a way to design the play.'

Magda Willi, his designer, had flown in from Berlin for four days. Three have gone by.

'We've been working really hard. So I should warn you, which is why I'm calling, that we might end up with nothing.'

He laughs like a starter motor turning over.

'It's not easy if you've done the play before. Don't get me wrong, it's truly great to have this opportunity. You can come back to *Streetcar* again and again. I love it even more now it's defeating us. But it's so deep, it has so many layers, psychological, spiritual. We're looking for something entirely different from what Magda and I invented last time, though equally special.'

I'd been at the Berlin Schaubühne to catch a new show devised by visiting Israelis and Palestinians mixed in with the Schaubühne acting company. When it ends, as I come out into the spaceship circular foyer, there's my friend Tobias Veit, the executive director.

'If you hurry, you have just five minutes, you can see another.'

'Really?'

'It's an excellent *Streetcar* by one of our younger directors, Australian actually. I somehow feel, you know, with all your interest in our German style of production' – he's grinning, only the English think there is such a thing – 'of course that's quite a generalisation but, even so, perhaps Benedict is one you should get acquainted with, maybe. Now you have three minutes. What do you think?'

'Wow, well, thank you, I'd love to but it's late and my flight's at seven in the morning.'

'Well, of course it's up to you.'

'Oh fuck it. Thank you. Where do I go?'

When Gillian and I agreed we wanted Benedict for *Streetcar*, she didn't know he'd directed it before.

'But then would he have any interest in doing it again with us?'

Years go by, you change, the world changes, the play's changed but has it changed enough? You can't fake your response to a great work and you sure can't repeat.

On the phone I say to Benedict

'Your first *Streetcar* had almost nothing, a bare stage that revolved, a table, a chair, a bowling ball, a door that opened onto the actual street. It was a fabulous design.'

'Yes, well, thanks but now we need a totally different almost nothing – though *which one*? I don't want to worry you. What we're searching for is a design that works precisely in your theatre, that's open, that's expressive of the whole of Stanley's apartment. Magda and I feel we need a certain amount of detail this time that evokes the grit, the terrain of the journey – philosophical, emotional, whatever name you put to it – that Blanche, no, that Tennessee, our playwright, was on.'

'Sounds great.'

'Easy to describe. We're so far from achieving anything.'

So what do I do? Cancel the show? Obviously no and it's too late, anyway, it's been on sale for weeks. Should I get angry?

'We'll keep working obviously. But I thought – we know each other well enough – that I should warn you.'

'You do have one more day.'

'I know but I'm not hopeful.'

The French Quarter of New Orleans. Blanche is hoping to find a home with her sister and brother-in-law, Stella and Stanley. Creditors have taken her family home in Mississippi. She's in her early thirties. She's broke. She has nowhere else to go.

We're in the theatre rehearsing on the full set for the first time. Gillian/Blanche enters. Her filigree gold hair. Her pearly white, tightly tailored suit glistens. She drags behind her a suitcase on wheels, her ball and chain. What you watch are her eyes wide as the sky, peering through lenses of burnt crimson. She steps out, knees raised high, a length at a time, like a pavane.

> **Eunice** What's the matter, honey? Are you lost?
> **Blanche** They told me to take a streetcar named Desire, and then transfer to one called Cemeteries and ride six blocks and get off at – Elysian Fields!
> **Eunice** That's where you are now.

Ma is crying too much to drive. She pulls over. To look at me in the back seat she has to swing her body right round making little hillocks in the dark cloth of her dress. Her breast presses into the firm car cushion. In the light of the street lamp her face is furrowed.

'But if that's how he behaves to me, how can I . . . ? I don't know how to . . .'

She cries. She can't speak.

The windows are rolled up. It's steamy in here. Will it seem unfeeling if I—?

'Say it, Ma.'

'You don't seem to realise.' She's shouting. 'It's hard to talk about these things.'

'I know, Ma.'

Forget the window.

'We're married thirty-five years. I want to be loyal to him. It's hard for me.'

The shouting seems to have relaxed her but there's no sigh, no release. I wind down the window.

'Don't do that.'

'There's no one to hear us.'

Even past midnight it's a busy street.

'How can I play the wife to him . . . ?'

'If?'

'What?'

'If what, Ma?'

'If he . . . Don't be stupid. You're not a stupid person.'

'Ma, I can't help you if you don't tell me what's upset you.'

'I'm not asking for anyone's help.'

'Do you mean is he . . . ?'

'You *know* he is.'

'I know nothing, Ma.'

She lunges away squealing with humiliation, pulling the cloth of her dress straight, pressing her face onto her knees.

'Ma, he wouldn't talk to me about what he gets up to even if he is.'

'Liar! What are you laughing at?'

'I'm not laughing. But I'm so surprised you say that. You know he never talks about anything to me.'

> **Stanley** My clothes stickin' to me. Do you mind if I make myself comfortable?
> **Blanche** Please, please do.
> **Stanley** Be comfortable is my motto.
> **Blanche** It's hard to stay looking fresh. I haven't washed or even powdered my face and—

'Gillian.'

'Yeah, Benno?'

'Can we try that one more time?'

'Surely we *can* try that one more time. I'd *like* to try that one more time. Especially if I can have a pair of shoes that don't *squeak*. Though I adore my shoes. Do you adore my fancy shoes? Is there a way I can somehow keep the shoes and lose the squeak?'

Even without the dog tag dangling at his neck you'd know Ben Foster's Stanley is an ex-soldier. The natural stance of his tanned, muscled torso says 'I've seen worse, I'm ready, for you, for anything.'

'Ben.'

'Benno?'

Benedict's up on the stage which is placed at the centre of the auditorium with the audience on all sides. As the story plays out the stage revolves. The audience see into the kitchen, the bedrooms, the bathroom. No aspect of Blanche, Stanley, Stella's lives is concealed.

Benedict calls up into the flies

'Can you kindly stop this damn thing turning? Thank you.'

Ben and Gillian are sitting on the bed. Benedict leans over them whispering, almost nuzzling them, his hands moving like he's scooping milk.

I can see Ma in the rear-view mirror staring through the wind-screen straight ahead.

'He doesn't *talk* to me, he doesn't *connect* to me in any way whatsoever.'

'Is it worse than it was?'

She throws her head back like she's acting laughter in a play.

'Ho, ho, ho.'

'Don't do that, Ma.'

'Oh, it's funny.'

'What's funny, Ma?'

'Everything. *I so don't want it to be like this!*'

Stage manager: 'Where shall we go back to?'

'Let's pick it up from just before we stopped. Alright with everybody?'

'In the evenings, I've never any idea, none, what time he'll be home, ever. In the morning as he goes to work I ask shall I make dinner for him. In the afternoon, I phone him to check, things change, important meetings come up, I'm not a selfish woman.'

'I know, Ma.'

'He has a phone on his desk, the old kind, heavy, black, you know what I mean.'

'That phone doesn't work, Ma.'

'It works, I've seen him use it. But he never answers when it's me. His secretary says "Yes, Mrs Lan, I'll tell Mr Lan you phoned but Mr Lan has an extremely full day." How do you think I feel? Should I wait for him? I read but I have to read the page over and still I don't know what's happening in the story. I hear his car coming up the drive, I want to run out the back door—'

'Ma . . .'

'He doesn't look for me, he doesn't call my name. He walks in, goes upstairs, gets into bed, doesn't even take off his clothes, well, his trousers and shoes, he pulls the quilt up over him, reads his *Time* magazine.'

'He's depressed, Ma.'

'You think I'm stupid? I know he is.'

'Is he drinking badly?'

'There's always a bottle by his side of the bed. I clear it in the morning, I don't want the maid knowing anything.'

At the first technical rehearsal, when the set first began to turn, the speed that was set was too fast, you couldn't connect to the actors. It span like a top, a whirligig.

Benedict edged up.

'Is this whole idea a fuckin' disaster?'

'It'll work. Just slow it down.'

'The idea we've been working on is it should sweep by.'

'I think try it slower.'

Stage manager: 'Benno, like so?'

'Try even slower. Can they play a scene?'

'Gillian, Ben – would you . . .'

'Sure thing.'

> **Stanley** If I didn't know you were my wife's sister I'd get
> ideas about you.
> **Blanche** Such as?
> **Stanley** Don't play so dumb. You know what!

The stage revolves more slowly and more slowly. Suddenly there's form, outline, definition. Then . . . snap. Focus! That's it.

'Great! Will you mark that?'

'I've marked it.'

'Is it ok, do you think? It's so much slower than I imagined. Whew! Gillian, Ben, at that speed, it's wonderful. We can edge it up and down a wee bit but we've cracked it.'

Then to me

'You're sure it's going to work?'

'It's working.'

'Whoops, almost lost it for a moment there I did.'

'You didn't really.'

'No, I didn't really. It's good, no?'

'It's great.'

He's in need of a hug so I hug him.

The Life of Galileo
by Bertolt Brecht, directed by Joe Wright

2017

'I'm sure it's all my fault.'

'Yes, David, it is.'

'I can't work out how our dates got muddled.'

'I can. You said you'd keep the end of the year for me.'

'Well, if I did—'

'You did.'

'Then I'm useless. I apologise, ok? Either it slipped my mind or, dunno, I offered those dates to someone else forgetting . . . or their dates moved and I tried to fix that by . . . never mind, if you thought I was keeping them for you—'

'That was my slot or so I believed.'

'We don't have slots, Joe. That's too, I don't know what, mechanical?

We're not a factory. I try to produce shows at the ideal time, for a long run or a short run, in whatever way's best for that particular show.'

Ok, bad moment to try to suggest what a creative producer I am.

'God knows what happened, I haven't a clue. I'm rubbish, ok? But *can* you do it in September?'

And he said, as they all do,

'It depends on when my film starts shooting. Their dates keep moving. And the script's not ready. It's not *bad* though actually it's not very good. Yet. But . . . So no, those dates aren't fixed. Almost. Not absolutely. They must be soon! So it could work. Possibly.'

He laughs. I especially love him for this way he has of swinging one-handed off the planet. It has to work out. We'll go down every route, we'll try everything.

In late summer I visit him in a small palazzo south of Florence that belongs to his old close friends. Warm-hearted, intellectual *mamma*, towering sons, exotic daughters, aged aunts and uncles have been gathering to this shady cradle since the dawn of time to eat ragù and gaze down at the sun-splattered valleys. High rooms lined with history and sketches, my bed up a rickety ladder through a trapdoor to a whitewashed cell not too far below the sky . . .

We stroll through rye fields, wade through dusty olive pathways lined with stands of plane and pine and burst out into sunlight. Joe rhapsodises . . .

How to drench a theatre in ideas and feeling. How to place the cosmos on a stage.

Quite by chance, nearby is a monastery where Galileo was a student. In this tidy, pebbled courtyard edged with ancient, deep-scarred wooden benches, he stared up at the stars and planets, 'starry messengers' he called them, whose revolutionary messages are

Everything that can move does move.

God's not in heaven, he's everywhere.

Nothing is chance, everything has meaning. Everything's part of not a cosmic plan but a cosmic pattern.

To see this pattern you must stand back quite far.

I'm standing, back pressed to the wall of a ramshackle hall in Islington. The stage Lizzie Clachan has designed is the rim of a circle wide enough to almost fill the whole of the YV auditorium. Most of the audience will sit around it on tiers with fifty or so of them perched on cushions in the epicentre. The story will unfold on this circular track, the actors revolving like planets or stars. High above, the heavens, space, infinity will be projected onto a vast dome.

> *Galileo and the boy Andrea appear. From the ceiling hangs a model of the universe according to the Ptolemaic system. Andrea takes it down.*
> **Andrea** What is it?
> **Galileo** It shows how, according to those who studied these things long ago, the stars move round the earth.
> **Andrea** How does it show that?
> **Galileo** Let's take a close look. Begin at the beginning. Describe what you see.
> **Andrea** In the middle is a little stone.
> **Galileo** That's the earth.

Wearing white T-shirt and jeans, straddling a high wooden stool, somehow facing forwards and backwards at the same time, Joe has full command of the room. He brandishes a loudhailer but it's self-satire: 'Here's how we do it in the movies', an outsize cardboard prop, amusing only because it's the opposite of how he relates to his actors, constantly nipping down to be with them in close-up, intimate, bare feet padding the track alongside Galileo (Brendan Cowell) and Andrea (Billy Hoyle), cheek to cheek, arms stretched around their shoulders, provocative, confident, loving like the potter loves the wet clay on his wheel.

> **Galileo** Do you understand what I told you yesterday?
> **Andrea** No. How do you expect me to? It's very difficult and I'm not even eleven till October.
> **Galileo** I want you to understand, you particularly. That's why I buy expensive books instead of paying the milkman, so people like you can understand my discoveries.
> **Andrea** But I can see *with my own eyes* that the sun's now in a different place from where it was this morning. I don't care what you say, it *can't* be standing still.

We're on the way home but Dad suddenly swerves into a slip road. Sonny grabs the front seat.

'No, Dad, please not Granny Golda now!'

'What's the matter with you? This will only take five minutes.'

'With you, Dad, nothing's ever five minutes.'

In Granny's kitchen he gently clears aside the bowls of flour and jars of oil and guides her through the shop's weekly accounts speaking, as he always does with her, in Yiddish, his first language. He learned English before either of his parents so even as a young child he was king.

Decades later, Golda's daughter Becky tells me her mother was all her life virtually illiterate. So who read the thick volumes on her shelves by Ben-Gurion and Abba Eban?

She feeds Dad barley soup with *kreplach*. Sonny and I won't eat anything.

'Even one mouthful, Dovidol, Soningka, sweetheart. Why? You're not so happy with mine cooking?'

Out in the garden, we hold a summit under the date palm. Cars whizz by, whizz by on their way home.

'His mother is his wife, his brothers and his sister are his children, so who are we?'

We've never before landed this thought so daringly. It makes us heart-sore and breathless. We parrot the few mish-mash Yiddish words we know and chortle till we hear Granny's beetroot voice outraged at some detail, full-throated, yelling. It's funny but horrifying.

'Oy, it's *tsuros* now they're *hukking*,' Sonny whispers but the pleasure's gone out of it.

The *kreplach* Granny's made are spread out to dry on windowsills. She stacks some into a biscuit tin.

'Give it your ma, she likes how I make it. Jossie, now I'm angry with your kids. Dovidol, take the tin for your ma! Soningka, give your Granny a kiss!'

Brendan has the bounce of a wrestler and a rocker's sensuality. His Galileo uncovers truths about the cosmos with his nervous system, his muscles as though sprinting up a mountain or battling a strong wind.

> **Galileo** Nothing in the universe is fixed in one place!
> There are other suns!
> **Sagredo** Calm yourself. You think too quickly.
> **Galileo** Excite yourself, man! What you saw no one has
> ever seen before!

Brendan pounds the track, fists thrust above his head, a winner on a victory lap, exultant thought made flesh, truth lived through exhilaration. God is in us or nowhere.

> *The Medici Palace in Florence*
> **Virginia** Father, I'm afraid.
> **Galileo** Don't show your feelings. We won't go home.

We'll go to Voli, the glasscutter. I have an arrangement.
In the yard next door he always keeps a wagon with
empty wine-casks ready to smuggle me out of the city.
They start to leave.
A High Official Signor Galilei, it's my duty to inform
you that the Court of Florence is no longer able to resist
the urgent demand of the Holy Inquisition to examine
you in Rome. The Inquisition's coach is waiting for you.

A deep rumble. The wall of the auditorium drags open, a bank of
steep stairs is shoved in. In his light summer clothes, which now
seem to leave him naked, Galileo lumbers towards the thick smoke
and the columns of light jutting in. Drumrolls. He mounts the
stairs, looking over his shoulder at his child. Is this the last time
he'll ever see her? As he climbs, he glares back at us accusingly.
Why in God's name does it have to be him?

Late in rehearsal I watched a run and afterwards talked about it to
Joe in a way that upset him. Next day, a Sunday, he called – or did I
call him? – and said in a strong though wounded voice that I'd been
too harsh, too unforgiving. But, he said, he'd written about it in his
diary and, looking back to notes he'd made last time we worked
together, found that then I'd done the same thing.

'But when you remembered that, did it make you feel better or
worse?'

Better about himself, *A Season in the Congo* had been a big hit,
worse about me. Generously, he asks the question I can't ask.

'Or is it possible that if you hadn't said what you said last time, even
though it made me deeply unhappy, that show wouldn't have . . .'

Neither of us can finish the sentence. Possibly. Unlikely. Could
be. Who knows?

It all depends. Am I as insightful as I think I am in those moments in the dark when what seem to be 'insights' come? Longer, shorter, faster, slower, cut this, add that, it doesn't make sense, start the story at the end. It isn't asked for, it's a spasm, it's neurology. Sharing the hunch is as intimate as sex. It's a fledgling you nurse in warm hands before releasing into calm air. It's one to one, it has to be. And we're best of friends, aren't we? For this time of our lives there's no one closer. I trust you. Trust me.

He'd called – if it *was* him and, yes, it must have been – because he wanted me to know that though he *was* hurt by my roughness, abruptness, whatever it had been, it was alright between us, that perhaps – deep breath – some of it had been almost kinda useful.

Or maybe, Joe, I screwed up. I screw up all the time. I talk and talk. It doesn't mean anything.

> *1640. Galileo now lives in a house outside Florence, a*
> *prisoner of the Inquisition.*
> **Andrea** Your book will found a whole new science of
> physics.
> **Galileo** Stuff it under your coat.
> **Andrea** And we thought you had betrayed us! My voice
> was raised loudest against you!
> **Galileo** And quite right too. I taught you science and I
> denied the truth.
> **Andrea** This changes everything.
> **Galileo** Does it?
> **Andrea** You *concealed* the truth. From the enemy. Even in
> the field of ethics you were a thousand years ahead of us.

Why is it, Dad, that musing on a mash-up of you and Galileo reminds me of a tiny, elderly headman who lived in the Valley in the village of the lepers. Apart from the pillbox hat he wore perched on one side of his hairless head, he owned nothing, no land, not even chickens. His village being far from a river, he couldn't grow maize or melons. His hut had no table, no chairs, the mud floor was cracked, the roof fallen in. His vest and shorts had gaping holes, *were* gaping holes. The mat on which he slept was terminally tattered.

From time to time an elephant would wander south, tread on a landmine left over from the war. The 'boom' would echo across the breadth of the Valley. He'd borrow a bicycle, hurtle towards the crater, gather flesh and still be sampling it weeks later though by then it was wormy and rotten.

But here's the thing. When I first cycled down the track to his village, he didn't ask me for cash or for employment as so many other impoverished people did. He welcomed me with a gift. In a twist of newspaper he'd wrapped a paste of wild herbs which, he said, if you rub a little on your forehead brings you great good fortune.

Yerma
by Simon Stone after Federico García Lorca, directed by
Simon Stone

2016

One summer in France we gathered a small flock of mallard ducks. I fell for them, their cockiness, their easily faked-up rage, how they square their haunches and hold their ground, their lightning reactions. Throw a nut at a mallard, if the core is good they nip it out of the air, if it's rotten they don't even shift their feet. So when the lights went up on Simon's Melbourne production of *The Wild Duck* and the first thing you see is a lonely mallard in a vast glass box, I think

'Well, I know at least *one* of the actors.'

As soon as it's over I scurry upstairs, down corridors, out into the cold and swerve right to the stage door. I don't even know what he looks like.

'So what do you think? Will you do a show for me?'

'Definitely.'

'When are you free?'

'I've got lots on. I'll let you know good dates as soon as they're clear to me.'

I scooted round Europe where other shows of his were playing. In Paris a five-year-old *Thyestes* also from Melbourne, at the Amsterdam Toneel Groep a *Medea* newly created for them.

'After that I quite fancy doing *Phaedre*.'

'Racine or Euripides?'

'Well, Racine, no? Though Euripides is good.'

'I once did a version of the Euripides.'

'*Hyppolitos*?'

'Yup.'

'Directed?'

'No, wrote.'

'Oh, did you now? Interesting. Full of jokes, isn't he, Euripides. Funny old bugger. Yes, I quite like him. The Racine's the bigger challenge though.'

'Is it?'

'No question.'

'I guess it is.'

'Yeah, *huge* challenge. It's a cathedral.'

'Let's do it then.'

'You think it's the right idea?'

'Let's do the Racine.'

'Simon, I hear Warlikowski's *Phaedre* is coming to London.'

'Is it now? That's damn annoying. Especially as it's magnificent.'

'I haven't seen it.'

'Oh, wow, you haven't? You should. It's always on some place. Of course it's not only Racine. It's Sarah Kane, it's Wajdi Mouawad, god knows who else he popped into the soup . . . He's a master chef. Well, that's torn a hole in it.'

'Do you think?'

'I do.'

'It's on for only four days.'

'Yes, but once it's happened it's happened. What's your opinion?'

'Let's have another idea.'

'I'm sure that's right. I'll have a think.'

'There is one I could suggest right now.'

'Oh there is?'

'I've been saving it up for a long time.'

'Oh, intriguing.'

'Or do you want to have your own think first?'

'No, now I have to know what *your* idea is.'

'Do you know *Yerma*?'

' . . .

. . .

. . .

Fuck me.'

Yerma is a childless woman living in Andalusia in the 1930s. She's desperate to have a son. Her husband Juan isn't interested.

> **Juan** Life is easier without children and that's how I like it.
> **Yerma** You'll never change your mind?
> **Juan** Never. Get used to it.

In the last scene she strangles Juan.

> **Yerma** Yes, I've killed him. I've killed my son.

Try to recreate Lorca's imagistic dialogue in English and you sense at once the translation's inauthenticity. Whose crazy poetry is this, Lorca's or the translator's? So should you abandon the idea of staging *Yerma* in English? That would be a tough decision. A woman and a man scrapping over a son, even one that doesn't yet exist. For me, it's *the* masterpiece.

'Can I visit your rehearsals?'

'Any time.'

'That's ok with you?'

'Honestly.'

'I'll sit at the back and keep quiet.'

'You don't need to give me any warning, you're the boss, just drop in.'

Of course I've forgotten the code to the door. Don't think about it, just press four buttons. *Click.* Through one door, down a short passage, gently edge open the swing doors. Oh, are they on a break? The big room is empty. No, there they all are down the far end in an odd sort of huddle. I take a seat against the wall up this end and imagine I'm anywhere else. It's a touch embarrassing because all they seem to be doing is giggling, no, snorting with laughter. They're laughing so much some of them get to their feet. Simon waves the length of his long arm cheerily like he's on a train pulling into a station.

'Hello producer.'

All the actors, Billie Piper, Brendan Cowell, Maureen Beattie, John MacFarlane, Charlotte Randle, Thalissa Teixeira wave, all on the same train, all cheery.

'We're not doing any actual acting today.'

'Oh right.'

'So there's nothing for you to look at.'

This comes with Simon's goofy, warm, affectionate grin which today seems to mean

'You won't believe how amazing it is, what we've got going on over here but there's no way I'm ready to let you find out what it is.'

'I'll come back tomorrow.'

'Great. Or next week even. Come back next week.'

From week three of the five they have in the rehearsal room, they break early each afternoon so Simon can go back to his hotel room and write. He brings in fresh pages each morning.

'Can I read . . . anything?'

'Ummmm . . . no, actually. I mean, yes of course, but much better to leave it till I've got a bit further down the road.'

When I run into the actors they're blissful, which is not always a good thing. It's not part of the deal that actors should be happy *all* the time. At the beginning and at the end, yes, you work for that, but there has to be some long moments of

'Fuck, we've got in too deep.'

These actors are permanently blissful. But I've begun to understand how it works, what he's up to. The play he's writing is emerging out of *Yerma, it's a Yerma for these actors,* using everything he's learning about them through all that huddling in corners as individuals, as personalities, as friends. He doesn't want them to rehearse, to do acting in any formal way. They're exploring the *Yerma* situations through their own experience, what they think about them, what they feel, intimately, profoundly – and he's listening and remembering and then going back to his hotel and writing it, not inevitably using their own words but offering back what he believes these actors can act better than anyone else in the world because these characters that Lorca imagined are now, at the same time, *them.* Perhaps this is how Shakespeare did it, or those few great writer-directors who also reworked existing plays, working closely with companies of actors, as Molière did, as Brecht did.

I visit on the Friday of the fifth week. Billie and Brendan are sitting on wonky metal chairs at either end of a small side room.

'You guys alright?'

'We're great!'

It's like I've blundered in on some druggy cult.

'We're fine, so bugger off and let us get on with learning our lines. We only got these this morning.'

'We're doing a run tomorrow. Jesus!'

'Not *a* run, *the* run. Our one and only. So what Brendan said is correct. *Jesus!*'

Because the play will happen inside a sealed glass box and therefore all the actors will be miked, when they rehearse they keep their volume as low as they will when they're performing, as delicate and intimate as 'real life'. Others watching this run are laughing – and they're gripped. I'm gripped but, as I'm somewhat deaf, I hear almost nothing.

Dad brakes hard.

'*What are you doing?*'

Ma's throat is jammed but her cry bursts through.

'Let me out of here!'

He swerves to the side. The door hurls itself back on its hinge. She tumbles out, gets to her feet staggering.

Sonny is squealing 'Ma! Ma!'

Dad clambers out. Sonny wants to go after Ma. Dad pushes her back but with tenderness.

'You both stay where you are.'

Sonny yelling 'Tell her she's bloody crazy!'

Dad's found Ma. I can barely see them in the dark. He's calming her down. She gets back in the car, her face set hard.

'It's ok, kids, nothing to worry about. Ma's a bit upset, that's all.'

He searches his pockets, can't find the key, stands there outside the car not moving. Ma reaches her arm through the dark, gropes for Sonny's hand, touches it, brushes mine.

'So, Dave, you'll have some exciting moments to put in your plays, won't you?'

On stage there'll be machinery enabling scene changes to be so speedy they'll seem magical. We can't replicate this in rehearsal but, of course, I know the plans and can follow how the stage will change from interior to exterior, from one room to the next. In Simon's *Thyestes* a full-size grand piano appears out of thin air and vanishes just as magically.

After the run I say

'It's going to be great – but where's the grand piano?'

Simon thinks about this for no longer than a mallard would and nips it just as neatly out of the air.

'Yeah, I see what you mean.'

To achieve the super-speedy changes in the dark, we'd tested and then bought yards of 'intelligent' glass which flips from transparent to opaque when a switch is tripped. The first sheet is screwed in and tested. It's clear it *almost* works, the glass is almost but not *quite* transparent, it will be annoying and distracting to the audience, so we junk it and order ordinary glass. While waiting for it to arrive, Simon, Lizzie Clachan (designer), James Farncombe (lighting designer) and the production team come up with a way of achieving a perfect black out behind the glass, with the audience on both sides just inches away, so the scene changes can occur at super speed invisibly. Also Simon has invented an equivalent of the grand piano – a room full of furniture which arrives on stage, as the piano did, out of thin air, and then disappears magically.

Sim-salabim!

All challenges have been met, everything's in its proper place. The dress rehearsal begins.

> **Her** You get home at three, fall unconscious, what am I supposed to do? I've been fucking sitting up waiting because you *promised*—
> **John** That's life. Things like that happen.
> **Her** You promised things would be different.
> **John** And you promised you would stop obsessing about this shit, you promised to give me a break from all this, you promised me a fucking moratorium on this—

Billie and Brendan purr, tease, taunt, torment, punish, brutalise, terrorise each other's hearts out. They're caged, they're miked, it's totally artificial, it's totally real, it's not acting, it's living, but who could live like this with all the dials turned up to maximum intensity?

> **John** Did you miss me?
> **Her** Of course I did. I just moved us into our house all on my own.
> **John** I'm sorry babes.
> **Her** Don't say that. Don't call me that. I'm serious.
> **John** Me too. I'm sorry. I shouldn't have left it so late. Barry organised us a meeting with the financiers at the last minute and it's a once in a lifetime—
> **Her** I'm happy for you.

I start awake. Through the thin wall between my room and theirs I hear a *crack*, not a splintering, as though a slate has been snapped.

'There! I've broken it!'

What did Dad break? Ma's dressing table mirror? Her heart? Her spirit? Overhearing grown-ups quarrel in the next room is how theatre begins.

Five

Comrades

London, 1972

My second day in England. Boxing Day. Nick and I spend the afternoon with Caryl Churchill and her family at their home in Islington. For me, every aspect of everything is new, the intensity of the cold, the rituals of the season, but for them it was just two days after the last performance of *Owners*, Caryl's new play directed by Nick, so the air was flavoured with melancholy. The ghosts have packed their suitcases but are sitting in the corners having a last look round before stoically exiting the room.

Over the decade, time and again Caryl and I would say

'Wouldn't it be great for us to write a play together?'

'Oh yes, what a good idea,' we'd say.

1986

'Actually, you know what, maybe there's something in spirit possession.'

'Oh, *I'm* interested in spirit possession too. And other kinds of non-hierarchic power, *anti-hierarchic* power, the power of marginalised people.'

'Women?'

'Obviously women. Yes. The different sorts of power women have or that they discover they have when they're under enormous pressure. Like thought transference, for example, ideas travelling over vast distances directly from brain to brain. You know the kind of thing I mean.'

'Oh yeah, like mothers lifting trucks out of the way to rescue their children.'

'Well yes but that's common or garden. It's a far richer field. That's women doing things you'd expect men to do, imitating male qualities, physical strength, rather than women performing actions only they can perform, the extraordinary things *they would be able to do* if left to themselves.'

'Collectively?'

'Meaning?'

'No, what do *you* mean?'

'I mean without men.'

'Ah yes, obviously.'

'No, I can put it better, the things that women *do* do – actually do, we just don't know about them – when they're not under male scrutiny.'

'And gay people.'

'Yes! *Their* special powers.'

'Oh, do we have any?'

'And marginalised *peoples*, whole peoples, oppressed populations and cultures.'

'Like spirit possession in the struggle against colonialism.'

'Oh yes, I think I saw there's an interesting new book about that.'

'I just wrote one.'

'Oh, so you did.'

'Well, that should be enough for a play.'

'Or two.'

'Or two.'

During our times together we laughed about everything.

'I wonder if it would be easier for us to work together if we started with a play that already existed.'

'Well, yes, I was wondering how exactly we were going to do this.'

'And we could adapt it.'

So we read widely and settled on the one great play about spirit possession that already existed: *The Bacchae* by Euripides.

Our adaptation was commissioned by the Joint Stock Theatre Company and Birmingham Repertory Theatre. Following the by then well-established Joint Stock method, as Caryl, though not I, had done many times previously, we researched and improvised with a company of actors. Then we wrote a mosaic of scenes, each with different characters, marginalised people discovering the extraordinary powers their place outside the institutions of power unexpectedly lent them.

We wrote the scenes separately and agreed that we wouldn't reveal who'd written which, which I was (and remain) keen on as it was obvious hers were more resonant, more poetic, *better* than anything I was capable of. Together we wrote some terse, allusive choric moments which told the story of the seduction of Pentheus (insider) by Dionysus (outsider), or sort of did.

We had a director, Les Waters, and a choreographer, Ian Spink. We found our title *A Mouthful of Birds* in a description of schizophrenic experience in a journal of psychiatry – 'It felt as though my mouth was filled with birds . . .'

Birmingham Rep was hoping for a follow-up to *Top Girls*, Caryl's recent hit. During the Birmingham run and on the subsequent tour the show evolved and found itself so that, six weeks later at the Royal Court, it was a fair-sized hit, but at its opening it was a series of jagged, rowdy moments interspersed with jagged, rowdy dancing. The Birmingham marketeers wrote to their patrons

'We know you've bought seats in good faith but if you'd prefer to exchange them for another production later in the season . . .'

We knew we were making something, though we knew not quite

what. Most days were invigorating but often the work seemed incoherent and outlandish. Amongst the company were broken romances. Fractiousness set in, then turbulence and now even Caryl and I couldn't agree about anything. It boiled over during a technical rehearsal—

'The lighting's so fucking dark all the actors will crash right off the fucking stage!'

and I thought

'One writer is plenty',

abandoned the theatre and set out into the big city. After a while I wandered into a street market. Amongst many stalls was one selling classical music cassettes. Fumbling through the boxes I found a symphony by Charles Ives whose music I knew pretty well. On the same cassette was a piece by Ives I didn't know existed called *Robert Browning Overture*.

'That's odd', I think, 'why've I not heard of this? I wonder what the occasion was for writing it. Hmmm. Dum ti dum. Interesting.'

I bought it and wondered on.

Hey ho. Ding ding. Time's up. Better head back into the room and face reality.

As I walk into the immense foyer, leaning against the mile-long bar is Caryl buying herself a drink. She's a close, dear friend whom I love and at the sight of her all my anger decays. I'm no longer resentful about anything. I walk across and am about to tell her this when she holds up her hand.

'Why am I thinking this?'

'What?'

'Shush. For what possible reason has this come into my mind?'

And she quotes the last line of *My Last Duchess*, the best-known poem by Robert Browning.

Which Claus of Innsbruck cast in bronze for me!

Angola, 1987

Central Angola, Huambo province, in an armoured jeep slicing through burnt dry brushland into the blinding. It's superb guerrilla country. Under cover of the sun whole armies might be hiding. The inscrutably plate-glass glaring light is unmatchable but, even so, we're not filming. This is a research trip with my producer Adam Low to persuade the BBC there's a story here in the refugee camps some miles (and miles) up the road – or perhaps they're *there*, obscured by eye-high grass and scrawny trees staggering in the glare, the glare, the razor glare and glistening.

Days before, my friend Gerald who has HIV/AIDS wrote to tell me how sick he is – but how sick *is* he?

Mile after mile of harsh red cracked red mud red track. Namibia is fighting for its freedom from South Africa. The tortured of the border regions have fled here. How can there fail to be a story, if we can unearth it? Has to be.

If he can write, lick, seal the envelope, how sick can he be?

Civil war rages also in this country but to the north and in the south. Here in the central provinces it's peaceful now or so they tell me. Even so, our guide rides shotgun in the jeep that leads. Behind, armed guards interrogate the sun from armoured jeeps.

The sun.

The sun.

The darkness.

In the camp, doctors in white coats politely ask if we'll stay in our tents. The people here don't want to see white faces. Ever? Well, at least, comrade, until we tell you otherwise.

So what to do now? Write to him.

The town's besieged. As night falls,
from each other's beds our soldiers rise
to guard each other's bodies. The high grass crawls
with enemy platoons, fire in their eyes.
At dawn strangers like us stroll into our sight.
Our men interrogate them, feed, strip, lay them down.
By noon we're dead. Under cover of light
the enemy has taken the town.

Namibia, 1989

North near the Namibia/Angola border on a gravel road that blends into the endless gravel plain, spiked here and there with silver-grey *miombo* trees like needles stuck up into tapestry that stretches north south east west endlessly.

We're endlessly improvising and re-shooting a conversation between two young refugees who've spent two years in a camp in Huambo province. Now the war is over and their country's free they are heading home on foot when we run into them.

'We're making a TV film about refugees returning to their home-land. Will you talk to us about how you've kept alive all these years and what you've seen?'

'For filming of us two? Oh, we can do that, yes, sir, why not?'

'Oh, that's great. We're grateful. Thanks so much. We really need you. Our film will be called *Welcome Home Comrades*. Possibly.'

'Oh? That's so nice. We've seen so many rough things, honestly. Which ones do you wish to hear of first?'

Now it's late afternoon, the sun is weak and some of the team are saying

'Enough already, it's freezing, you knew this idea would be hard to pull off, poor guys, they're great but they're not actors, give them a break, come on, let's pack it in.'

But some of us can only think: much of our interviewing has been, how best to put it, unrevealing. It's not easy for exhausted, frightened people to speak freely, feelingly. If this idea works, when we come to cut our little drama-doc, we're going to need this scene.

'Hey, team, we're offering them a good deal, a lift all the way to Windhoek which will save them days of walking. Comrades, where were you planning to sleep?'

'Oh, sir, we don't know that. Just somewhere in the bush.'

'We'll get you a nice hotel in town. Are you ok to try this one more time?'

'Oh yes, we're so, so clear now what you want from us.'

'You are?'

'Oh definitely. And we very much want to do it. We want that your people overseas know very, very clearly what happened in our country.'

'Get ready then. Ok, guys? Everyone set?'

'I'm set.'

'Turn over.'

We shoot them sharing memories of their journey fleeing north as now they're driven south a mile or so in the back seat of our battered blue Volkswagen. For authenticity, we want the whole two-hander in one take.

This time it's lively, coherent, quirky, deeply moving.

'Checking the gate . . . It's clean.'

Hugs and beers. We pack up, board our bus. Comrades and crew sprawled out across the seats, our cameraman starts filming, getting shots that in the final film we edit in, as we head on down the endless gravel track across the gravel plain heading south to Windhoek where they live.

Ma phones.

'Is it Dad?'

'Can you come home?'

'Not really but yes of course I will. Is he in pain?'

'Come. Quickly.'

Cape Town, 1989

By air, home is two hours. At the airport he waits in the car. It's startling, I've never seen him in a passenger seat. He unfolds like a robot manufacturing a machine. Somehow he's taller. His hair, never long, now flows over his collar stylishly but randomly blotched with grey, his cheeks grey under the red and hollow, his tanned neck scraggy and lean. Shame seems to dull his eyes like a boxer who has lost a fight the world believed he'd win.

He's stretched out on his bed, on his right side, head on his out-reached arm, striped pyjamas loose around him, still a big man, big as a Verdi or Puccini tenor. I stretch out beside him holding his ivory hand, my mind still out there on the gravel plain.

'We want the whole two-hander in one take. For authenticity.'

'I want you to know I understand now what you have with Nick is a better, a stronger thing than what there was between your ma and me. It was good on some occasions, I'm not denying that, in the beginning, in the early days. We danced, we went on picnics, we read the same magazines . . .'

He frees his hand.

'What, Dad? I can't hear you. What do you want to tell me?'

He shakes his head.

('I have nothing more to tell you.')

He shakes his head.

('And if I had I couldn't find the way to say it.')

It's winter but it's warm on the white sheets.

Intuition

Nick is invited to the Royal Court 1995 Christmas party. I've had nothing to do with them since they turned down my play *Desire* six years ago.

'You go, I don't want to.'

'You've got to get over this negativity about everything and everybody.'

'It's *not* negativity. I don't want to be there. I don't know anyone there anymore. What will I *do* all evening?'

At the party I run into Ian Rickson.

'Oh, I was going to get in touch. Would you read a play I'm directing in the New Year? It's by a young writer called Jez Butterworth. It's his first play. Stephen (Daldry) wants it to go on the main stage.'

'Really? That's bold. I'd love to. What's it called?'

'We're not too sure about the title. I'll tell you though it's quite likely to change.'

I spent much of 1996 on *Mojo* – before rehearsals, during rehearsals, as it opened, when it moved to the Duke of York's in the West End.

Doing what, exactly?

For example

'Jez, your play has four acts. Acts 1 and 2 and the last are set in a Soho club, Act 3 is in its basement. The interval comes between Acts 2 and 3. If the design is in any way realistic, and your stage directions suggest that you want it to be, there'll need to be a longish pause between Acts 3 and 4 while the stage is reset. That will screw up the rhythm of the evening. So, is there a way Act 4 can also happen in the basement?'

Jez thinks about this for two seconds.

'Possibly.'

Artistic director Stephen asks me to join his team as 'writer in residence' which makes some sense as I have a great idea for a play but I can't write every moment God sends, can anyone?

I attend the Court's famously febrile 'script meetings'. Each week the group's opinions on eight or ten new plays are solicited and meticulously marked up on the multiple columns of a complex grid. It's quickly obvious that, agree or disagree, grid or no grid, the only accurate indicator of future seasons is which plays Stephen pops into his cycling bag and takes home with him.

The job description he gave me, never written down, was 'do what you like until you meet resistance'. So if I liked the sound, the aura, the style, (the director), the feel of a new show that the theatre was producing I'd attach myself, read drafts, suggest revisions, sometimes sit in on auditions, watch many rehearsals and all the previews. Some shows I only dipped in and out of because more wasn't welcome or I had no special feeling for the subject or the artists. One show I feared would crash (weak play/ wrong director) I rewrote from start to finish over a weekend, my version going (inevitably/correctly) into the bin on Monday morning. No deal was ever made. As soon as writer or director had had enough of me, I'd be out of there/back to my own play.

But why should any director put up with this?

I guess because one never said or implied (or even thought) 'if I were writing or directing, here's how I'd do it'. What one did was intuit, if one could, what the writer or director was working to create and have ideas on how they might better achieve what they'd imagined. Possibly.

Together, Stephen and I watched every first preview.

When you direct, you usually do trade-offs.

'I'd like you to do this particular thing which you don't want to but you agree provided *I* agree to let you do some other thing *you* want to do which I *don't* want but which, provided you do the thing *I* want, I say yes to.'

Or . . . the director says

'I know the table we're using is totally wrong but the carpenter came in to make it on a Sunday morning when her child was ill.'

It's useful for someone to say

'It doesn't matter what you previously agreed and I know you've already exceeded your budget but the actor with the lisp has got to fix it or be replaced. And that blue wall at the back has to go red.'

One says

'Be strong. Go further.'

I was in Provence near Avignon working on a screenplay with my friend Peter (the film was never made). We took an afternoon off from musing with our feet up in a garden and visited the Cistercian abbey Notre-Dame de Sénanque. In front of the cheerfully magnificent though austere twelfth-century building is a vast rectangular field planted with lavender, rows and rows of lavender, nothing but lavender, it was in full flower then, row upon row of purple lavender and more lavender and nothing else. And I thought

'That's it, that's the secret. Decide what you're going to do and *just do that.*'

The Royal Court literary department hands me a play that everyone's read and enjoyed. It tells the tale of a crisis in the lives of a Pakistani–English couple, largely from the viewpoint of their kids. It's so full of life, originality, wit, insight it's obvious we have to do it but the drawback is . . .

In the play, a painful argument breaks out when the Pakistani father discovers that his youngest son hasn't been circumcised.

He's humiliated in front of his co-religionists and furious with his English wife because she hadn't noticed.

I say

'Sorry, I don't believe it.'

'But it's all true. I didn't make it up. This is about my own family.'

'A mother bathing her baby son, adoring every tender part of him, not noticing whether or not he's circumcised?'

'But she *didn't* notice. Honest. It's what she told me. That's why my father was so angry with her.'

'I'm guessing, of course, what do I know about your mum – I know my own mum and dad but that's another story – but try this thought. Perhaps she knew and didn't tell your dad because she was angry with him for some other reason . . . ?'

'No, no, despite everything she loved my dad.'

'I don't doubt she did, but love and anger sometimes, often, usually, go together.'

'But if she'd known about it . . . And she hadn't told him . . . Oh, my god, yes – and if she *was* angry with my . . . um, with the father in the play for some *other* reason and deliberately concealed that the boy wasn't circumcised . . . But that would be a terrible thing to do. Oh, yes, fuck, oh god, got it. Fuck, yes, oh I *see*.'

There's the play – and there's the invisible play.

There's the play you know you're writing, that you want to write and then there's that other play that will write itself if you get out of the line of its trajectory, that will flee if you pursue it or try to shepherd it into a fenced-off field.

Even though you believe you chose and therefore know the subject of your play, a play arises from a contradiction or dislocation of which you know nothing. It can only be released, though not resolved, by writing the play.

For these reasons, the playwright is the last person who can explain to you the meaning of their play.

Playwrights write to reveal what they think and feel but also to repress, to conceal.

There's the play – and then there's the hidden play.

The Court, purported to be falling down, was scheduled for a major renovation. Over a year I filmed for the BBC everything to do with the redesign – debates, consultations, interviews, design sessions, trailing around behind, mostly, Stephen and architect Steve Tompkins, the fundraising, the PR, the board deliberations, Kensington and Chelsea council meetings. My camera was the size and weight of two large bricks. By year's end, for *Royal Court Diaries* we'd rescued from oblivion seventy hours of great minds thinking, sketching, arguing, intriguing.

Halfway through the edit I had news that Arthur in Australia was near the end. I took off two days and went to see him. He was in a special care ward so I spent my single night in Sydney in his tiny pad on Manly Beach, a whirring flock of green and red parrots nestling, as he said they did each dusk, outside his third-floor window in a palm tree.

'You know, I could go on taking the fuckin' medicine but I know what I've been through and sure as fuck I know what's coming and I've had my fill of it. I don't know you that well, David, but I love you if for no other reason than that you've come all that fuckin' way to see me. What a fuckin' nutty thing to do. I'll always remember this.'

And he laughed and cried because there'd be no always. But then, despite our efforts, there never is.

Cruel and Tender

by Martin Crimp adapted from Sophocles, directed by Luc Bondy

2004

His name seems to designate a species not a single human being. I'd never seen a show of his. Nick had seen his *The Winter's Tale* with Michel Piccoli at the Paris Odéon. I'd read about and seen pictures of his *The Triumph of Love, John Gabriel Borkman, The Sea.* He'd directed *Don Carlos* at the Royal Opera House. I'd ask

'He's special in what way?'

Humane. Delicate but deep. The Spinoza of the stage. Who said that about him? I tried to read Spinoza to find out what that might mean. The *Ethics* defeated me but it seemed that he believed something like

'If God is anywhere he's in us, in our bodies, in our experience of being human.'

That sounds like theatre. I liked the sound of him.

Ruth Mackenzie, who had invited his *Playing with Fire* by Strindberg to Nottingham, told me

'Even if Luc is interested, it will take at least two years to land him.'

I wrote to him. I heard nothing.

I went to the Edinburgh Festival to see his *The Seagull* from Vienna's Burgtheater updated to the 1930s. It seemed perfect to me, each of the characters enchanted by each other's sensuality. The long evening overflowed with an urgent, clawing need for tenderness, for reassurance that, however destructive our emotions may be, they are our struggle to be fully alive, a struggle to the death, possibly.

I hurried to the stage door.

'M. Bondy has left the theatre.'

In Vienna to see his production of *Anatol* by Arthur Schnitzler at the Burgtheater. His staging was all interiors cut into exteriors, each opened-out space hinting at some deeper, darker enclosure. I tracked him to the canteen, his attention given entirely to being mobbed by his exhausted, glistening actors. After an hour

'So, my friend, why you say nothing? You don't like my performance?'

A few weeks later he called.

'I hear from my English acquaintance your theatre is not so bad. I make a performance for you.'

He was living in Paris in a rambling house in Belleville in the east. We sat out one evening in his flower-filled yard with Marie-Louise his wife, his twins and Geoff Layton, his ever-present friend and long-time assistant. The subject was what play should Luc direct as his first show not just for me but in the English theatre. Everyone chipped in.

'Molière?'

'In English?' Raucous laughter. 'Strindberg can be in English, Molière never. I make you *The Father*. Gert Vos can play him, he'll be marvellous.'

'Oh, great, yes. How's his English?'

A silence to consider this.

'Or . . . we find a marvellous English actor. We ask Daniel Day Lewis. You know him?'

'Or what about Schiller?'

'Yes, yes, English is the only language for Schiller. In German Schiller is kitsch.'

'Great, so which one? *The Maid of Orleans*? *William Tell*?'

'No, no, pardon me, in fact Schiller is kitsch in any language.'

He staggered down from his study bearing in twelve volumes the complete comedies of Eugène Labiche and began to read in French, which I don't speak, what he said was the funniest play ever written, perched on a low stool, eating complicated food, drinking his favourite Bordeaux, declaiming, spluttering.

Everyone knows that Labiche in England is always a disaster.

'Yes, that sounds hilarious, Luc, let's do Labiche.'

Each meeting was a festival of laughter, every phone call a comedy. You always knew that he was talking to someone else on one of his other 'handies' giving you just enough attention to keep the conversation you were having more or less coherent and avoid some, never all, misunderstandings before abruptly ringing off.

'Bye bye, David, bye bye, bye bye.'

When he was working with me I'd often find him outside on the pavement having a quick smoke, always a chance to tell his latest joke. Ruth told me that when Daniel Barenboim told her a joke she'd said

'That's marvellous. I must tell Luc'

and Barenboim said

'No, it was Luc who told it to me.'

There's this promising young composer. A director asks him to write music for a film. 'Can I see the film?' 'Not necessary. Just write some music, it has to be so and so long, it has to sound so and so.' The composer needs the commission, he writes the music. When the film is finished he's invited to a showing. There's no one else in the viewing room but an elderly couple. The film begins. Oh my god, it's a porno. And, even worse, his music accompanies the sex scenes. And it's not just a porno, the couple are having sex with a dog, a big grey wolfhound. It's torture for the composer but it's the only chance he'll ever have to hear his music. When it's finally over and they're leaving, the old couple ask 'So what is your connection to this film?'

'I wrote the music.' The couple smile very proudly. 'It was our dog.'

So, of course, for Luc's English theatre debut we chose a play with almost no jokes.

One day he called.

'I have the answer.'

For the Aix festival he was directing Handel's oratorio *Hercules*. It's based on Sophocles' *Women of Trachis*.

'Read the Sophocles. Tell me what you think.'

It's intellectual melodrama powered by the heroine Deianeira's fury at her betrayal by her husband Hercules who's fallen for a younger woman. It's rarely done. There's a whizz-bang translation by Ezra Pound and a few by academics.

'Crimp can make us a new version.'

He'd directed Martin Crimp's *The Country* in Vienna. They'd got on famously.

We could only afford *Cruel and Tender* by co-producing with the Vienna Festival of which Luc was director. He's a super-star in Europe so other co-producers quickly joined in as well as Chichester Festival Theatre which was then run by Ruth. We were deep into preparations for the opening when we had a visit from two Vienna Festival producers.

'We have such a serious problem.'

'I'm sure we can find a solution.'

'This *Cruel and Tender* is a show of Luc.'

'It is.'

'It absolutely must *premiere* in Vienna.'

'Ah . . . no, we've been planning this for two years. It's opening in London.'

'No, no, what we say is crucial. You must listen. You can have perhaps some preview performances, eight or even ten, but the European press must see it first in Luc's own city. If you open this production here they will all fly to London to write about it which for the festival, for Luc, will be *Katastrophe*.'

'But how do we get an audience even for ten previews for what is, in effect, a new play directed by someone who, to be blunt, no one in London's heard of unless we open it in our theatre and get the reviews?'

Much head-shaking and whispering.

'It's Vienna! It's Luc! It's highly political, so political it's hard for a person like you to understand. So believe what we tell you. *You know how much money the Festival is spending on your production.* For Luc's sake you must give in.'

Beneath the fancy eighth-arrondissement tailoring, the dash, the *savoir faire*, Luc's a punk at heart. Drugs and sex and taking chances, making rapier-sharp interventions, where's the next thrill? When he took control of the Odéon, one of France's national theatres, it was said to have been sewn up for him by Sarkozy, his drinking pal. When the design for his shows burst our budget, I'm invited for fine dining in a pricey Knightsbridge restaurant with one of Luc's shadier acquaintances and – hey presto! – our budget is in the black again.

Our last performance of *Cruel and Tender* was our last before we closed the theatre to rebuild. Over the next years I saw everything Luc directed – *The Chairs* by Ionesco, *The Maids* by Genet, *Viol* by Botho Strauss, *The Second Surprise of Love* by Marivaux . . . We'd meet in Paris round his Boulevard Saint-Germain kitchen table, Peter Handke, Roman Polanski, or at the 'Blue Diamond', his favourite Chinese restaurant in Soho . . .

We searched for the next idea. *The Merchant of Venice*. He had a great idea for Shylock. I was dispatched to New York to give Wally Shawn the news.

'Luc . . . thought of . . . me . . . for Shylock? Well, what can I say?

I'm kinda flattered. Kinda. How well do I know Luc? I think, no, I'm sure I have definitely shaken hands with him . . .'

We planned *A Long Day's Journey Into Night*, William Hurt as James Tyrone, then the rights were whipped away by a producer who'd stage-managed the first ever production which gave him, so the agent said, the stronger claim.

'This is serious,' said Luc. 'But we go ahead. Why not? America is far away. What can they do?'

Sweet Nothings
by Arthur Schnitzler, adapted by David Harrower, directed by Luc Bondy

2010

From a technical perspective, here's how rehearsing used to be. You're doing *Richard II*. In the show there'll be a throne for the king. You don't need that throne in rehearsal. You have a chair, possibly a big one, but if there's a throne in the play, well, imagine it. You'll get the actual costumes, the real shoes at the dress rehearsal. For the main weeks of rehearsals the focus is on the actors. Having created an effective structure with them, you have two or three days in which the light, the sound, whatever goes up or down or turns around are introduced.

Luc says

'That's ridiculous. Good for you, perhaps, but not for me.'

From day one of rehearsals he wants everything to be real or as real as we can afford to make it.

'How many weeks can I have for rehearsalling?'

'Five is what we offer.'

'It is impossible to make a production in five weeks. Good for someone else, perhaps, but not for me.'

'Ok, how many do you need?'

'Maybe eight, maybe nine.'

For me that's challenging. If Luc has maybe eight, maybe nine how do I tell another director they can't have it? Does it even make sense that the really experienced director gets more time than the kids who are just beginning? Yes, because you have to know how to *use* maybe eight, maybe nine, you have to have maybe eight, maybe nine weeks' rehearsalling *in you*.

'How many stage managers will you need?'

'What's a stage manager? I understand nothing of this. No, I don't need a stage manager, whatever it is.'

'Then who's going to run your show?'

'Explain to me what you mean.'

Ok, our director wants eight weeks of rehearsal and no stage manager. How do we organise everything else, *everything*, the budget, the scheduling of the theatre, the working hours, the expectations of the production team and all the other people who work in this organisation to make this feasible?

Our mantra is

'We give our directors what they need.'

You can't say to an artist

'Direct a show for me but I'll make it impossible for you to function in the way that enables you to create the work for which I hired you.'

At the same time, it's quite a big deal to say to your production team who pride themselves on their experience and expertise

'Put aside everything you know. This time it's going to be totally different.'

Luc says

'The artists I bring with me are my assistant, my dramaturg, my choreographer, my designer, my designer's assistant, my lightening designer, my lightening designer's assistant, my sound designer, my sound designer's assistant. And I need to have them in the rehearsal room beside me.'

'Beside you?'

'We make a good long table.'

'The whole time?'

'The whole time, of course, what do you think?'

I watched him rehearse *King Lear* in Vienna. A cavernous studio, a vast trestle stretching the length of the room, designers, assistants, more designers, more assistants, all sitting to attention intently facing the platform that had been thrown up at the other end. There's a lighting grid with thirty lamps burning, columns of speakers playing some sort of droning atmospherics. I arrived after the session had begun. They were halfway into the scene where Regan plucks hairs out of Gloucester's chin.

> *By the kind gods, 'tis most ignobly done*
> *To pluck me by the beard.*

The acting is forthright, elastic, shameless.

'When do you open?'

'Excuse me, my dear friend. How do you mean?'

'It's really great, Luc. When's your first performance?'

'We started our rehearsalling on Monday. This scene we began ago one hour. You think it's good? You don't know nothing of anything. Wait! Wait! Wait! You will see something.'

David Harrower wrote us a sprightly adaptation of *Liebelei* by Arthur Schnitzler, retitling it *Sweet Nothings*.

'How long can I work each day?'

'How long do you need?'

'Well, I lose the actors each day at four.'

'No, they can work with you from ten to six.'

'They're not playing in the evening? None of them? Ah, of course, it's not a company, it's not repertoire. Here you make *en suite*. Very good. I like it.'

Two weeks into rehearsal . . .

'But these actors arrive on time. They're not doing someone else's production at night. I like very much your people and your way of working.'

It's why directors in Europe want to work in the UK. They know how rigorous and muscular our actors are and also how subtle and quick.

Four weeks in . . .

'My actors are so good, they work so hard, I love every one of them. I think we're ready to open in one more week. Can you arrange everything so we open two weeks earlier, please?'

Luc's directing of his young quartet of actors (Natalie Dormer, Tom Hughes, Kate Burdette, Jack Laskey) radiates all his love of ambivalence, of contradiction, of flirtation, of hanging about in rainbow-lit cafes with friends and lovers, of wine, of good food, of laughter, his love of love – feel it, almost touch it, breathe it in.

Early one evening we're all sitting outside a pub in the Earls Court Road. Luc needed to visit some particular pharmacy to pick up some particular prescription for his diabetes. His sister Beatrice is with us and the ever-present Jeff. They chatter away in French and then there's a burst of laughter. As always, I need translation.

'Beatrice, what did Luc say?'

'He says one thing he is not is homosexual, never, it's not possible for him, but if he were he says he would take an interest in you.'

Even louder laughter. They're bouncing up and down, howling.

I Am the Wind

by Jon Fosse, translated by Simon Stephens, directed by
Patrice Chéreau

2011

He strides, head low, his wrestler's shoulders piled up like a bull. He spies me on the far side of the square and veers, moving with such impetus it needs a wide curve to reset his target.

What am I fearful of? His anger? Worse, his disappointment. I know I have to see him so I chose this wide square at the centre of Vienna's Museum Quarter in the early-morning sun to have my *Milchkaffee* and croissant but now I wish I were in some dark *Kaffeehaus* down some blind *Gasse*. As on every day his wardrobe is superb. Today it's a dark suit, funereal, white cotton shirt, string tie. A wad of papers clenched beneath an elbow, loose sheets of an orchestral score scratched over with his writing. He drags a chair out with one finger, seats himself, cocks his head.

'Tell me the truth now. Can he do it?'

'Patrice, I'm sure he can.'

'But he didn't finish last night. I know because I went back to the theatre late, after you had left.'

Damn, I knew I should have stayed until the very last moments of the session.

'What is the actual problem with him?'

'With who?'

'You know who I mean.'

'I don't know this for sure, I think he's a depressive.'

'Agh! I knew it. Alcoholic also?'

'I don't believe so.'

'Yes, I do believe so. And not only alcohol. Don't bother to shake your head, you have to protect your people, of course, I respect that.'

He's not one of my people. I don't know who employed him or how he came to be part of the team. I don't admit it. In my job I'm supposed to have a grip on everything.

'Listen, David, I have good experience of this, too much, believe me. I know the signs of depression among stage technicians.'

He brushes the back of a finger under his nose.

'We all know how they deal with stress, who will admit it? We ask too much of these people, on this subject I'm an expert since I was young. But did they finish?'

'They did.'

'Honestly? The job is done?'

'It is.'

'It works?'

'I went into the theatre the very first thing this morning. Yes, it works.'

'I couldn't bear any more last night, sitting there so impotent, waiting, waiting for news but, of course, when I got into bed I couldn't sleep. I read all night.'

'What were you reading?'

He scowls. Why? Was that a stupid question? Oh there's the waiter. I wave to him.

'You summon him in such a British way.'

'I'm actually not British. Well, I am but—'

'I know, I know, you told me, you're African. But whoever you are it's impolite. He's a worker, a professional.'

The worker

'Ja?'

'Patrice, will you have something?'

'No, no.' He waves him away. 'Thank you, you're taking care of me, I know. I had a strong coffee an hour ago. I've been up since sunrise, before even. What did I read? It's ridiculous, I read to relax, a stupid thriller, but I get annoyed by the bad writing, you know how it is. It works?'

'I watched them make it work this morning. It works now. Honestly.'

A smile floods his face, a smile I recognise from all the black-and-white photographs of the dark-angel genius aged twenty-three I used to see in German theatre magazines. Then it's gone. He taps my hand. An infinitesimal shake of his head. He's sorry he was rude. He knows only too well how tough it is.

There's a time slip. He didn't rise but he's standing next to me.

'It has to work tonight, you know that? Perfectly with no possibility of error. That's what you promised me.'

I cross the cobbled square between the high escarpments of arts buildings towards Halle G.

What made me think that I could do this job? Cobbles, cobbles. Why am I here? What do I know about anything? Cobbles, cobbles. Who the hell do I think I am? Cobbles, cobbles. Who the hell does he think he is?

I sense deep shadow. The towering dock door leads down into darkness. I go in.

The performance that night is a triumph. The dreaded mechanism works like a dream. As it ends, the audience are silent for what seems the longest moment, long enough for your heart to wither, then they rise with a trumpet blast of cheering. And go on cheering. The actors bow, Patrice strides on, grasps their hands, more cheering. As he takes one on his own the clapping falls into a ritual tribute to the god. Now they're stamping. With muscular swoops of his arms he commands the actors, Jack and Tom, to join him, beaming at them, adoring them, making circling gestures so the audience knows he knows that they're divinities let down from heaven. They retreat to the back of the stage, Patrice, the actors, all the designers, light, sound, costume, set, then all rush down like drunken children, like gallants in a painting by Watteau, garlanded with invisible threads of roses, clasping hands and raising them above their heads as though they're drowning, all of them, in the wonder of it.

London, 2004

When Luc directed his first show for me, his old friend Patrice Chéreau came to London to see it.

I'd known about Chéreau since I was a kid, his *Dido, Queen of Carthage* staged on ships in a flooded theatre, his 1968 *Ring* cycle at Bayreuth set amongst early Ruhr industrialists.

Expecting an instant refusal, I ask

'Why don't you do one too?'

Pause.

He cocks his head.

Aix, 2007

One step beyond the shade the light explodes – a sunflower punching your face. An out-of-focus stone street leading from the central square, at its end the opera house. It's new, it opened last week. This evening is the premiere of Chéreau's first collaboration with Pierre Boulez since their *Ring* – Janáček's *From the House of the Dead*.

Patrice had called me.

'If you have time, why not come? It may be interesting and you know how it is with opera, you reach a certain moment where everything you have made has become so complex even if you want to it's impossible to change anything. Though I find it's good if I make a big surprise change at the last minute.' He laughs. 'But anyway, if you can make it, we may find a moment or two to talk about things.'

A young man who was at the next table in the square is following.

'You're looking for Patrice but you won't find him.'

'That's ok. I'm not in a hurry. I thought I'd look at the new building.'

'He won't want you to see a rehearsal.'

'Honestly, I haven't come to Aix for that.'

'I know what you have come for. I'm one of his assistants. Come.'

A quarter-mile away is the villa where the festival has put him up. Does Chéreau stay here too? All the shutters are closed. It's a relief to be in darkness. As my eyes adjust I see how luxurious it is. He shares it with other members of the team but they're all at the rehearsal which was called unexpectedly.

'He doesn't need you this afternoon?'

'No, no. Yesterday he fired me. It's ok. I've worked with him so many years. He does it to make the others pay attention. And I get the day free.'

In the walled garden is a stone pool. We swim. We hang around in the cool. He has a battered old car. We drive back into town haltingly.

'Don't worry, you won't be late for him.'

'I don't have a time arranged to meet him.'

'Oh yes, you do. What am I here for, what did you think? He's expecting you in fifteen minutes.'

As he drops me off around the corner from the opera

'Don't say anything to him.'

'About what?'

'He can get anything out of you. He's so curious about everything.'

The cafe is scruffy. We sit outside in the heat, Patrice nursing an espresso. It's all mildly ridiculous, in a film for kids, like he's having a serious talk with a koala bear. I ask about the Janáček.

'You'll find out all you need to know when you see it, did we make something or will we be disgraced? I'm used to the boos, it's a natural sound, like wind howling through trees. I heard it, as you must know, when I brought my Marivaux, my *La Dispute*, to the National in 1974.'

'Is that why you've never directed in England?'

'No, no, I've never directed in England because no one ever asked me. Now, let's be practical about my situation. I don't make many things. I need much preparation. I work extremely slowly. Even so, I don't say it couldn't happen, possibly, in a year or two, if you are not afraid of the boos.'

'I'm not afraid.'

He laughs.

'That's what they all say before it happens. But we must think hard, both of us, what could the play be?'

Thessaloniki, 2008

Patrice is to receive the main prize of the World Theatre Forum. That I'd been asked to come means something – but what?

I walk into the vast, domed hall on the seafront to discover I'm on a panel of producers scheduled to discuss their experience of working with him. But that's absurd.

'Don't make a problem. Just give your impressions.'

'But I've never worked with him!'

'How can that be? He particularly asked that you should speak.'

Perhaps a hundred pairs of eyes gaze up at the improvised stage. I sit at one end of the group of producers and point at the elderly academic at the other end.

'You must see this as a tableau. George Banu represents the past, what has been, I represent what will be. I've come from the future to tell you of a production Patrice has yet to do.'

A feeble joke, especially as I still have no idea what the production will be or even if there's going to be one.

Someone asks the inevitable.

'But England has always ignored Chéreau. Tell us, why do you want so much to work with Patrice?'

London, 1974

Peter Hall's National Theatre invites Chéreau's *La Dispute* by Marivaux from the Théâtre National Populaire in Villeurbanne to play in the Lyttelton for four performances.

I remember a vast box hedge, a pool of water, a large woman – was she Congolese? – singing in a deep, rich mezzo, the intensity of the handsome actors playing the children. I remember the long stretch of music – was it Monteverdi? – that we heard before the performance started.

Thirty years later I ask him

'Was it twenty minutes?'

'Seven and a half,' he answers loftily.

I'd prepared by reading the play – but what was this?

It was the play but unlike any performance I'd ever seen. It had an extraordinary freedom. It somehow suggested the complexity of everything, the contradictoriness. It was the truth as two people knew it – Marivaux and Chéreau – but the total truth, for that brief moment anyway. Who knew you could get that amount of life onto a stage? It was thrilling.

Ever since, when the lights go up and I see a settee or a bench in the centre of the stage, I want to leave. If you've put furniture in the middle of the stage, where's the space for the vast box hedge? There's no room for the Congolese lady to sing.

London, 2010

A taxi draws up. Patrice stumbles out. I try not to stare at a scab across the bridge of his nose.

'I am so stupid. I got drunk in my hotel room and fell onto the minibar.'

Uh huh.

Later I notice one of his front teeth is loose. He takes it out and waves it about, grinning.

'I look like a *clochard*.'

He slots it back into his face.

'What will you drink, Patrice?'

'A strong Bordeaux.'

He had a way of drawing all the light in any space towards him. Dressed in costly dark colours, he seemed to burn with an intensity that needed fuel of many kinds. He often seemed about to blow up – with anger, with hilarity, with incredulity, you never knew what was coming. When he heard Patrice was to direct for me, a French festival director looked aghast.

'But he will explode your theatre!'

And in a way he did.

We half-hid at my corner table.

'I have made up my mind.'

'Great!'

'I want to make *Macbeth*.'

'Fantastic.'

'Yes but there is only one actor I can make it with.'

'We'll get him.'

'Yes, but he is very angry with me. I know he will refuse.'

'We'll persuade him.'

'You think it is ok for me to make Shakespeare as my English debut? Is my English good enough? You must tell me the truth.'

'It's a great idea. You should do it.'

'But how to do the ghosts? When I did *Hamlet* at Avignon, I thought – how to make the ghost extremely frightening? I had the idea for it to gallop in on a horse.'

'My theatre's not quite big enough for that.'

'But I've staged so many fights in my life, I'm sick of it. But I'll do it if you say so. I trust you.'

Oh Jesus, don't trust me.

As predicted, the only possible actor was angry with him. So we met others and soon Patrice had found the only other actor who could play the part.

After one such casting session he called me from the Eurostar on his way back to Paris.

'You know I am doing a play by Jon Fosse?'

Yes, it was to be performed in a gallery of the Louvre and then all over France. In Europe Fosse was the most performed living playwright. His subject, time after time, is 'the dark', the bitterly hard-won survival over despair, the self-destroying side of life we can't avoid or explain.

'His agent has sent me another one. It's crazy, they always do that. But I like this new one better than the one I agreed to do. You know, it's ridiculous for me to make my English debut with Shakespeare. Read this Fosse. Say what you think but if you like it I will make it for you.'

Tel Aviv, 2010

I'm here to watch rehearsals of Amir Nizar Zuabi's adaptation of *In the Penal Colony* by Franz Kafka which we're going to bring to YV. Sprawled on a pavement in the sun outside the Hotel Galileo I read *I Am the Wind*.

Two men meet. They decide to get into a boat and row out to sea. One drowns himself. 'I am the wind,' he says. The other drowns in grief.

I liked it but it seemed slight, the pages so empty, almost white. Would I have said

'Ok, let's go'

to any other director? Unlikely. Who in London will want to see this play? London theatre doesn't really know Jon Fosse but what it knows it loathes.

Patrice.

Patrice.

Patrice.

Ok, let's go.

London, 2011

I took him to see Room 7 at the Jerwood Rehearsal Studios, one of the best in town, high ceiling, flooded with light. On the way out, I lost him then found him contemplating a little fountain by the entrance: a rectangular block of thin stone very low down with water gurgling round it. In Richard Peduzzi's design this became the 'boat' on which the two men set out to sea. A simple rectangular platform, perhaps six inches thick. Operated by a special metal arm cunningly manufactured in Italy, it rose up out of the wide pool of water that suddenly gushed into and filled the room.

The moment when this 'boat' first appeared was exquisite conjuring. There's nothing on stage except a few inches of water covering a big seaweed-coloured canvas. And then – whoosh – up it came, parting the waters, and the two men were out there in the middle of the ocean riding the waves. Perfect. Poetic. Existential. But also just a piece of wood steered by one man somehow sailing another over a darkened stage.

A crisis came when the technical rehearsal began and the stage manager put on her cans so she could speak to her assistant who would operate the lighting board. Patrice caught sight of her.

'What are you doing?'

'Oh, sorry, I just wanted to . . .'

'But why on earth are you doing that? Take off the cans. Do it.'

'But I need to give Sophie the cue . . .'

'I don't want you to cue anybody.'

The stage manager walks steadily down to the stage watching her feet.

'Ok, Patrice, whatever you prefer. You tell me when you want things to happen, I'll write it down and then as we rehearse I'll use the cans to tell the people who are actually going to operate . . .'

'Listen to what I say to you. No, never mind. Who is operating? Sophie, is it you? You are a full member of the company, have you got it? I want you to watch the show very carefully as you did so well in rehearsal each day, to *feel* the show and press the button at precisely the correct moment which you will know because you will *feel* it with your whole body. You don't need anyone to cue you about anything. Now shall we get going please? You're wasting my time and you know in this theatre I don't get a lot of it . . .'

The stage manager looks at me. I look at her. 'Let's do it.' She's happy to. But then Dominique Bruguière, Patrice's long-time lighting designer, edges over to me.

'I just want to say in my opinion your system is better. Of course Patrice is Patrice and he works the way he always has but I like the way you do it.'

Oh no, so now what do we do?

Sometimes, inevitably, the cunning Italian metal arm malfunctioned. On press night, I stood at the side of the stage and prayed to all the gods in whom I don't believe.

Long afterwards, a critic who had loved it told me that as they took their seats a number of his colleagues chortled in anticipation of an evening of tedious pretentiousness. Many of them were bemused. Even bored. And even some of my friends didn't get it.

Jon Fosse himself had seen a late rehearsal. He arrived early in a good state but by the time the run began he'd had a few.

'This always happens,' his agent whispered, 'he gets so nervous.'

Somehow by the end of his play he'd sobered up. He padded across the vast, still damp acre of canvas into the *trompe l'œil* far distant horizon and put all three of his arms around the actors, Tom Brooke, Jack Laskey, and Patrice.

'You have made it a love story. I adore it. It's great, it's great.'

It was great. I have no doubt of that. We'd judged the number of performances well and it more or less sold out. Many people said to me

'That's the best production I've ever seen.'

Or 'one of the best', let's not go crazy.

Or let's go crazy.

In Barcelona at the Teatre Lliure, the man who operated the many delicately timed subtitles collapses with exhaustion at the end of a performance, flat out on the floor, hyperventilating.

'I got it right! I had to! I love it so much.'

In Paris at the Théâtre de la Ville, as the show ends, a man stands up, starts shouting. Oh my god, is he booing? It's not until the applause at last dies down that we hear the words he's howling across the emptying theatre.

'*Merci! Merci! Merci! Merci!*'

London, 2011

Before he started rehearsals, Patrice told me he had cancer.

'I have to tell you because you are my boss. Don't worry, I won't let you down, it will be fine. I have to return to Paris every weekend for treatment. But it's ok, I can do it. Please don't tell anyone.'

It was often obvious that he was in deep pain. The actors and his long-time choreographer Thierry Niang knew everything. Was he going to die? No. Was this a play about a man dying?

Once, sitting outside the theatre he suddenly went white, staggered, half fainted, hauled himself up, recovered, sat still for a moment, went back into rehearsal.

I'd fetch him in my little white car from St Pancras whenever he returned from Paris and the chemical onslaught. As I drove him to his hotel, he'd sit in ghastly silence clutching his translations of Conrad's *Lord Jim* and *The Mirror of the Sea* which were part of his research. One day as he arrived on the station concourse he told me at once that the cancer had got worse. It had spread to his liver.

Driving to the hotel, he examines a proof of the programme.

'She calls herself a make-up artist? Even after all these years I wouldn't call myself an artist. Can you tell her to stop doing that?'

I start to explain but give it up.

'Yes, Patrice.'

Patrice, Patrice, Patrice, Patrice, Patrice . . .

2013

In June I emailed him. I didn't hear back. In August an answer came.

'Hi David! I didn't answer you because my summer has been quite strange and very agitated. I am sorry. I worked very well at *Elektra* in Aix. The production was good, I guess. Then I went to Spain and suddenly, with the heat, I discovered how exhausted I was. Now I am in hospital recovering from strong anaemia, dehydration etc. Nothing very important. The illness seems to be stopped, under control. I hope to leave this place at the end of the week and have some days of holiday finally. Lots of love, p.'

With Patrice, always the small p.

New York, 2013

My iPhone buzzes in my pocket. It's a text message from Katie Mitchell.

'I've just heard some sad news and wanted to check you knew . . .'

Paris, 2013

The massive grey church of Saint-Sulpice dominates this part of the Left Bank just behind the Odéon, the most beautiful theatre there is. It's round the corner from where Patrice grew up in a family of artists, painters I think. Now he lies in front of the sepulchre in his shiny black box, a muscular socialist under a mountain of Bourbon lilies.

As the owlish President of the Republic looks on, a young priest clouds the air with rose incense. Later, his friends object.

'Absurd! Patrice was an atheist!'

The pallbearers heave up the heavy box and lug their burden the long, long distance down the crowded nave towards the towering doors. Suddenly someone in the shadows claps. My heart stops. At once the hundreds gathered start to applaud. It echoes, swells, deepens.

As the vast doors are wheeled open, there's a roar from the crowd outside.

We stand in the crowded square in the rain, crying, greeting his friends and ours, smiling, holding hands with handsome old people we hardly know, rows of tragic young faces glistening with tears, straight-backed, stoic, embracing each other, unable to say anything.

We took taxis to the Père Lachaise cemetery. Drenched, we dawdled, stopped off for soup then got stuck in traffic. By the time we arrived, the coffin had already been cemented in. A workman with a bucket was clearing his tools away. It was still raining, though lightly now. Thierry Niang looked at us, eyes washed with tears.

'Now Patrice is the wind.'

A View from the Bridge
by Arthur Miller, directed by Ivo van Hove

2014

The Vienna Festwochen. We're opening *Sweet Nothings*. After the first performance there's a jamboree in one of the cavernous concrete halls of the Museum Quarter. Luc makes a bad boy, uproarious, no-one-but-Luc-could-get-away-with-it thank-you speech.

I have one more day in the city. The Festival is at its height. What should I see?

Roman Tragedies is *Antony and Cleopatra*, *Julius Caesar*, *Coriolanus* played out in a TV news studio, cameras zooming in and tracking every which way, streaming to a massive screen high above and the length of the huge proscenium, the audience intermingled with the cast, elbowed out of the way of the cameras by stagehands or watching from auditorium seats, getting wide shots and close-ups simultaneously, or moving as they choose between the two. The actors are subtle, elegant, full-throated. Nothing is resolved, nothing is explained, all of life and much death, it's urgent, jagged, glued by the exultant energy that flows when artists know the quality of the work they're making. It's a masterpiece.

Next morning I run into some of the actors in the street.

'How did you do that?'

'Everything was prepared for us. We arrived, all the camera moves were already rehearsed. We just fit into place and do the acting, not a problem. So you liked it? Ivo will be pleased.'

Over the next months I saw everything of Ivo's that was playing. *The Misanthrope* at the Paris Odéon, *Edward II* at the Schaubühne Berlin, *The Antonioni Project* at the Barbican in London.

A year later we open *I Am the Wind*. Ivo comes to see it. Afterwards

'Chéreau is my god. I see everything of his. I don't care where it is, I have to go.'

'C'mon, Ivo, if Patrice will do a show here . . .'

'I tell you, I'm booked up for centuries but, ok, let's find out what's possible.'

He slides from his leather jacket a little hard-backed notebook, then slips it away again.

'I'll talk to my people who manage my diary. Meantime see if you can come up with an idea for me.'

I only ever had one idea for him. *A View from the Bridge* is Miller's least resolved play. His other great works are scarred by his tendency to nip in from the wings to tell us how to think.

'People must pay attention.' (*Death of a Salesman*)

'He has his goodness now.' (*The Crucible*)

In *A View from the Bridge*, who knows why Eddie Carbone is so obsessed with his wife's niece, why he betrays the two immigrant longshoremen? Push him to explain his crazy behaviour, he'd rather be dead than analyse it.

As Miller tells it in his autobiography *Timebends*, he heard an anecdote about a Brooklyn longshoreman who betrayed fellow workers to the immigration authorities. It was McCarthy time, so that's what this new play will be about – loyalty and treachery, an urgent political theme. But as he wrote, the play circled in on something unexpected, a different order of integrity, which is what I thought might interest Ivo.

I suggest it to his close colleague Wouter van Ransbeek.

'You may be onto something. Yes, this may be good material for him.'

The only other play we considered at all was *A Game of Love and Chance* by Marivaux. Ivo and his designer Jan Versweyveld didn't know it and were intrigued. But I think

Hardly anyone in London knows Ivo. Hardly anyone knows Marivaux. If they see Ivo's Marivaux they'll think

'So that's what Marivaux is.'

They know Arthur Miller. If they see Ivo's Arthur Miller they'll get the heart of the play because Ivo will show it to them but they'll also see the kind of director he is.

'Ok, we'll do it. How long will I have to rehearse?'

Each director has their preference as to, say, length of working day, how much technical back-up they want in rehearsal, and so on. What they all want is time. Our offer was five weeks of rehearsal with the actors, a week of technical rehearsals with the full set on stage, a week of previews. That's seven weeks from day one to opening. *All* directors want more and if they *really needed it*—

'The usual will do,' says Ivo.

In his home city Amsterdam, Ivo has long worked with the same company of actors. He knows few in England apart from movie stars but hates auditioning, the artificiality of it. Through most of our auditions he examines his feet.

'Ah fine, today I have on my feet my nice brown shoes.'

Mark Strong isn't free which we're sad about but we get over it and start looking for someone else to play Eddie Carbone and then some television schedule gets altered and he's in. Nicola Walker, Phoebe Fox, Emun Elliot, Michael Gould, Luke Norris – the company comes together quickly.

Jan and Ivo arrive with a model of the set. The published text describes various locations – the Carbone home, the streets, the office, the phone booth, the prison. In plays of this period such descriptions are often not what the writer imagined while writing but how the original production was conceived. Likewise published stage directions often describe the moves made by the play's first actors.

Jan has modelled a bounded emptiness, a sculpted arena. A low transparent wall frames a bare thrust stage. At the start, a large box obscures everything. It rises as the play begins and at the end is lowered obscuring everything.

It's more than a design, it's an aesthetic philosophy. If I don't agree with it, I've chosen the wrong team. It's a throne room for the common man. It's magnificent.

A week or so later I get a phone call.

'Look, David, I'm sorry if this is a bit of a shock. I have a problem, not a big one and we can easily fix it. But . . . I forgot, damn it, I'm an idiot, in our second week of rehearsal I have to be in Australia.'

Pause.

'*What?*'

'Yes, we do *Roman Tragedies* in Adelaide, it's the premiere there and whenever we do that show, it's so complicated, you know that, you've seen it, I have to be present, they do need me actually but it's in the contract anyway.'

'And *our* contract?'

I don't say that. I don't know if we actually have one yet.

'I can go and be back in three days. Or four. Surely not more than a week.'

'And our rehearsals?'

'My associate director Jeff James can work with the actors, he's very good, thank you for finding him, they can learn their lines, there's plenty for them to do, it will all be fine, believe me.'

A few days later . . .

'I have a new idea about our rehearsals.'

'Oh good.'

'I'm coming to London. We can talk about it when we're together.'

We're together.

'This is how it will be. In the second week I'm in Adelaide, so we won't rehearse that week at all. And now what I think makes much more sense is if we don't rehearse the previous week also. It's much better not to have a break. We'll start our work for real in what *in your schedule* you call week three.'

'Really, Ivo? Is that enough time? Can you do that?'

And this was the only time my dear friend Ivo got annoyed with me.

'I'm enjoying working in your theatre, the production team are excellent, Jan loves them all, but you are now coming too far into my territory. It will be fine. Take my word for it.'

I know the quality of his work so I do. But how will I explain this to the actors?

Day one, I hang about outside the rehearsal room in case there's a problem. What could happen? The actors rebel – 'we have to have longer rehearsal'? Unlikely but the actors will surely be anxious. I've seen at least six of his shows. None of them have seen anything.

They emerge incandescent. It's the best first day of rehearsal they've ever experienced. Ivo showed them the model, explained to them that that's all there is, no props, not even shoes. Their bodies, their clothes, that's it.

'But I'll have a knife?' asked Emun who, as Marco, stabs Eddie at the end.

Ivo shrugs.

'We'll see.'

Most of the actors have learned their parts before rehearsals begin. From the first moment they're on their feet. Ivo speaks very little. The rules of his game seem to be that the actors should do precisely as they feel, the assumption being that whatever they need to play their part is already in them and unlikely to be buried deep.

A full-size mock-up of the set has been built. He'll dart on stage, stand close to one of them, share a quiet thought, an approach, a possibility. He's effortlessly cool and intimate, hour after hour, with the whole group and with each actor individually. Little talk, no character analysis.

'In a play, as in life, all there is are relationships. Don't think too hard, you already know all you need to, just do it. What's to lose?'

At the end of week two, I drop in. Ivo pulls a sour face.

'Honestly, David, I don't know what to say to you. This play . . . It is what it is.'

'Which means?'

'You know this, don't you, I hope you do, it was your idea to do it. It's nothing special, it's just a play by Arthur Miller, that's all it is.'

New York, 2016

After playing the West End, our *View/Bridge* has been on Broadway. I'm back for the Tony Awards. Ivo is up for Best Director, *View/ Bridge* for Best Revival. In case we win, I write an acceptance speech about the value of immigrants and refugees to American society. I email it to our adventurous Broadway producer Scott Rudin. A nanosecond later my mobile rings.

'The revival Tony is a producer's award so if we win I'm receiving it, ok with you, my friend? And anyway that speech you've written is one hundred per cent inappropriate. No one speaks like that at a Tony ceremony. Ok with you, my friend?'

Ivo wins. We win. I troop on stage with a crowd of folk most of whom are new to me, our Broadway investors –

'Really lovely to meet you too . . .'

– alongside YV producers and the Broadway team, as well as Ivo back again . . .

Scott, centre stage, is saying something, I'm gazing out into the auditorium and barely listening and then – damn!, what's happening?

'We looked after it on Broadway but this is the team who nurtured it, who made it happen. David?'

I blunder over to the microphone.

'Scott said he wouldn't do that.'

A laugh – of recognition perhaps? Of sympathy? Quick precis of my speech.

'This tale of immigrants, of economic refugees coming from Sicily to this country is a great song of the great people of New York. It's been our privilege and our enormous pleasure to bring it back to you.'

Somehow Ivo has ended up with both Tony statuettes. His agent commandeers them and shares them out

'One for you and one for him.'

And yet somehow that was the last I ever saw of either of them.

The Jungle
by Joe Murphy and Joe Robertson, directed by Stephen Daldry and Justin Martin

2017

In the early spring of 2016 two young playwrights, Joe Murphy and Joe Robertson, took a ferry to Calais, then travelled on to the informal refugee camp that had sprung up on filthy wasteland close to the entrance to the Channel Tunnel. Moved and intrigued by what they'd read and heard, all they intended was to see for themselves and perhaps find out if they could help in any way.

Especially, but not only, after websites and newspapers across the world featured photographs of Alan Kurdi, a Syrian child who drowned while crossing the Aegean and was washed up like a sacrifice on a Turkish beach, others from the UK did the same. When the sun went down and the winds blew in off the channel most visitors went home. 'The Joes' stayed. They heard music, watched dancing, realised that, however calamitous life in the Jungle might be, however clear it was that, as a priority, all these eight, nine, ten thousand people should be sheltered securely and comfortably, what they *as theatre people* could do was create a space where, through music, dance, martial arts, poetry, the sharing of personal histories – '*and this is what happened to me*' – some of these desperate folk might reclaim a glimmer of their old selves, of their true lives' meanings, might regain, if only for a moment, some of the autonomy that had been stripped away from them on their perilous unintended journeys.

With encouragement and cash from Stephen, Sonia Friedman and others, they bought a second-hand geodesic dome, took it to the camp and erected it with the help of new friends from amongst the refugees and older friends from the UK, amongst them Tracey Seaward and Amy Reade. They'd heard refugees speculating about whether or not on some particular day they had 'a good chance', *bonne chance*, of making it to the UK through the Eurotunnel, either walking or hidden in a truck, so they called it the Good Chance Theatre. It was *terrain* without nationality, a no man's land where strangers might meet, a 'town hall' to discuss issues of urgency and a 'theatre' in which they could entertain each other with their remarkable and varied skills. And for many in the UK with the desire or need to ease some of the suffering on our national doorstep it was a way in.

The Joes said to Stephen

'We have an idea for a play'

and he said

'Write it and I'll direct it.'

He gave a Sunday tea for many of those who'd worked with Good Chance in what had become known as 'the Jungle' or had visited them. I knew if I wanted the play I had to be there but I'd come down with flu, pretty badly, as happens to me once a year at least. I knew that Rufus, now director of the NT, *would* be there and, given half a chance, would commission it. And fair's fair, he'd gone out to Calais, Paul Handley, his head of production, had put in time on the team that erected the dome, whereas, though my adventurous YV outreach team held many workshops there alongside the Royal Court, the RSC and other UK theatres, I . . .

'I'm sorry, I know I said I'd come tomorrow but an actor's gone off sick, we have to put the understudy on' or 'they've moved the dress rehearsal' or 'I promised to see so-and-so's show and tomorrow's the last performance . . .' Until I had a free weekend and 'Oh, don't come now, nothing interesting will be happening, can you come next Thursday?'

And then the Jungle was gone.

Fragile shelters, shops, cafes, churches, mosques in flames – a war zone of its own – bulldozed by the French riot police, thousands of refugees with not a thing and nowhere to go scattered to the autumn winds, amongst them hundreds of solitary children . . .

They wrote their play.

Two members of the NT board who were especially moved by the prospect of the show put up money to ensure its production but the NT commits to its seasons way ahead and couldn't find a 'slot' for this one in the foreseeable future (or something). So, in the way of things, as if by chance, *The Jungle* came to me. Inside Miriam Buether's recreation of 'the Afghan Cafe', it played with us, it played in the West End, then at St Ann's Warehouse in New York, then San Francisco and then, or so we intend, the world . . .

Sim-salabim!

November 2017

Watching Stephen direct I'm struck (again) by the way this famous charmer headlocks a room. His domination is absolute, like vodka in a vodka tonic, like honey in tea. If you direct, the power of your personality is your primary tool. A show is the consequence of everything that happens between its director and her or his actors, writer(s), designers, stage managers, producers, assistants, scene builders, front-of-house staff, publicity people, old Harry who's been an usher at this theatre thirty years. The director's tone, their style, their habits, conscious and otherwise, all flow into the show. Every colour of every shard of glass in the kaleidoscope of their individuality all seep in and flavour it far more than the show's design or how it's lit. It's Bondy's roguishness, Chéreau's romantic fascination with power, Katie Mitchell's profound anger, Van Hove's fatalism, Richard Jones' compassionate sense of how ridiculous everything is.

With Stephen it's tough love. Because his default response to any situation is to laugh, his rehearsal room is ankle deep in laughter, which doesn't mean, of course, that he finds everything a big joke, far from it. His laughter is a 'first response unit'. Laugh, then we'll all be in a fit state to triage the difficulties.

Though I have known exceptions. I happened to drop in on the New York remount of *Billy Elliot: The Musical*, a smash hit in the West End. They're in, perhaps, their fourth week of technical rehearsals. The auditorium and all adjacent corridors, apertures, crannies of the Imperial Theatre on Broadway are littered, cluttered, piled ceiling-high with flying cases, boxes, trunks, thick metal cables, obscure equipment, dismantled technology. Perhaps a hundred exhausted folk are draped over rows and rows of seats, some fast asleep, or dead possibly, sprawled on the scarlet-carpeted floor like bayoneted soldiers in Goya's famous etching *The Disasters of Remounting a West End Smash on Broadway*, though in fact when it opened a few weeks later it was the runaway hit of the season.

And way down there at the far end of an endless aisle, as long and scooped out as a *piste*, is Stephen in mustard-coloured corduroys, tensed up and glaring at the stage, both palms resting on its edge, with the entire male chorus, policemen, coal miners, lolling, wilting, melting or espaliered against the back wall waiting to be given an instruction, any instruction. But Stephen isn't saying anything. The princess has pricked her finger on a spindle and the entire palace, enchanted, has fallen sleep.

After the longest ever silence, the stage manager winds her slim, cardiganed arm gently through his.

'Stephen, sorry to disturb your thinking, precious, but can we skip over this, can't we move on and come back to it some other time?'

'No,' says Stephen. 'I need an idea. I haven't got the idea. We can't move on till I get the idea.'

The air in the palace pullulates with sighs. I know it's the wrong question but someone has to ask it and I'm expendable, I'm an interloper, I can leave.

'Umm, but what did you do at this point in the show last time?'

'Who gives a fuck what we did last time? We're here now, aren't we? We're not there anyway. Fucking – stupid – fucking – infantile – question.'

And so it is.

The Inheritance
by Matthew Lopez, directed by Stephen Daldry

2018

In the late summer of 2016, Stephen and I spent a week in Cape Town working with the Isango Ensemble on *A Man of Good Hope*, their new co-production with YV.

The show is based on the life of Asad Abdullahi as recounted in a joyously grim blow-by-blow biography by Jonny Steinberg. A young

Somali who fled the civil war in his country as a child discovers his aptitude for business while working as a trader on the back of a truck in Ethiopia. He smuggles himself south, crossing border after border down the continent in search of a better life in which he can use his skills. He arrives in South Africa just at the time of a massive eruption of aggression against foreigners. It was while investigating this widespread viciousness that Jonny, originally a crime reporter, met Abdullahi and recorded the chronicle of his life as a refugee.

Stephen and I are waiting in Cape Town airport departure lounge for our flight home.

'I've been sent this new play. I think I'm going to do it.'

'Tell me about it.'

'I'm not sure I will do it, as it happens, but it's a great play.'

'What's it about?'

'It's the best new play I've read since I can't remember when. Ever!'

'Who's it by?'

'Don't bother to think about it, you've never heard of him.'

'Can I read it?'

'We did a reading in New York. Every actor I sent it to, they're calling their agents off the hook, yelling "Get me into this workshop."'

'Workshop or reading?'

'What time is it?'

He wanders away to look at the flight information display.

'Will you email the play to me?'

'I'm planning to do another workshop in a month or so.'

'In New York? Can I come?'

'Hurry or do you want to miss our plane?'

A year later. I'm in a YV board meeting describing our next season.

'. . . and after that we're doing this fabulous new play by Matthew Lopez in two parts.'

'Does that mean two evenings?'

'That means two evenings. It's called *The Inheritance*. It's about two generations of gay men in New York, the older having struggled through the agony of the AIDS epidemic and the younger intrigued about the past, not knowing much about it, but deeply preoccupied with working out who *they* are and what *they* want to achieve. It asks the question "how does one generation hand on their experience of struggle against the hostility of the world to the next – politically, sexually, emotionally, morally?" The cast isn't that big, it needs thirteen actors, a classic number, the number you need for almost any of Shakespeare's plays, but the event itself could be monumental. It's currently seven hours long though that will come down, I mean it's a *good* thing it's long, it's *great* actually, but let it be no longer than it needs to be. I'm confident it will attract a really wide audience. Everyone will see themselves in it, not just gay men, or so I think.'

Patrick (chair)

'That sounds expensive.'

'And it's going to be *hugely* expensive but – we have a commercial partner. And, oh yes, I should have said this at the beginning, it's closely based on E. M. Forster's novel *Howard's End*.'

'Which is in copyright,' says our entertainment lawyer and expert on these things.

'No, it's out of copyright. It is, I checked.' Pause for thought. 'Or rather, no, that's what Matthew Lopez's agent said. Or that's what I *think* he said. Perhaps he didn't.'

'You want to be sure about that. It might be out of copyright in the US, I believe it is, but I recently advised on certain contracts and . . .'

The room goes deathly still.

'Ok. Thank you. I'll check. And after Matthew's play . . .'

What's *Howard's End* about? Class and property and 'Who owns England?', and how experience will smash up life's jigsaw puzzle if we allow it to and, above all, the desperate need to act, to engage, to try to fulfil other peoples' contradictory needs. *The Inheritance* contains all this ('Who owns the US?') but, more than anything, it's a riff on love. To live without love is a killer but to live with it is also not so easy.

It was commissioned by the imaginative and courageous Hartford Stage, Connecticut which is, of course, in the US where, as our lawyer knew, you can do as you please with Forster's novels.

When he realised the quality of what he'd read, Matthew's young agent at CAA had passed it to a more senior agent who happened to be one of Stephen's CAA 'team', so he sent it to Stephen who, after various shenanigans (see above), emailed it in two massive files to me. But in the UK, as we quickly discovered, Forster *is* still in copyright. Though the play is not a scene-by-scene adaptation, it does depend on the book and explicitly owns up to this, so we in England can't do as we please.

We're doing *Cat on a Hot Tin Roof* at the Apollo Theatre in the West End. I spend much of the technical rehearsals outside the stage door in Archer Street on the phone, backwards and for-wards, agents, lawyers, producers, more agents, more lawyers, sometimes tetchy, sometimes despairing, occasionally hopeful. Days melt into weeks, the best part of the summer goes in untan-gling this . . .

With the expertise and good will of two big agencies, CAA and PFD, lawyers find a way through the maze. It's expensive but neat. And so, in fact by chance, two shows in a single season – as luck would have it, my last – were directed back to back by Stephen, though for *The Jungle* he was joined by his long-time associate Justin Martin.

Sim–salabim!

Producing in the way we did –
　　saying to directors
　　'Do the thing you've never done but long to'
　　'Take a leap in the dark'
　　'Do the crazy thing'
　　with our side of the deal being to say
　　'Yes'
　　to (pretty much) everything
– needed ever greater quantities of cash. That enough leaps landed made it possible for us to find a good deal of the money we needed (by fundraising, by holding starry galas, all the usual things) but if a show succeeded the worst thing you can do is think
　　'Ah, we now know how to do that kind of show'
and try to repeat. Ambition was always ratcheting up. To fulfil these ambitions required an ever more excellent, ever more experienced team. To hold onto our team, as led over many years by Lucy Woollatt, we had to pay ever more competitive salaries. For a number of years the amount we spent on core staff was, by chance, precisely what we received from the Arts Council but then, seemingly suddenly, it was much more.

'Oh no! Our team's now far too big.'

'But the shows you want us to produce are so demanding, if you want us to achieve these standards we *need* these people!'

You can't compromise on the shows. It's because of the shows the audience keeps coming. Across a year we filled ninety-six per cent of our seats. We kept seat prices low. Irrespective of box-office demand, we gave ten per cent free to our neighbours, not handed out randomly but targeted at individuals or groups to whom we'd otherwise be no more than a blur as they walked down our street. I wanted the people who walked *past* the theatre on our busy street to be the same as the people who walked *into* the theatre. You don't just make the show, you make the audience for it. 'Great shows for great audiences' was one of our slogans. *What are you saying? Who are you saying it to?* We wanted to speak to everyone: old, young, black, white, neighbours, tourists, the residents on the estates to the south and east of us, first-timers, theatre aficionados. By and large, we achieved this. And on top of box-office income, we raised as much from 'friends' – supporters and foundations – as we (gratefully) received from the Arts Council.

Frequently we'd aim to cut costs by co-producing but if you co-produce with theatres in other countries the show must be conceived and cast and designed and built in such a way that it can move. Instead of reducing costs you can easily double them.

I'd say to funders

'Yes, we want to keep seat prices low and do the adventurous things but we want to do them next year too, and the year after that.'

Each financial year but one of my eighteen we balanced the books – and the year we didn't (we'd followed a *Dido and Aeneas* co-produced with English National Opera with *Pictures from an Exhibition* co-produced with Sadler's Wells, both great to do but not so smart for a playhouse to schedule a dance piece after an opera) we'd found a supporter – thank you, Patrick McKenna, long-time chair of our board – who very generously plugged the gap.

('Um, it's a bit worse than I thought it would be. Well, yeah, thanks, it's *so* good of you, Patrick, but do you think we might go just a tidge north of that . . .')

I'd frequently ask Arts Council England for extra cash above the grant they'd allocated to us. We needed it, simply, to keep producing in the way we did and for a few years they found another ten per cent through various schemes designed to enable and reward excellence and internationalism.

Two or three times over the years I'd thought it was nearing the moment for me to move on. Not everything we did worked out but we pulled off most of it. One danger 'success' can bring is you start to think you know what you're doing and how to do it. And one knows, on first principles, that a show only has a chance if you go into it with the cool comprehension that you've no idea how to produce it. Did I now think that I knew? Yeah, I did. So, was it time to blow it all up and start again from a different premise? No more hotshot directors, no more blowing all your cash on long 'rehears-allings' and 'European' design. I thought so. But all those years in, though I still had stores of energy for travelling to find the new, the amazing, the challenging, for producing, for fundraising, did I any longer have the *need*? Is making theatre any longer – for me – *the most important thing*? If it's time to go back to beginnings wouldn't someone else's take on the ways of the world be more convincing?

I talked to Patrick, as I so frequently did.

'I think if I keep going I'll destroy it.'

'I don't see what you mean.'

'Well, the way you run these publicly funded organisations is you pick them up, you run with them for as long as you can keep going, then you hand them on, hopefully in a better state than you found them.'

'I don't agree.'

'You don't agree?'

'Not at all.'

Which was surprising. Patrick and I agreed about most things.

'You can do with your theatre anything you decide you want to. You can develop it, change it, expand it into whatever you have the imagination to make of it.'

'Really? Can I? Is that true?'

It is, actually.

And yes, indeed, I still had plenty of crazy big ideas for shows I hadn't yet got round to. But one day, for no particular reason, all the choppy waters in my head suddenly stilled and I thought

'No, that's it.'

Nothing lasts for ever and why should it?

An irony of my last season was that it was produced in a similar way to the early ones, with other people's money, though to everyone's advantage naturally. *The Jungle* was paid for in part by the NT, *The Inheritance* largely by our commercial co-producers, my good friends Sonia Friedman and Tom Kirdahy.

'Stephen, everything in my book is recreated from memory but, bizarrely, though we've been talking pretty much nonstop for twenty-five years, I find I can't remember ever having asked you the questions I want to write about. If I make it up you'll say it's all wrong. You'll probably say it's all wrong whatever I write even if I write down exactly what you say.'

'Rubbish.'

'Nonetheless . . . I want to record your answers, then I'll transcribe them. Ok?'

'What do you want to talk about?'

'Directing.'

'Get on with it.'

'Technical things. When you are directing actors, what are you looking at?'

'What am I looking at? Or what am I listening to?'

'What are you looking at, what are you listening to? What are you *doing*?'

'Trying to give it life . . . Trying to find where the play *is* in the scene, trying to find the incident in the scene. If you work out what the incident is, then you can work out what the life is of that scene. If a scene doesn't have an incident you have a problem because you can't direct it.'

'If it doesn't have an incident?'

'Yeah, a justification for the scene. Once you discover that . . . It's a complicated question you've asked, isn't it? Which means this needs to be a long answer.'

'Go for it.'

'What am I looking at? I'm looking at a million different things. You're looking at how is the scene going to come to life. How will it be believable. It's an artificial context, it's not real, but you're trying to create a real conversation or situation, something based in what the actors are *doing*. And, I suppose, in trying to direct you have to get specific very quickly . . .

'If you take a scene from one of the two plays we've just done, if you take the first scene of *The Inheritance* where right at the start there's a group of chaps sitting about, that took ages to get right because we couldn't work out what the contract was with the audience, what's the premise, what's going on in the scene?

'Watching it again today, it's still not quite right. Because something in it is contradictory in a way that's confusing. What is the premise? "We're a group of young men and we are now going to make up this play?" Is that it? Are they *improvising* a play? Or are they *writing* a play? What's going on? Working out all that took ages. By the end, we'd spent *weeks* on, what is it?, three minutes?, maybe less, of little set-ups. What are the detailed inter-personal relationships between the young men that bring the scene to life? And the core question turned out to be: what is Adam's role in this? He tells us right at the start that he can't write his novel, he doesn't know where to begin. So is it "Oh I see, it's *Adam's* play"?

Actually what we discovered is *it is* but it took us ages to realise that.

'A good deal of directing is trying to structure *what could be*, trying to structure the basis of the evening.

'In our other show *The Jungle*, if we're talking about what the underlying structure is, it was your idea to start the play at the end, to begin with chaos, organised chaos in which we introduce all the characters in a Spielbergian way. *Raiders of the Lost Ark* was the first one, wasn't it, where you start at the last beat, with the *dénouement*. It gives a huge injection of energy into the opening moments. That was an intensely complicated scene to orchestrate and thus far not, in my view, entirely successfully achieved.'

'Ok so you've described your intention. Now forget your intention. What are you actually *doing* when you're looking at the actors?'

'You're trying to watch as though you've never seen it before. You're trying to work out whether it's interesting. Trying to be objective. Trying to find the tensions and what I would call the *jeu*, the game, the "play". Trying to find out where the ball is. Once you've locked onto where the ball is you can play with it.'

'And how do you do that?'

'You listen, you watch. You're trying to have an idea. You're seeing what something *could* be. You're looking for opportunities.'

'And when you start a rehearsal do you have all this in mind?'

'It's much more exciting if you have the idea in the room. I can only do it in a relaxed state. If you're tense and you're trying to force something or push an idea you've had previously onto an actor it's rarely any good. You have to just work with what the actor gives you and with what the text yields in the room, in that moment, on that day.'

Amir Nizar, my writer-director friend from Palestine, was in town for a few days. I arranged for him to see *The Inheritance* and afterwards, as he'd been deeply moved by it, standing in the wide alleyway outside the stage door, we talked about love – love in life, love in the play.

'My father loved my mother so much. Even to his last day he was so bound up with her. He adored her mind, her body, everything about her. He once said to me "Do you know what love is?" And I said "No, Father. Tell me what is love." "It's paying attention," he said. "It's paying endless, very close attention. That's what love is."'

───────────

Art is a struggle against death we always lose. Theatre *is* death, it implies death. Whether it lunges or glides or saunters towards its end, though while it lives it's wound as tight as a ball of plastic thread, though an inexplicable richness throngs together while the light is burning, the darkness is this side of the horizon. Theatre is ending after ending until it ends.

Dad never saw or read any of my plays. Ma gave them pride of place in the bookshelf in their bedroom but – perhaps in part for that reason – they didn't interest him. And I'm certain he didn't read more than a page or two, if so much, of my book about my time in the Valley – though once I glimpsed him holding it over his head and turning it ever so slightly so its glossy cover glinted in the sunlight.

I'm the last one left in the graveyard. The drizzle is now a downpour and the others are sheltering. I see myself from a distance, in long shot, as though from the back of a theatre, in the long black coat I found in his wardrobe, facing into the darkness, the rain thundering, shovelling sodden earth into his grave, backlit by lightning.

Six

The Room

Anton Chekhov

1967

This is the tree-lined pavement I hurried along after watching a performance of *The Seagull* by Anton Chekhov, after waiting for the actor I slightly knew in the pebbled courtyard outside the stage door. He emerges, blond hair tucked behind his ears, wearing a pale trenchcoat like in the Truffaut movie *Jules et Jim*. I think I've caught his eye. He gives a sprightly wave. What did it mean? 'Thanks for coming' or 'come with me'? Or was he greeting the bronze-faced kid, charcoal-stubbled, kohl-ringed eyes, hovering on sandalled feet? Desire like spice in the late-night breeze.

I'm burning to be welcomed, wanted, even just included in *whatever is happening*. Is it a wild party he's now striding towards far ahead along this fractured pavement shadowed by high trees?

There's where I watch him enter *that* squat block of flats, *here's* the ground-floor window in which a soft light flicks on, snap, out, darkness again. And when I steal across the grass and sally past the window glancing in – could it be him *already* on the bed with who?, that kid? – a blind is jerkily let down.

Let me into your room! Let me in!

1968

I was having mild sex with a teacher, not from my own school, in his flat in a bland new block on the slopes of the mountain just below the trees. I tell him my tale of woe. My father had struck me across the face with a leather glove because, in his professional view, the red curtains Ma had run up for my room were made with too little fabric, they didn't hang as full as they should, and I'd disagreed.

'Actually, he's correct about the curtains but I had to say I liked them. He hates it if I take her side but to slap me across the chops like a Prussian swordsman? Is he challenging me to fight him? What does it *mean*? Honestly, he's driving me crazy. Ok, both his sons are disappointments – one's a cripple, one's a *moffie*. Not much to boast of with his golfing friends but it's not my fault, is it?'

He tops up my Bacardi with a slosh more gin.

'You know, if you really can't take it, if you can't *really—*'

'You think I'm pretending, acting?'

'You'll have to think hard about this but . . . you can always come live with me.'

So I had to choose – or believed I did. Or at least evaluate things. Who am I? What do I care about? Who needs what? What do I need?

Dad and I talked about everything so I told him I was leaving home and going to live with the teacher. Yes, I was still at school but I was grown-up, sixteen. Somehow Dad found out where he lived or where he worked, I don't know how, he didn't tell me.

It seems to me I'm transcribing from the copybook of memory. I hear, rehear, rehearse in an inner auditorium not words or sentences but scenes in multiple dimensions, expertly lit. Plush red curtains rise, then the one behind flies out, then another divides. Unexpected depths of stage are revealed. The back wall recedes and recedes. The light brightens exposing ever sharper detail, connections and disconnections. As I write it *feels* real.

But of Dad and the teacher I've nothing. I can't even picture it except as a B movie.

'Now listen, fella, and listen good. I'm only going to say this one time.'

When Dad came home, or whenever I next saw him, there must have been some kind of scene. But open the trapdoor, edge your way down the dark steps into the cellar, there ought to be bags of grain and jars of wine. There's nothing.

1969

Crossing that pebbled courtyard, I enter the stage door to start rehearsals for another play by Chekhov. Most of the actors in *Three Sisters* are professionals.

> **Olga** Father died a year ago, one year to the day. The
> snow was falling, it was bitterly cold. Now we look back
> on it all quite calmly.

I'm a first-year acting student. I've very recently evaded being a soldier but I play . . . the soldier Fedotik who's in love with Irina, the youngest sister. He has three lines.

> **Fedotik** This is for you. A spinning top. It makes a
> terrific racket.

One week in, some crisis causes the actor playing the aged servant Ferapont to leave the cast.

Our director:

'Some young actors can be rather good at playing elderly men.'

So *here* in the darkened wings in straggly beard, ill-fitting wig, night after night, I breathe the oxygen of a masterpiece.

> **Ferapont** Some people say there's a rope stretched right
> across Moscow.
> **Andrei** Tiresome idiot.

1970

These were our haunts when, strawberry-haired, decked in tones of red, Nick came to direct Anton Chekhov's *Uncle Vanya*.

On *this* beach amidst a muscled mob we lay on fiery sand, the sea a swaying glistening icy sheet . . .

On *this other* beach rough winds beat warm waves high. Surfers swagger along the furthest end where the shoreline bends, then bends again . . .

In the courtyard of *this* run-down hippy house, thick walls stand high so at night we get high in the open air and, lying flat on flag-stones, drop acid, star gallivanting . . .

In *this* bedroom of a rented tin-roofed shack abandoned party guests glimpse us in bed which seems a victory . . . Over who? Dad? The kohl-eyed kid?

1998

Katie Mitchell asks if I'll 'translate' *Uncle Vanya* for her to direct for the RSC at YV. I'm delighted and say yes with one proviso, that once our 'version' is achieved her actors use it. To write a 'version', to try to conjure into English another writer's world, all you have is your own sense of fit. If you combine translations, mix and match, it falls to pieces.

'Agreed?'

'Agreed.'

We commission a literal translation (from Helen Rappaport) which arrives complete with reams of notes, subtle, insightful. I keep the Russian near at hand and explore each thorny sentence. It's interesting to see their shapes, some long, some short, some-times many short ones in a row, some words stand alone. Where he has three dots between phrases I do the same.

Sonya We sent you everything, Father . . . We earned
the bread we ate. No, I'm not getting this right, not
saying it well. Try to imagine our lives, Father. Try.

I imagine Anton Pavlovich at the other end of the room, patient,
amused, sucking tea through a sugar lump clenched in stumpy
teeth. It's . . . what's the ideal word? . . . intoxicating?

In Stratford-upon-Avon Katie is mid-rehearsal for some Samuel
Beckett plays. We're side-by-side all weekend. The work is pains-
taking, each phrase weighed for implication and cadence. A few
weeks later we work through it again. There's barely a word that
doesn't cry out, like Yelena

'Leave me in peace!'

that doesn't yearn, like Sonya in the last scene, for the day they
can cease their toil and sleep.

I'm away for the first weeks of rehearsal. As I walk into the room
during week three, actors and director, in a circle, kneeling, hear
footsteps, glance up – scurry, scurry – five other translations van-
ish – *whish* – beneath rehearsal skirts.

Leaving at the end of a preview, I say to Nick

'Well, that was awful.'

He stops. The streaming audience bump against, then edge
around us.

'Why do you do that? It's self-indulgence. The production is terrific. So she asked you to rewrite some of it . . .'

'*Some* of it!'

'So? Are you an artist or what are you?'

'That's the wrong question. The correct question is: am I a hack
to simply do as she instructs me.'

'Oh, she instructed you?'

'Well, no, but with Katie how do you refuse?'

'Why would you want to?'

That's not the fucking point!

'It's way the best *Vanya* I've seen.'

'Oh? You think it's good?'

He's had his fill. He strides on.

'And I couldn't hear my fucking words!'

'So what? And anyway that's *your* look-out, deafo! I could hear everything!'

'Lots of people were complaining about it.'

'Lots?'

'The people behind me. No, be fair, what's the point of my spending those *months* . . .'

'Self-obsessed . . .'

He's off again down the street.

'Please! I need to know! Did you like it?'

It's absurd. We're both in tears. Because . . . because it's Chekhov. Did we arrive even close to where the god lives? Did he peer out through a high window and beckon us in?

Over the run I watch it again and again. Like all his last plays, it seems the best there is and Katie's production is deeply serious yet light-of-heart. And Nick is correct of course. To create something *truly* intoxicating, water of life, an *aquavit*, herbs, spices, roots, fruits must yield up their distinctiveness, suffer ego loss, dissolve into a potion like Buddha into nirvana or beetroot, carrot, potato, bay leaf, onion, dill, celery into the borscht which, as Granny Golda made it, had a thick but smooth consistency, the colour of old wounds and a fragrance that was sweet but peppery.

2000

Trevor Nunn saw our *Vanya* and asked me to do an English *The Cherry Orchard* for him. At the National, Vanessa Redgrave and her brother Corin play Ranevskaya and her brother Gaev.

The first day of rehearsals is a week to the day after I start at YV. I beetle over. Sitting at a desk at one end of the room, Trevor is mid-describing how he's imagining it all when he's cut off by Corin's marmalade baritone.

'Our translator is making an error using the word "slave" for "serf". From historical and political and economic points of view, they're utterly different phenomena.'

Oh Lordy, here we go.

'I did give some thought to this. We call Russian slaves "serfs" because they're "white" people, it sounds less brutal, but the land-owners owned the peasants body and soul. A small proportion were clerks and administrators but by and large their only value was their labour.'

But I quickly give it up and make my excuses. My work here was finished long ago. I have other fruit to stew.

2012

I call Benedict Andrews in Sydney.

'What about *Three Sisters*?'

> **Irina** I've never loved anyone. I've dreamed of love, I've longed for it all my life, night and day, but my heart is a piano that's locked and someone's lost the key.

Baron Tuzenbach, a lieutenant in a Russian army brigade holed up in this provincial wasteland, owing such existence as it has to its military base, strolls over to the piano, lifts the lid . . .

But where are we exactly? Watching or reading the play you've no idea. Is it a way station for troops heading north to capture, torture, exterminate Siberian nomads? Or is this town on the long trail south to the Caucasus where these soldiers will 'pacify' Chechens, Georgians, Azerbaijanis and secure the Russian empire's outer extremes?

Either way, the soldiers are from Moscow and they're stalled and bored. The only local entertainment, for officers at least, is the genial household of the Prozorovs, three daughters and a son of a general who died 'a year ago to the day'. There they flirt and fall in love, perhaps have a little sex with the sisters – probably not actual fucking but Chekhov loved fucking (read the Donald Rayfield biography), so yes, middle sister Masha and Colonel Vershinin probably did – dine in the open air, have their photographs taken, get rat-arsed . . .

So at a certain moment Tuzenbach wanders to the piano and folds back the lid. He ponders. What will he play? A sprightly tune of 1901, the year of the play's premiere? A bagatelle by Rimsky-Korsakov, a waltz, let's go, two, three and . . . But no, the riff he plays is jazzy, bluesy, raucous, contemporary with the moment the play is being performed a hundred and eleven years later, now, today, this instant, this very evening.

Between acts we hear 'Smells Like Teen Spirit' by Nirvana.

I first heard this during a technical rehearsal, got it, loved it but had no idea what it was. Actors, stage managers, crew were bopping along. How can I do this job, I asked myself, if I'm so poorly plugged into popular culture? (Even members of the Critics' Circle who for this show chose Benedict as 'Best Director' revealed in their reviews they knew what they were listening to.)

The set, designed by Johannes Schütz, consists of seventy-nine square wooden tables, all the same size, all painted grey-blue. When laid out in rows they form a squared-off, jutting plane on which Acts 1 and 2 are played. In Act 3 a fire rages through the town. While this is happening, soldiers carry out the tables, all seventy-nine. By Act 4 they're gone. The last scenes happen on the flat earth floor.

Surely this massive metaphor would jar against the delicacy of the naturalistic scenes but by some alchemy there is no *I* or *you* or even *we*, there's only thought and feeling dismantled in the flow of action – the show, the event, the experience, the thing.

While the fire mutilates the town, the oldest sister, Olga, gathers clothes to give to her neighbours who are suddenly bereft of everything.

> **Olga** They can have this grey one . . . and this . . . the jacket as well . . . Nanny, take this skirt . . . Take it all, we don't need any of this, give it all away . . . Just sit quietly for a minute, my darling . . . You're exhausted, poor thing . . .

Olga's kindliness floods across the deep distress caused by Vershinin and Masha's adultery, the duel that masks a murder and a suicide, brother Andrei's savage depressive loneliness, his wife Natasha's vicious bullying, the alcoholism, the brutal stupidity . . . Out of her kindness to her sisters, to the world in which she lives, Olga struggles to articulate a hope in which, I think, she can't believe. At the play's end, as the soldiers abandon the town, their band strikes up.

> **Olga** Dear, dear sisters, don't think just because they're leaving our lives are over. Not at all. We'll live. Listen, they're playing a jaunty tune. It's so odd, I feel as though if only they played a little longer we'd make sense of why we're here, of why we suffer. Oh, what joy it would be to understand everything.

> Chekhov said – and no one had said this before, not even Tolstoy – that first and foremost we are all of us human beings [. . .] and only secondly are we bishops, Russians,

shopkeepers, Tartars, workers. Do you understand?
Instead of saying that people are good or bad because
they are bishops or workers, Tartars or Ukrainians,
instead of this he said that people are equal because they
are human beings.

Vasily Grossman, *Life and Fate*

To us, Chekhov's plays are as unlike any others as to Christians, perhaps, the gospels are unlike other biographies. We long to be kind to them, to restore them to life with all the shocking vigour, the acid wit, the black enriching depressiveness *we believe* they had when they were first seen. We weren't there, we can't be sure of anything. We pore over his short stories and letters looking for hints and clues but the house is dark, you feel your way with fingertips from door to door, from room to room.

2014

There's the side window of the little house with its slender metal bars through which you can easily see, though you may not enter, the whitewashed room where Chekhov wrote so many stories and his final plays. A narrow metal bed. A shallow desk with inkstand. A rust-green statuette, is it Tolstoy or could it be Shakespeare? Its domed head is turned upstage. Turn *your* head and deep below is an inlet on the coast of the Black Sea. A rocky bay. What's changed, what's the same? Waves tumble in. Is that a new wave or the last one draining, folding, whitening, pouring back in?

On an anniversary of his death, in Yalta with a group of theatre folk from Russia, France, Italy, Germany, we promenade along the bulky seafront, strolling beside the five-branched lamp posts topped with shades like cloves of garlic and the swaying palm trees. The air is hot. It's drizzling. We gather in a coffee shop hoping, we laugh,

240

to glimpse 'The Lady with the Little Dog', the heroine of Chekhov's famous tale, first sighted by its hero where we now sit.

> He'd run into her at least once a day in a park or in a
> square always on her own, wearing the same beret and
> walking a Pomeranian.

We visit his house in town, his lush garden stocked with ferns, rhododendrons, azaleas. We wander in. There's the grand piano Rachmaninov played. There's the telephone on which his wife, the actress Olga Knipper, called from Moscow after the first performance of *The Cherry Orchard*. She played Ranevskaya, owner of the doomed estate. Her cherries were not the sweet red fruit of

> *Cherry ripe, cherry ripe,*
> *Ripe I cry*

but rather *griottes,* sour cherries.

> **Firs** In the old days, forty, fifty years ago, the cherries
> were dried or marinated or pickled and they made jam.
> Then there was money to burn! The dried cherries were
> soft and moist, so sweet, fragrant . . . In those days they
> knew how to do it.
> **Gaev** Shush, Firs.

Chekhov had been too ill to make the long train journey to the capital – or did he just loathe first nights?

'Go on. The line is good. I can hear you.'

'The audience called us back again and again. Each time the curtain rose they clapped still louder. We wept and bowed and waved to our friends and bowed again. The curtain calls were more exhausting than the performance.'

'They liked it?'

'From the back row someone cried "Author!" Then they were all yelling for you "Author! Author!"'

'But did they laugh?'

'Everyone says to tell you it's your finest play.'

'But what I'm asking you, Olga, is was there laughter in the theatre?'

'Don't shout, dearest, I hear you perfectly.'

'That fool director never understood it's a fucking comedy!'

His long leather coat hangs in his bedroom cupboard like a corpse. Theatre programmes. First editions of collections of his stories. *In the Twilight. Motley Tales.* Fat medical books with broken spines. His stethoscope.

I'm studying a sepia photograph of him sitting in his garden with Maxim Gorky on a wooden bench. Young, punky Tanya sidles up. She's a St Petersburg critic with long black hair cut in a crisp fringe.

'Everyone stages Chekhov, Chekhov like no other Russian ever picked up a fountain pen. Explain why you never produce Gorky? I don't say his plays are better. His is another mood entirely. Chekhov's world-view is extraordinarily harsh but underneath flows a sparkling stream of kindliness. He wishes us well in our bone-headedness. Gorky is not so sure our souls can be redeemed by a few good deeds. As things turned out, his view was the more realistic, don't you agree?'

Arm in arm, we stroll back into the garden. There's the wooden bench. Somebody's painted it a poison green. We perch on it. At the far end by the gate, facing a metal bust of the playwright on a plinth, the leader of our group holds his hat high and makes a speech. We feel awkward, as though we're claiming a place in history, so wander off, disagreeing and gesturing, back along the narrow path that edges the giddy cliff and leads to the whitewashed room where the writer-doctor no doubt screwed his Olga, regretting, no doubt, the narrowness of the bed, jotted down plots of stories, wrote and wrote and mused and gazed out of his window and took the heartbeat of the sea.

Towards evening, back in town, we gather in a wood-panelled room high up in the Theatre Anton Chekhov. Artistic directors, directors of plays, theatre administrators, critics, academics . . . Tanya chairs the conversation. The hot topic is the Berlin Volksbühne's *To Moscow! To Moscow!*, a mash-up of *Three Sisters* and a short story 'Peasants'.

'But I'm compelled to ask a simple question. Is it acceptable if half the audience walk out?'

'Not at all, not at all. But you can't instruct an audience on its behaviour.'

'We're discussing aesthetics not good manners.'

'Friends, we have much to share this evening. Let's move on.'

'No, no, Tanya, dear, this production is worthy of the most detailed analysis. It has energy flowing through it! To keep the work alive, alive is our number one responsibility.'

'But is it Chekhov?'

'An unanswerable question.'

'Why "unanswerable"? I am willing to give you an answer.'

'Every word on each actor's lips was taken from Chekhov's writings, from his mind, from his heart.'

'So here's my answer—'

With her scarlet smile, Tanya imposes order.

'Shut up, you!'

They're good friends so everyone laughs and then the angel of silence descends.

'We'll go round in a circle. Each delegate should make a contribution but, I ask you, briefly, please. We don't want to delay the special dinner they're preparing for us.'

Some applaud, others rock to and fro like greedy children.

'On the other hand, we've all travelled far to be here so when the microphone is in your hand, speak as you feel, the floor is yours.'

I'm not expecting this. I'm certain that as soon as I begin—

'But he's a charlatan!'

'He knows nothing about Chekhov!'

'Or any kind of theatre!'

My fall-back is a note I wrote to my 'version' of *Uncle Vanya* years ago. I rehearse it as the microphone circles . . .

'Now our one colleague from England. Of course it is for your benefit we're all speaking English.'

Laughter. Is it mocking? I think it is.

'Ok. I'll be brief.'

'No need.'

'You said—'

'I know what I said.' The scarlet smile. 'We're all so anxious to hear you.'

Remember – breathe.

'People tend to divide Chekhov's plays into three groups – the one-act *vaudevilles*, the three early full-length plays, the four late works.

'But I'd categorise them differently. *Platonov*, *The Wood Demon* and *Ivanov* are Chekhov's versions of the nineteenth-century Russian theatre tradition of Ostrovsky and Turgenev. You know those plays – doomed love affairs on country estates, many sharply drawn characters, you're made to feel as though a whole society is on stage. From his letters we know Chekhov felt none of his attempts at this kind of play was successful.'

'But he didn't give up!'

Whose growly voice is that? I can't even tell where he's sitting.

'Then in *The Seagull* he wrote the perfect version of that nine-teenth-century genre. And then he moved on.'

'Naturally he moved on – into the twentieth century.'

Laughter.

Who is this person? What's going on? Tanya is laughing. At him? At me?

'*Uncle Vanya* is an altogether different kind of play. Its strongest characteristic is its ambiguity. It's true that, like the earlier plays, it's set on a country estate but now the surrounding forests are being cut down by starving peasants in need of firewood. Industrialists are logging on a massive scale. It's gone so far the local climate is affected.'

'My dear, Doctor Astrov who makes these claims describes everyone who lives in this backwater including himself as a *chudak*.'

'I'm aware of this.'

'Well then.'

'No, this is my point. *Chudak*, as I understand it, means crackpot or weirdo.'

More laughter but now, I think, on my side.

'Yes, "weirdo" is good.'

Then a new voice, elderly. I think it's the woman who's run a Moscow theatre for children for forty years.

'The word is untranslatable but in my opinion "crackpot" is good.'

'Ok, friends, crackpot.' This is Growly. 'But Astrov admits he is a crackpot himself. So why take what he says so seriously?'

'"Nincompoop" is even better.'

This is Tanya. The group practise their English slang. 'Nincompoop, nincompoop.'

'So are the Russian forests really under threat or is this simply the obsession of a – whatever translation you wish to use?'

During dinner, I share a table with the Russian minister of culture who was due to make the opening speech but has just walked in. He sports a thick moustache and a heavy charcoal suit. His skin is dark as teak with painful-looking crevices. After the soup he hoists himself onto his shiny shoes.

'It is of course my pleasure to welcome you to this gathering and to hope you will find time – I know your stay is brief – to enjoy some of what our world-renowned coastline . . . of what Crimea's world-renowned coastline has to offer even so late in the season. And now I ask that you fill your glass with some of our . . . with some of Crimea's marvellous red wine . . .'

Over the carp, I put the question Tanya and I prepared for him.

'Minister, if I may ask, what's your opinion? Chekhov was born in Taganrog, just a few miles from here. So was he Russian or Ukrainian?'

'Chekhov wrote the most perfect and precise Russian, diamond-sharp but with a good melody which brings tears to the eyes of all who hear his words across the world. Now try some of our . . . try some . . . These *pierogi* are delicious. Flatter me by filling your mouth with them.'

We flow back into the wood-panelled room for coffee. A stubby man pads across to me. He has spiky hair like one of those natty Swiss hedgehogs my grandmother Golda used to keep on her mantelpiece.

'Interesting to hear your opinions.'

It's Growly.

'So it is your opinion that Chekhov's last four plays are stylistically different, one from another? You've studied them for many years? Obviously.'

'In *Vanya* everything we're told by one character is contradicted by another. In fact, the play is so constructed that at the end all you're left with is contradictions. This is true also of *Three Sisters* but not, it seems to me, of *Cherry Orchard*...'

He has turned away as though something arresting is happening through the window at the other end of the room. When I break off there's a silence, then he turns back.

'These plays are important to you as the director of a theatre, someone who has to make decisions about what will attract an audience, what will sell and what will not, or to you personally?'

'I don't make that distinction.'

'Aha! A fortunate man. Who in this room can say what you have just said? Believe me, they appear to be free beings with wills of their own. In fact they're puppets, slaves to their finance directors while their finance directors are slaves to the few wealthy men and women, mostly women, who sit on their boards. No one else is interested...'

'Is that really true?'

'You've lost me. What is your question?'

'Is what you said true of everyone?'

'Forget about it. Say more about Anton Pavlovich. For you, his plays, especially the final ones are great, yes, but are they great beyond anything?'

'I don't understand what you're asking.'

'Ah, box and cox, is that how you put it? You do understand but now *you* wish to avoid *my* question. I want to know if in your opinion they are greater than the greatest Englishman, William Pavlovich Shakespeare. But you're English so for you no one can be greater than William Pavlovich. Am I correct?'

'If you're asking me—'

'I am asking you.'

'For me, Chekhov's plays are what a play *is*. Every play is good or bad or *is* what it *is* in comparison to them.'

'You go extremely far, further than I imagined. I'm deeply concerned by what you tell me. And you speak fluent Russian?'

'Not at all.'

A throaty eruption of laughter. He throws his hands in the air.

'So what are we talking about?' This is to the whole room. A few of the group come closer in.

'Actually, my grandparents were Russian.'

Shit! I've wrong-footed myself.

'And so? This means?'

'Almost Russian, spoke Russian. Lithuanian, Latvian.'

His attention is caught again by what's happening outside the window. It's raining heavily. He shivers.

'But you speak . . . ?'

'My mother's mother's family were from Vitebsk.'

He swings back.

'Ah, Jewish, no?'

'I'm Jewish, yes.'

'So your first language was Yiddish?'

'My father spoke Yiddish before he spoke English but his parents spoke Russian as well.'

'But not you?'

'Not me.'

'You didn't pick it up?'

'I didn't.'

'Not one word?'

'I know *panima* means "do you understand?"'

'It doesn't. Not at all. And anyway that's Russian not Yiddish.'

'I know that.'

'And do you regret this?'

'Regret what?'

'Your ignorance.'

Someone murmurs 'Gregory' and touches his elbow.

'Of course.'

'How much?'

'Deeply.'

'And yet you venture to speak about Russia's finest playwright. No, no, please, I'm not the chief of police, no need to confess to me. Vitebsk was the home of many marvellous artists. Chagall. El Lissitzky. Plenty of smaller fish. This is your heritage, no?'

'No, not really.'

'You don't admire Chagall? You find him kitsch? You've made *Fiddler on the Roof*?'

I laugh. 'I haven't.'

He laughs too showing porcelain teeth. He lays a brotherly hand on my shoulder.

'You've visited Vitebsk?'

'I haven't.'

'But why not? Why not, my friend? These days it's so easy. A cheap flight, a few hours from London, you don't even notice how far it is.'

'Even so.'

'So, with deep pan-Russ artistic culture you have no, how best to put it, intimacy? Except with Chekhov. Him you are expert in.' He makes a jerky gesture with his hands. He repeats it. 'Fascinating!'

An acre of gleaming parquet floor. The room feels windswept.

'Who are you?'

Oh Jesus.

'No, I'm asking. *Who are you?* You come from South Africa. Now, there's a country to which you could make a contribution. But you're too highbrow, too sophisticated, is that it? No, let me speak.'

Tanya is stroking his back. 'Gregory . . .'

'What's wrong? You want to censor me? He comes here, tells us we understand nothing, makes infantile distinctions . . . Do you direct plays, you yourself?'

'Occasionally.'

'Hardly ever and quite right too in my opinion. I googled your wiki, I've seen the kind of reviews you get.'

'There are no reviews on my wiki.'

'Don't pick straws, my friend. What is actually your function at your theatre? How does it work with you people?'

'My job, the way I see it, is to create the best circumstances . . .'

'So you're a kind of midwife?'

'You could say that.'

'Bullshit. This is your way of avoiding responsibility for the disaster that is the British theatre.'

With all my heart I long to leave.

'You have brothers and sisters?'

'I do.'

'Which do you know better? Chekhov or your siblings?'

A titter.

'If you're asking me . . .'

'Yes, I spoke quite clearly. I'm asking you.'

More tittering.

'Then I'll say truthfully I feel, yes, I feel I have more understanding of these plays than of my brother and sisters.'

'You agree there are certain distinctions to be made between a play and a human being?'

'There are more contradictions.'

It's like I'm in a fucking nursery school.

'Even more contradictions, precisely.'

He strolls towards the window, spins back, light on his feet.

'No, what you say is not at all clear to me. In which are there more contradictions? In plays or in human beings?'

I so don't care. I've totally lost it with this conversation.

'Yes, I also don't have the answer. This is our tragedy, we people of the theatre. Nothing is real to us. We care more about heart-rending suffering in made-up stories than what goes on right out there beyond that window in the rain, in the icy gutters, on the hard pavement, in the squalid street. The beggars, the, the, the homeless. Have you noticed how many there are? Tell me, be courageous, don't conceal anything, did you see them this afternoon out on the so-famous "Little Dog" promenade? I counted more than a dozen. I gave away thirty euros.'

'Rubles.'

'Rubles, thank you, Tanya. Yes, that's not a great deal – but even so. It's shameful. It shames us. I speak as a European. Where's the fucking minister when we have something meaningful to say to him and not just to *lécher son cul*?'

He drubbles his tongue against his upper lip. The small crowd bristle. Where's he going with this? I think he's going to spit at me.

'*Like you did!*'

'Honestly, Gregory, I hardly said anything to him.'

Tanya says 'Stop it now. I suggested he ask that question.'

'Oh yes, the poor are simple people, they have simple meanings, why should we spend our energy to analyse, to make distinctions about them? But great stories! Marvellous plays! By the way . . .'

He's been haranguing the others, now he's back on my case.

'I too am Jewish. All Jews love Chekhov. My mother used to read all the stories 1888 to 1904 from start to finish every summer. Nothing special in this. It's in our DNA. You can claim no credit for it.'

'But I don't claim anything. Tanya passed me the microphone, asked me to speak. I would have preferred to say nothing.'

'Oh ho! So that's how it is.'

He claps his hands. Game over. That's it. I've lost, he's won. Tanya tuts at me.

'If you attend a conference you must expect to speak, to make a contribution. It's part of the bargain, no?'

She puts an arm round Gregory's meaty shoulders. He gives her a quick kiss, then another not so quick, then, holding her tight round the hips, he smirks at me.

'And she's *my* girlfriend. You get it?'

He snorts, laughs, looks at me, then I'm in his arms and he kisses my cheek. And we're all laughing, we're all well-meaning colleagues, all at peace and all united against the tragedies that roam the hills beyond this room which if you'd asked me yesterday did I want to enter, to join this European literary elite, I'd have answered

'Yes, yes, me, me'

and which now I ache to leave.

'So, Mr African homosexual British Jew, do you have plans for producing any of these brothers and sisters whom you know so intimately? Give us insight into the wonders you will offer the world in your next remarkable season.'

2018

I'm on the RER B travelling between the Aéroport Charles de Gaulle and the Gare du Nord. Sitting on the opposite bench is a skinny young man in camouflage trousers and tight blue corduroy jacket, no more than eighteen or nineteen, reading the final pages of *Le pouvoir du moment présent* by Eckhart Tolle. On my mobile I google 'power' and 'Tolle'. It sold billions of copies in multiple languages, it spent a decade on the *New York Times* bestseller list. I watch him concentrating so hard you could lose yourself in the furrows of his oh-so-smooth forehead.

He turns the last page, shuts the book, screws up his little tortoise face, stares out the window. He sighs. All his dilemmas are resolved. It's true what Tolle says. Past and future *don't* exist. *All there is is now,* this train scurrying on *this* track, *that* view of the harsh, angular urban periphery, *those* clouds like silver feathers, *this* tight warm space in which he's constrained, *this* tiny snatch of the infinite, which is not infinite, which has no length or depth or any quality, which barely exists except at moments of intensity – like now. NOW! *NOW!!*

But now it's then. We're pulling into Paris. The train stops. Time flows again. The boy is on the move. Where did I stash my shoulder bag? Will I need to show my ticket to the guard? How long until my first meeting?

The Room

Nick and I had argued about something that seemed, mid-argument, of huge importance but, as we both knew, wasn't so at all. Who had done what or hadn't done and why they had or failed to do it even though the other had or hadn't wanted them to.

'But *you* said *you'd* . . .'

'No, *you* said *you* . . .'

And on and on, digging into each other ever more hurtfully. Even while we were arguing, standing so angled and so intoxicated by the articulacy of our rage, so poised, trembling with the tension, darting dark-eyed anger at each other from far sides of the room, not daring to get closer because we were so in love and, in particular, so loved each other's bodies that if we did stagger closer we might fall into each other's arms and the argument would decay. We knew we needed to stay on the high wire because underneath our words, below the detail of this triviality, was a crucial conversation which must be had.

Perhaps it was whether we wanted to go on living together. Perhaps it was the fear that if, after so many years, we continued this love affair, we might never have any other, we would never share love or life with other people, this would be all we ever had, ever, ever.

So it was fear about limits to life. Was this all our life would be, what would we have missed, how might we have grown? It wasn't just sex, though sex was a part of it. It wasn't just that we knew there were others we might, we would want to roll around with, cuddle up against or fuck, or go much further . . . It was fear that perhaps the person we were with was wrong, that that person would limit us, that we would never become the person we were capable of being because this love affair, would be, would be . . . and not knowing what it would be, the razor slash of fear of never knowing is why, I think, the argument had become so brutal, so nasty . . .

No, this is it. The fear was that the other's limitation would be a limitation for them.

Then Nick said

'Oh, come on, let's stop, it doesn't matter that much, does it?'

Or Nick said

'I can't bear this. It drives me crazy. We can't go on like this.'

And I thought

'But we always will.'

And even so, thinking that, I left the room where we were arguing and went to my own room.

It was late. The argument had gone on for hours and all the time I'd known I have to end this, I must go out and meet the man. And is that why we were arguing, why I was, to make clear how impossible this was, to give me a good reason to break free? *But it's so late.* Time's run out. I can't be late for him. Will he wait for me? I don't know if he will wait. But I know that if I go, when I come home, if I come home, this that I have, this love affair might have ended.

But also I know Nick wants me to go, does and doesn't, loves me with so much kindliness he wants me to be free, to be totally free (dream on) to become the person I am, whoever that is, we don't yet know. But if he loves me that deeply, how can I do what I know, or think I know, no, *know, I do know*, will hurt him, even if he wants, or thinks he wants me to do it, or says so.

So I long to go but I can't go. And I long not to long to. But I do. I struggle with this but all the time my body knows what it will do.

It's already sensing the edges of this room and the corridor and the front door and the steps down into the street . . .

Nick's writing in his room. Or probably. Or is reading? He's not listening to music, I can't hear anything. He went in and closed the door. He's writing probably so I don't want to disturb him though he always says he never minds being disturbed. By me.

Before I dress to go out, I take Nick a cup of tea, strong like he likes it. He is writing. Well, he's at his table with a pencil in his hand. He looks across dry-eyed, quizzical but there's pain there, I can see. By his elbow is a half-drunk cup of tea.

'You already brought me one.'

As I leave, I ask

'Would you like some more?' then stumble into the door, spilling what I'm carrying.

'Just leave it, alright?' Harshly.

I fetch a cloth from the kitchen, wipe it up, go to the bathroom, shower, dress in tight jeans. I can't go out, I can't go, I have to. I have to. He doesn't want me to. Whatever he wants me to do, I'll do. I have to go, I hate to.

I pick up a chair, a bentwood with curly arms and a curly back that bends right round the seat. I hold it over my head, shove it back and forwards through the black air, smash it, smash it hard against the wall. The back splinters, a leg cracks, the seat falls out. Again! Bits of wood litter the floor.

I slip out of the house. *I'm so late.* I hurry to the Underground, then, fuck it, a taxi's rising up the street, no, let it pass, as it passes I hail it, it stops, dash down the street, travel at speed through the empty, glistening late-night city streets, through streaky jets of neon. It's drizzling.

Outside the club a juddering line of boys is heading in, tight packed, their desire pushing them closer to each other's bodies and the way in, security rough-checking for drugs, knives, open popper bottles, thwarting it.

There's no sign of him. He hasn't waited, why would he? Has he gone home or in? I pay, get wrist-stamped with a purple duck, go in. My god, the heat. I should put my jacket in the keep but *is he here?* It's far too dark to see. If not, I won't stay. Possibly. The swirling heat, the thumping, the flock of cawing, crying creature-birds. I gape through crowds. I know my spirit's wrong and out of rhythm. This is the land of cool, of want not need. I'm anxious. I move with the wrong kind of forcefulness. He's nowhere. Am I certain? How can I be?

Should I just melt into whoever? Into the dark mass, the hell-hole corners, the herd of dancing T-shirts, jeans, no T-shirts, no jeans . . .

I'm outside in the street, waiting, waiting. Fuck it, everything's wrong! Wherever I turn I do the stupid thing. A taxi stops, lets out three glittering skinny kids, lighting up the sky. I half change my mind. The taxi's waiting, I clamber in. We drive two blocks. In the driving mirror I see a flash of green.

'Stop! Please. Sorry. I have to go back.'

I pay speedily, rush back, get there just as green shirt reaches the head of the line and slips in. I show the purple duck and follow, see him wandering and then take up with . . . But does he know him? Or is . . . ? I watch. I have to see it happening. He kisses him. A deep smile, deep embrace. Then he leaves him, moves on, puts his arm around . . .

Back on the street. Another taxi, I'm just about to get in. Green shirt is next to me.

'I'm so sorry to be so late. I was at a dinner party and you know, all at once I realised I was in love with the person I was with. I hadn't expected it. It never happens but that's what happened. So I couldn't leave. I so apologise for being late for you. Why didn't you go in? Why are you leaving? It's great in there. We can't stand here, it's freezing.' A depth charge smile. 'Come, come, come. Let's go in.'

I close the door of the taxi, I name my street.

I unlock the front door. I go in. The light's on in the passage. Lock the door, go to my room. All the wood fragments have been cleared away. The tea cups have been washed. They're drying on a dishcloth neatly spread out at the edge of the sink.

I hover in the corridor.

I go into Nick's room. He's fast asleep. He's not asleep. He pulls aside the blanket.

I take off my clothes.

I stretch out in the bed without touching him.

He turns onto his side and puts an arm round me.

3

The Lemon Tree

It was her maid's day off. As I imagine it, she was kneeling on the black earth, loosening it with her trowel to bed in fresh cuttings of 'Busy Lizzie' after watering her bird-of-paradise, her agapanthus, her lemon tree.

A neighbour

'I thought it was a cat whimpering. First it really got under my skin, then I thought I'd better investigate what is the trouble with the poor creature. I carried the ladder out of our shed, it's not that heavy, looked over the wall. I simply couldn't believe it when I realised from where the moaning was coming. I have to tell you, these days we complain about our services but the ambulance pitched up in minutes, literally.'

How long had she been stretched out there? Hours? Possibly.

For days fury possessed her. Her skin suddenly pitted, powdery, blotched with red, she lay shrivelled under her rose-pink quilt, her hair a hedge, choked by rage, thunder in her eyes, despising everyone and everything.

The doctor from across the street

'She's an old soul, folks. From a medical standpoint, our choices are down to single digits. With the best will in the world, there's no way back from this.'

In the hospital, she flew at elderly patients, scratching them with jagged nails she wouldn't let her nurse trim, gripping their spongy flesh, biting it, tearing from their necks their necklaces, their jewellery. When Sonny and I walked through the door she lurched up from the bed they'd caged her in and pressed a poor, red, swollen thumb on the metal rail.

'I want you all right there under my thumb, that's where I want everyone!'

Her doctors titrated her medicine. Then she sat as if enchanted day after day under the window in her sunny, tidy, mockery of a room in the hospice making lists in a notebook, numbers and signs, numbers and signs, her hand scuttling crab-like down and down, columns of numbers and signs down the left-hand side, turn over, numbers and signs, numbers and signs.

'What are you making lists of, Ma? What do the signs mean?'

Bent tight to her task, she swivels her head towards me like a woodland creature, her hooded eyes smouldering.

———————

With his engraved silver *yad* the rabbi deftly points my way through a thicket of Hebrew. Despite having gazed at these words all year, they still mean nothing to me – sounds without resonance, phrases without shape or sensuality. I've half-heartedly learned them by heart. That I'm faking is clear to everybody.

Even so, as a gift, not just for me at my bar mitzvah but for the whole family, Dad brings home the *Encyclopaedia Britannica Great Books of the World* – fifty leather-bound volumes from *The Iliad* to Sigmund Freud by way of Plato, Dante, Galileo, Newton, Shakespeare, Adam Smith, Marx, *The Brothers Karamazov*, Darwin, *War and Peace*, each with a finely woven edging, green for literature, red for science, blue for philosophy . . .

When Ma was in the hospice which we knew she'd never leave, Sonny sorted out her house. In a little-used upstairs room, there they all are – never opened, never read, barely touched, sweaty, fifty silent heroes locked for eternity inside a walnut bookcase Dad made in his carpentry class at school when he was fifteen.

The surf comes rolling in. It crashes against me. I stand my ground. Far out beyond the breakers, skimming the heaving swell they swim like water spiders, pulsing, pulsing. They wave, then one by one head out towards far deeper waters.

Bye bye, Arthur. Bye bye Luc. Bye bye Patrice. Bye Golda and Mottle. Bye Jeff. Bye Ma. Bye Dad. See you soon. Next summer. Possibly.

Seven

Directing

Captain I'll be no more,
But I will eat and drink and sleep as soft
As captain shall. Simply the thing I am
Shall make me live.

All's Well That Ends Well

2012

It's a blissfully warm evening. A fruity hum rises up to my desk in the general office. I look down through the high, wide window, past the young birch trees on our garden terrace, into the bar/cafe and across into the street. It seems more like a club than a theatre, every level alive with people of all hues and ages sprawling on sofas, drinking, eating – actors, directors, neighbours, flirting, cruising, auditioning, interviewing . . .

When the building reopened I came across two young folk on a sofa superglued to each other, lip to lip. This was our christening.

My mobile buzzes in my pocket. I don't recognise the number or even the country prefix.

'Hello?'

'I need to speak to Mr Peter Brook.'

'I'm sorry, he's in the middle of a dress rehearsal.'

'It's extremely urgent.'

'I understand but I can't disturb him.'

'Can't?'

'Who actually wants him?'

'Please, my friend, don't muck about. You're boss, or so I believe. Of course your phone number is confidential. If I say he is needed, take my word for it.'

Peter, in his mid-eighties, is the most famous theatre director in the world. He told me once that when he went 'up to Stratford' in 1946 aged twenty-one to direct *Love's Labour's Lost*

'The full extent of rehearsal I was given was—'

He holds up four fingers.

'Four weeks?'

'Not at all. Four afternoons.'

Now his shows are worked and reworked over years but his rehearsals are closed. This is not unusual. Few directors are easy with visitors wandering in and out or even silently observing but in Peter's case there are scores of actors, directors, theatre journalists, academics clambering to get in.

'The door is shut,' he says, 'not because there's anything secret going on – my recent book is titled *There Are No Secrets* – but because actors are more willing to go too far, to tumble, to stumble, to seem to make fools of themselves, though nothing they do is foolish, if they aren't observed by anyone except those they trust to go as far as they themselves are willing to.'

'But who shall I say . . . ?'

'Time, my son, is precious . . .'

I head out through the door, sharp turn left, down stairs, past the poster of 'Tobias and the Angel', wary as though I'm crossing into enemy territory. Down, down, down . . .

On the first landing. What do I feel? Vulnerable? Naive? Out-manoeuvred. Casually interrupting a director mid-rehearsal is an obvious blunder but if it *is* an emergency and I fumble it . . .

Down, down . . .

More hesitation in the blue-lit corridor that circles the auditorium. I gently edge apart the swing doors but can't prevent the lip-smacking *smooch* as layers of rubber acoustic separation pull apart. I enter the room . . .

Murk, like a rain forest under a leaf canopy. Disembodied heads fixed on the spikes of their own shoulders. A rich, soupy silence.

On stage, *The Suit*.

A newly married couple live in Alexandria, a black suburb of

Johannesburg that was destroyed by apartheid decades ago. While the husband is at work, the wife makes love to another man. The husband's friends tell him what's going on. He hurries home. The lover escapes through a window, abandoning his clothes. The husband makes no complaint but instructs his wife to treat her lover's suit as an honoured guest. The suit is introduced to their friends, is fed at meal-times . . . In the end, the wife can take no more of this torture and ends her life. A heartbroken, heartless joke ends in catastrophe.

It's played on an empty stage. A simple clothes rail doubles as the bedroom window, as doors and as the clothes rail on which the suit lives. Peter throws handfuls of colour and sound at the stage. Nothing fits and everything does.

'Look, my hands are empty. And now . . . here's a glass bowl with a goldfish swimming in it.'

Sim-salabim!

I spot him on an aisle, crouch at his side, mime a telephone held to my ear. Alarm tightens his eyes, he lays a finger over his lips. Oh fuck, I'm rubbish. I leave. Damn whoever he is. I knew I was doing the wrong thing.

The rehearsal is over. When I find them again, Peter is giving notes to his actors.

'Ah dear David. Perfect timing.'

Just behind him sits a tall man, very dark with long swept-back silver hair, a silver cross perched on his chest.

'Peter, sorry I disturbed you earlier. Someone phoned and said it was urgent.'

'Well, I didn't know which was the correct door into the theatre.' The tall man leans forward, his hand on Peter's shoulder.

'You were inside the building?'

'One prefers not to stumble about in darkness but when one is put to it one finds the way.'

271

'And the rehearsal, Peter? How did it go?'

'Well, I believe in your beautiful theatre we may . . .'

The tall man makes quick little shakings of his head.

'You are right. Let's not tempt fate.'

So this man knows fate's secrets. And what do I know? An actor is whispering in Peter's ear.

'Ah, yes, David, we were all wondering whether in your cafe the actors get a discount on food and beverages . . .'

1980

I'm living way up in the north of Zimbabwe, in a village in a clearing on the edge of dense, descending forests of olive-grey *mopane*, massive *baobabs*, spiky dry *ilala* sixty miles from the torrential waters of the Zambezi.

In those days, tsetse flies which suck the blood of cattle and, in time, kill them were endemic in the Valley. The mud hut in which I lived was near the fly-gate where vehicles travelling in or out were sprayed to stop the flies advancing up the escarpment. Chikepe was a fly-gate man. Wearing khaki shorts and peaked cap, his job was to operate the wooden arm that blocked the road and spray clouds of sticky chemical all over trucks and jeeps and other vehicles.

He was in love with Rosemary but she was ill. After consulting a village healer, it was agreed that the cause of her illness was the spirit of her dear friend who had fought as a guerrilla in the war and been killed in action. The spirit wanted Rosemary not to marry Chikepe for, as everyone knew, during the war he'd been a 'sell-out'.

When the sun went down and the tsetse flies were sleeping, Chikepe would visit me.

'Even when the fighting was strong, I had to do my work, Mr Davey. I ask you, who else but the government would pay for me to do it? These people are very far from reasonable.'

Because he had been in work throughout the war, he was one of the few local men with any money. Is that why she'd agreed to marry him? How ill was she really? Even while the story was unfolding around me, I began to imagine a play about Chikepe and Rosemary.

1987

My play *Sergeant Ola and His Followers* about 'cargo cult' in New Guinea is in rehearsal off-Broadway at Soho Rep. Everything's in short supply, even a theatre in which to perform my play.

'Manhattan is real estate, that's all it is. Build, make a load of cash, knock it down, make another load of cash, build again. There's no room left for art.'

Some weeks earlier they'd been forced out of one space and were almost definitely moving into a fabulous new one just as soon as something complicated was sorted out by some or other administrative department of the city.

The artistic director Marlene Swartz took me to see a series of vacant rooms round the back of Bellevue.

'You know, this used to be the city's madhouse.'

She laughs but stops immediately. There's nothing crazy about making left-wing theatre in the US of the 1980s. It's a rational life choice. They saw my play as a satire on commodity capitalism, which it is, which is why they wanted to do it.

'So,' I say to Marlene, 'I know this is the most difficult question you can ask an artistic director but what shows should I see?'

A great hall at 'La Mama' on 4th Street in the East Village. Vast sloping, black-painted platforms are wheeled to and fro. The audience stands in whatever spaces are created and recreated and then, when you think you'll be safe in this spot for a while, they're recreated again.

Fragments of a Greek Trilogy: Medea and *The Trojan Women*, by Euripides, and *Electra* by Sophocles, all directed by the

Romanian-American Andrei Şerban. They're played one after the other by muscular, handsome, dark-haired actors speaking an invented language, part classical Greek, part Balkan laments, part who-knows-what, largely sung to a complex score by Elizabeth Swardos. At any one moment you've no precise idea what's going on but somehow in fact you do, you feel it all, disaster after disaster, whole planets of suffering and resilience, you live it, you get it, it's magnificent.

In its final moments, as Electra and her brother Orestes are joyfully reconciled, they each ring a handbell. The ringing builds towards a climax. Will it ever end? Ellen Stewart, the original mama of 'La Mama', trips in out of the darkness with her own handbell and rings the tone that completes this journey into the mystery of family and blood and violence and culture-destroying rage and desperately fought-for redemption – of history, of order, of spontaneity, of theatre, of play.

1989

The Almeida Theatre has new artistic directors, Ian McDiarmid and Jonathan Kent. They ask for *Desire*, my Chikepe/Rosemary play.

'Great!'

'Who do you want to direct it?'

'Well, two years ago in New York I saw this amazing production . . .'

I'm in Nice. Andrei Şerban is waiting for me in the glittering foyer of the world-fabulous Hotel Negresco.

'Ah, David! I feel it must be you. Who else can it be? Welcome.'

He's wearing shorts and a Hawaiian shirt. The day is sweltering.

'So tell me, what are you doing in this shitty town?'

'I came to meet you.'

'Ah, no, really? I'm deeply touched.'

Standing on the wall of the Promenade des Anglais, we look out at the lackadaisical waves of the Mediterranean.

'Can you see Greece? No, of course you can't. What a crazy idea.'

Dashing, muscular, swirling hair, tired eyes that ask without asking.

'Tell the truth, what are we doing here?'

It's almost lunchtime, his wife and sons are waiting in their house high in the hills above the town.

'Tell the truth . . . ?'

'I mean on this planet. Do we have a purpose? It's ridiculous but I always seem to ask this when I look at the sea. What's your opinion?'

His only production in England, a spectacular, warm-hearted *Turandot* at the Royal Opera House, has been revived season after season.

'Have you . . . ?'

'Have I what? A purpose?'

'No, have you read . . .'

'Naturally I've read your play.'

I've no idea what to say to him. He directed Irene Worth and Meryl Streep in *The Cherry Orchard*. He's the most distinguished avant-garde director in America. This was foolish. We stand gazing out at the Mediterranean. It's true, you can't see Greece.

1990

Andrei overturned everything I thought I knew about theatre. About *making* theatre. Everything I now know, or think I know, I began to learn with him.

That can't be true.

The week before I left Cape Town for London, I watched a Sunday afternoon try-out performance in an upstairs room of a new play by Athol Fugard and two actors from the Eastern Cape, John Kani and Winston Ntshona. *Sizwe Banzi is Dead* lasted an hour. When it finished the blankets were pulled off the windows, the sun streamed in. We were exhausted and exhilarated. It was obviously an immediate classic and we were amongst the first to see it. When I got to London, I told Nick and this was, I think, one of the reasons – I'm sure just one – that the Royal Court brought it to London and launched it on its world conquest.

I guess that what I've tried to do in this book is chart the growth of an aesthetic or, perhaps better, of an approach to aesthetics. Working with Andrei I *felt* as though I knew nothing. *It seemed to me* as though I was a blank sheet of paper, a newly sharpened pencil, an unopened, foil-wrapped moleskin notebook.

To Dad and my way of thinking, thinking was everything. You analyse, you discuss, you try to get to the bottom of things, you believe there *is* a bottom to things and one of these evenings, sitting up late, when you ought to be doing your homework you're bound to reach it. So if you happen, for example, to be directing a play, you wouldn't dream of facing your actors until you've learned everything there is to know about it, researched its previous productions, studied other works by your playwright, other plays of the period and the period itself from social, political, economic points of view . . .

Andrei just walked into the room.

Before rehearsals for *Desire*, did he actually *read* it?

On day one, the actors sat in a circle and read the play. Andrei laughed at the jokes. He winked at me.

'I wouldn't normally do this, it's such a waste of time and in this country you don't give much but it's your tradition to read the play together and it's good for actors to feel comfortable at least in the beginning, just as long as no one today tries to do any acting, when they do that I find it horrible.'

Years later he told me that before we'd strolled along the Promenade des Anglais he'd done no more than give the play a bit of a skim.

'I picked up the main conception. I formed a strong impression.'

'Then what persuaded you to take the job?'

'Our meeting.'

'Really? We barely spoke to each other.'

'No, David, honestly, don't you remember? You talked for hours. Oof! I thought my hearing would give out. But I had a feeling about it.'

'What feeling?'

'Well, how can I convey it to you? What I felt was something. It was more than nothing. You have to trust your instinct, don't you agree?'

I was shocked by his directing technique. It was clear I'd made a mistake. He didn't seem to form relationships with any of the actors. He made things up as he went along which the actors must have realised, how embarrassing. If an actor started a discussion, he'd go off to one side of the room, read a newspaper until the disturbance had blown over. When rehearsals ended, he didn't drink with the actors or even talk to them, six o'clock, time's up, he's gone. What was I to do? We'd employed a charlatan.

But day by day, scene by scene the actors became enchanted. They adored his openness to suggestion, his spontaneity, his sense of fun, the freedom he offered. He was creating with them, for them, on their bodies, as choreographers say. It was only *in the room* that he did his thinking.

We are the poorest of the poor and the richest of the rich. Precision is our only value – of feeling, of understanding, of expression, here, now, in this air that we all breathe together on this instant of this day, on this spit of the earth, in this bare room with everything to lose, everything to win.

Moments before each rehearsal Andrei and I would sit together and he'd ask me to talk about the scenes scheduled for that day. He'd scrawl in blue ink till there was as much of his writing on each page as my own.

'Yes, yes, I get it, wonderful, now I know what to do.'

Huge smile, an embrace. These were sensual moments. We were co-conspirators and, all at once, friends.

1991

The phone rang.

'Is that David Lan? This is Peter Brook. You know Andrei Şerban? He tells me you're good friends. Andrei and I worked together many years ago with Ted Hughes, I suppose you know what I'm referring to, in Iran. I have a small project I'd like to propose. I'll be in London in September for a day or two. Or do you ever come to Paris?'

I went to Paris. He had an idea for a film. A film, not a play?

'I'm a film-maker too, you know. In fact, I'm only a theatre director because that's how the cards fell. My intention when I was young was to make films, it was my great passion. And this idea which I have, about which I want to talk to you, is perfect for film. Not a large film. All my Hollywood friends tell me – and this is also my experience – if a film costs no more than three million dollars you have a chance, just a chance, that you can make the film you've dreamed of. The very instant you go over that sum the studios take control and that leads to disaster.'

So, a small film.

'Are you interested to hear more? I'll tell you the story and if it grabs you – it has to grab you at a deep level or we're going to get nowhere – we can commission you, not in a lavish way, and you can get going.'

He asked me not to repeat the story to anyone. I never did, or not frequently. Now Peter has, at last, made it into a play it's in the world, so here it is.

Afghanistan. Let's say Kabul. The 1960s. A young man commits a terrible crime. It doesn't matter too much for the story what it is provided it's bad enough. Let's say he murders his father. He's arrested, tried, convicted. The judges accept that there are mitigating circumstances so they don't sentence him to be executed. His punishment is prison for twenty years.

The young man is a member of one of the many Afghani Sufi societies. He has a spiritual master to whom he's close. The master believes him to be a person of great quality who would only have committed this crime if driven to it by exceptional circumstances. He and the judge respect each other, both follow the law in their different ways. He asks the judge for a tremendous favour. The prisoner, he says, is a young man of potential. It would be a profound loss to the world were he to rot in a cell, to suffer prison brutality, his body deformed, his mind embittered. Will the judge agree to release the prisoner to him? He won't set him free but will punish him severely in an appropriate way.

The master leads the young man out of the jail which happens to be on a busy street. They go no further than the pavement outside the prison wall. He tells the young man to sit.

'And there you will stay for twenty years. No one will keep you there but you yourself, your own will, your sense of discipline, your sense of justice. You are under no one's instruction but your own. You will stay there not because I have commanded you to but because you know that this is right.'

Peter was taken to see him sitting on the pavement in the sun.

'You can imagine the dust, the heat. He barely moved. But *I* was moved. I've been thinking about the meaning of his story ever since. If you look below the surface, there are powerful dramatic possibilities.

So we have to think: what's going to happen, will it be this or will it be that, do we shoot off in one direction or swerve round in another? However, in any good story there is always one central question. In our case it's this: what would need to occur before our young man would simply stand up, would get to his feet and walk away? Now will you get to your feet, go home and start work on the screenplay?'

What did we know about the young man? Nothing. So, first question: should the film be set in Afghanistan. Well, yes, that could be marvellous and original but, no, if the actors spoke Dari or Pashto we would never find the finance for it. And setting it in Afghanistan with actors speaking English would be ridiculous. So where should it take place?

Not Pakistan, same objections as above and far too difficult for Westerners to film there anyway but how about north India with their vast film industry?

Or could it be set in an English-speaking country? Could you believe that a High Court judge might hand over a convict to, say, an archbishop?

Perhaps we could set it before the twentieth century in some European backwater such as those to-hell-and-gone provincial towns in *Dead Souls*? Ah, Russia, let's think about that. If the characters are Russian we can certainly make the film in English, think *Doctor Zhivago*, that's not a difficulty. So would the story work if we set it within the Orthodox Church? We read *The Brothers Karamazov*, which seems apt because, amongst other themes, it's an investigation of a parricide. And we read explicitly spiritual texts such as the *The Way of the Pilgrim* and a collection of writings by fathers of the early Eastern Church, *The Philokalia*. Well, it's three stout volumes. I dipped into it.

In *The Way of the Pilgrim* the anonymous author describes how he learned the Jesus prayer, a technique of merging prayer with breathing so that, after much practice, every breath you take, in and out, becomes, without any longer being aware you're doing it, a prayer to Jesus.

'Lord Jesus Christ, Son of God, have mercy on me, a sinner.'

I'm not at all religious but I was intrigued. Does this degree of self-imposed discipline make you a good person even if you haven't committed a crime? And who hasn't committed some crime at some level of seriousness? I sensed a possible analogy to our young man so I practised. Eventually I could keep it up for, oh, seconds.

From time to time I'd say

'But, Peter, don't you think this *could* be a play? Then it would all be easy. An empty stage. You simply assert that an actor is a young Afghan student. This wall our wall, this pavement our pavement...'

But, no, he could direct a play any time he felt like it. At that time he was mid-rehearsal for *The Tempest*. No, no. A film. But wherever we eventually decide to set it, what does the young man actually *do* on his pavement? He can't just sit there. Or can he? Why *did* he kill his father? We need to think hard about this.

'Don't try to write the whole thing. Write fragments,' said Peter. 'We can work them up together with Marie-Hélène', his long-time closest associate.

Yes, great idea. I sat down to write fragments. But what of? The history of a man who murdered his father. Or perhaps he didn't. Perhaps he committed some other crime. He robbed a convent. He poisoned a well.

Wherever Peter was rehearsing or, as the summer wore on, wherever *The Tempest* was playing, I'd turn up, Marie-Hélène would check me into the five-star hotel in which they were staying, we'd spend hours in the hotel grounds with our feet up exploring this or that new hunch about how the story might unfold. Or if our rendezvous was in Paris, she'd book me into the famous circular room on the second floor of the Hotel La Louisiane in the Rue de Seine where Miles Davis and Billie Holiday used to stay, on separate occasions presumably.

'Disagree with me,' Peter would advise. 'The more you disagree with me the more I'll agree with you.'

A nice paradox. It didn't help me.

Once in Avignon I arrived as agreed only to be told there was an urgent meeting going on. Peter dumped a clod of typescript in my lap.

'See what you make of that.'

Thud!

Shakespeare and the Goddess of Complete Being by Ted Hughes, a profound, original and extremely thick book.

'It arrived this morning, almost broke the postman's back.'

And the subtext was? 'Ted is an unquenchable wellspring of poetry while, at the same time, writing studies as weighty as this. Whereas . . .'

One Sunday there was a large, boisterous, eat-and-drink-till-the-end-of-time lunch in glorious sunshine for the entire *Tempest* company – actors, producers, stage management – at the invitation of the director of the Avignon Festival. As the sun crossed the heavens and the shadows of the sheltering plane trees edged across the square

'*Ça bouge!*'

they cried and we'd pick up the laden tables and carry them bodily back into the shade. An elderly giant with crinkly grey hair rose and declaimed

'*Champagne et chocolate pour tout le monde.*'

For the entire world?

'It means for everyone who is with us at this table.'

282

I was with them at that table. It was where I wanted to be. The drawback was that I didn't really belong there because the story of the Afghan father-killer had defeated me.

Months went by. Why couldn't I write what was asked for? I came across a reproduction of Van Gogh's *The Potato Eaters* in a book called *The Class Struggle in the Ancient Greek World* and wrote a number of scenes about a young potato farmer. I thought they were rather good and still have them filed away somewhere but they had nothing to do with our convict.

Had they ever got round to sending me a contract? Unlikely. But even if they had, the money was peanuts. And that wasn't the point. I was a free man, wasn't I? I could admit failure, apologise, jack it in. I adored the company I was keeping. I would do anything not to be turfed out. But I couldn't write anything.

Le Costume/The Suit

2001/2012

At the time I landed the job of running YV, Peter opened *Le Costume*, the first, French-language, version of *The Suit*, at his theatre in Paris, the Bouffes du Nord. Of course I went to see it. I loved it. Shall we bring it? I phoned Marie-Hélène.

'But we would love to come to your theatre. Isn't it nice to be able to say *your theatre*? But can you pay for it? We are very expensive, you know that. For you we can make a special price but even so – ooh la la.'

The Arts Council found £20,000 behind one of their sofas. Sian Alexander, head of London theatre

'We want to help.'

Thank you, Sian, you did.

Le Costume was in my first season. Audiences loved it so much it was in my second season too. In later years we brought Peter's *Hamlet*, then his production of three short plays by Samuel Beckett, again for two seasons, then we co-produced *The Suit*, then his show about synaesthesia *The Valley of Astonishment*, then his meditation on the *Mahabharata* called *Battlefield*.

Whenever I could, I'd visit his rehearsals in Paris of whatever the next show was to be. He always asked for a tough response. At the end of every performance of his shows at the Bouffes the audience stood up. He disregarded this. He wasn't contemptuous of it, he just wasn't interested.

'Say what *you* thought about it. Is it what *you* expected? Ah, it wasn't? You were surprised?'

Wrinkly, twinkly smile.

'Good!'

Exit lines

2016

My mobile shudders. It's Marie-Hélène.

'David, you must come to Paris. Peter's going to do that story.'

'Which story?'

'Ah, you know, the Afghan boy outside the prison. You helped with it all those years ago. Peter wants you to bring whatever you wrote.'

'Marie-Hélène, you know over months and months and meeting after meeting I never wrote anything of any use.'

'It doesn't matter. Bring whatever there is.'

Don't say fragments!

'It could be helpful for us.'

'I've hardly told anyone but I'm telling you. Between us, Marie-Hélène, I'm leaving here.'

'You're leaving the Young Vic? *Merde!* I say that for good luck.'

'So I won't be able to co-produce or present your new show.'

'It's ok. We need you anyway. Come.'

As it happened, I couldn't make it to Paris when they were rehearsing. I visited one of their workshops in London.

Peter, Marie-Hélène and a few actors worked on some fragments a writer had provided. Scraps was all they were.

> **Man** Mother.
> **Mother** Yes, son.
> **Man** I'm going.
> **Mother** Where to?
> **Man** The vineyard.

Actually that's the opening of *Blood Wedding* by Lorca.

Why couldn't I have written something like that? That's all he needed to get going. It only takes five minutes and genius.

The hardest lesson for us without genius is

'It doesn't matter where you begin, don't think about where you'll end up, just start writing.'

2017

I call Peter to tell him that the next day we're issuing a press release announcing that I'm leaving.

'Now, I want to understand precisely your reasons for this. Is there a problem with your board?'

'Not at all.'

'Were you pushed?'

'It's entirely my decision.'

'Is it the funding? I know it's hell keeping a theatre open these days. Can't you play shorter seasons like they do in Europe?'

'I don't think so.'

'That would reduce your expenses.'

'No, it's nothing like that. The theatre's in good shape. Which is why it feels like the right time to go.'

'So this is entirely your decision?'

'Entirely.'

'Well, you have my congratulations. You feel it's the right time so you get to your feet and go. You're a free man.'

———————

At the airport on the day I left for London Dad said

'Ma's taking your going away very hard. I want you to write to her.'

'Yes, Dad.'

'She needs you to do that. Are you listening to me? Do you understand what I'm asking you?'

'Will I write to Ma.'

'Yes, at least once a week. Tell her what you get up to, will you do that?'

'Yes, sure.'

'Look at me.'

'Yes, Dad, I hear you. What I get up to. I will.'

Index of Plays

Permissions

Earlier versions of four brief sections were published in the *Guardian* and one in the *New Statesman*.

All translations are the author's own unless otherwise credited.

Faber & Faber gratefully acknowledges permission to reprint copyright material as follows:

From *Yerma* by Simon Stone after Federico García Lorca (Oberon Books, 2017).

From *Three Sisters* by Anton Chekhov in a version by Benedict Andrews (Oberon Books, 2012).

From *The Cherry Orchard* © Simon Stephens 2014, based on the original by Anton Chekhov, Methuen Drama, an imprint of Bloomsbury Publishing Plc.

From 'Portrayal of past and present in one', originally published in German in 1961 as 'Darstellung von Vergangenheit und Gegenwart in einem', translated by Tom Kuhn. Copyright © 1961, 1976 by Bertolt-Brecht-Erben / Suhrkamp Verlag. Translation copyright (c) 2019, 2015 by Tom Kuhn and David Constantine, from Collected Poems of Bertolt Brecht by Bertolt Brecht, translated by Tom Kuhn and David Constantine. Used by permission of Liveright Publishing Corporation.

From *On the Road* by Jack Kerouac, copyright © 1955, 1957, by John Sampas, Literary Representative, the Estate of Stella Sampas Kerouac; John Lash, Executor of the Estate of Jan Kerouac; Nancy Bump; and Anthony M. Sampas. Used by permission of Viking Books, an imprint of Penguin Publishing Group, a division of Penguin Random House LLC. All rights reserved.

From *A Streetcar Named Desire* by Tennessee Williams, published by Penguin Group © Tennessee Williams, 1947. Reproduced by permission of Shiel Land